More praise for *Coastlines*:

'[Barkham] engagingly interweaves his impressions with accounts of notable features and reflections on the hard battle to preserve our rich coastal heritage. A likeable as well as informative companion' *Northern Echo*

'Barkham is one of the most eloquent writers on these isles' *Suffolk and Norfolk Life*

'*Coastlines* is a must-read for naturalists' *Cornwall Today*

'A delight from cover to cover' *Norwich Evening News*

'In his previous books, Barkham has written beautifully about butterflies and badgers. Here he turns his attention to the 742 miles of coastline in the care of Enterprise Neptune, the National Trust's maritime arm. In a series of walks, he discovers the weird and the wonderful . . . and ponders how the surrounding sea has shaped our island life' *Sunday Express*

*Also by Patrick Barkham*

The Butterfly Isles
Badgerlands

# COASTLINES

**THE STORY OF OUR SHORE**

## PATRICK
## BARKHAM

*Illustrated by Emily Faccini*

GRANTA

Granta Publications, 12 Addison Avenue, London W11 4QR

First published in Great Britain by Granta Books 2015
This paperback edition published by Granta Books 2015

A CIP catalogue record for this book is available from the British Library

9 8 7 6 5 4 3 2 1

ISBN 978 1 84708 899 4
eISBN 978 1 84708 898 7

www.grantabooks.com

Typeset in Garamond by Avon DataSet Ltd, Bidford on Avon, Warwickshire

Printed and bound by CPI Group (UK) Ltd, Croydon, CR0 4YY

For Lisa

# CONTENTS

THE ATLANTIC

Giant's Causeway
Antrim Coast

Strangford Lough

Am̕
Kne

IRISH SEA

Cemlyn

Plas Newydd
The Llŷn Peninsula
Plas yn Rhiw

Dinas Oleu
(The Fortress
of Light)

Stackpole
(Broadhaven South)

Lundy
Island
Morwenstow
Crackington Haven

Penwith
The Land's End

The
Carrick
Roads

Wembur
Point

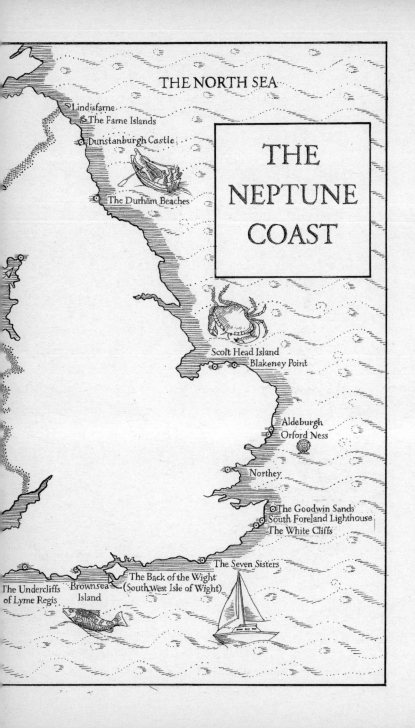

THE NORTH SEA

Lindisfarne & The Farne Islands

Dunstanburgh Castle

The Durham Beaches

THE
NEPTUNE
COAST

Scolt Head Island
Blakeney Point

Aldeburgh
Orford Ness

Northey

The Goodwin Sands
South Foreland Lighthouse
The White Cliffs

The Seven Sisters

The Back of the Wight
(South West Isle of Wight)

The Undercliffs
of Lyme Regis

Brownsea
Island

# INTRODUCTION

## The Fortress of Light

Dinas Oleu
(The Fortress
of Light)

No cars glittered in the large tarmac car park. Seafront razzle dazzle was locked away inside boxy grey amusement arcades shuttered for the winter. The little shops on the stone-and-slate high street betrayed a seaside town's weakness for punning: Born and Bread, Sophisticut and Cloud Nine. Opposite a derelict patch of weedy concrete, a tiny lane twisted upwards between dainty terraced homes, their chimneys pluming wood smoke from living-room fires. Five minutes and the old Welsh fishing village of Abermaw graciously gave way to gorse and bracken. A pause, breathless, where the slope softened, in golden sunshine, and the town of Barmouth was laid out like a miniature attraction below.

Stone cottages hugged the hill. Below them were dark, handsome houses with pointy gables that arrived with the Victorian holiday-makers. Behind them was a thin line of railway, its former goods yard filled with a supermarket; the ugliness of the amusement architecture and the deserted car park. Beyond them was a broad yellow beach and the strong blue Irish Sea filling the great expanse of Cardigan Bay. The Llŷn Peninsula stretched a hazy finger along the northern horizon; to the south, the swirly sand mouth of the River Mawddach met the sea; at its side was the old port, embracing boats with its stone arms.

This simple, easily earned view contained all the elements of the British coast. The fundamental ones – water, wind, rock and fire – of course, but their natural and human elaborations as well: mountain, river, harbour, beach, dune, seafront, bridge, car, boat. On one of those limpid days at the end of autumn, it also offered a vivid soundscape. Oystercatchers fussed on the mudflats. A corvid cackled. Beep-beep-beep went the warning sound of a lorry reversing towards a cargo bay in town. An amplified recording of 'Hark The Herald Angels Sing' wafted from the High Street, where Dolgellau Rotary Club were raising premature Christmas cheer. A jetski thudded on the sea. But none of these pinpricks of human bustle could detract from the mighty calm of a big sea view. Its peace quelled all dissonance.

The British Isles are more edge than middle. Our coastline spans 10,800 miles, longer than India's, and, however far we travel inland, we are never more than seventy miles from the sea. It has protected us from invasion and given us an empire. Our projection of naval power over the globe for a couple of centuries bequeathed us both unimaginable riches and the romantic notion that we are a maritime nation. But we are not, really.

Like a typical Briton, I grew up fifteen miles from the sea and spent my childhood holidays on a sandy, windy and occasionally sunny English beach. I can swim but I can't sail, I'm an appalling surfer, a bad birdwatcher and an enthusiastic coast-path walker. The beach clears my mind and cheers me up. I can't think of anything I dislike about the coast apart from nuclear power stations. I love old harbours, tacky resorts, big waves, sandy coves, humungous cliffs, oystercatchers, fish-and-chips, flotsam and jetsam, samphire, sunsets – but most of all I love the desolate beaches where I played as a small boy. The first thing I did when I had children of my own was to take them back there; someday, I'd like to retire to a cottage by the sea.

In this respect I am a typical member of a coastal nation, happiest when looking seaward with my feet placed firmly on solid ground. The line between land and sea has become our favourite playground, national park and retirement home.

It was not always so. For centuries, the sea was feared, a fickle, destructive god that brought invaders, pestilence and death on a whim. The coast was a place for fishing communities, military fortifications and lawless pirates and smugglers. The Romantics were in awe of its horror and immensity, even as they eulogised its beauty. The rest of us, even the wealthy, stayed away. We turned our backs on the sea until the eighteenth century, when Romantic sentiment and a quackish medical fashion for sea bathing saw prospectors rush to the beach as if the sand were gold, constructing the hotels, promenades, piers and attractions that created Brighton, Blackpool and Barmouth, playgrounds for working people enjoying their newfangled holidays. Time by the sea became an entitlement: in 1829 Dr Arnold, the founder of the public school at Rugby, observed that 'more than half my boys never saw the sea' as if it were an essential part of their education that they did. A few weeks' annual paid leave also came to be regarded as a basic human right and, by 1962, 30 million holidays were spent at the British seaside. The subsequent rise of cheap flights to foreign beaches with guaranteed sunshine caused many traditional resorts to struggle by the 1980s but the economic downturn in the first decade of this century saw a significant increase in domestic holidays, with long-term trends also showing people increasingly inclined to take short breaks on the British coast.

Our seaside has always been a place of extremes, of weather and landscape. We are naturally blessed with a greater diversity of types of coastline than perhaps any other nation: spectacular cliffs of granite, chalk, sandstone and a contrasting collection of other geological formations; coves, bars and spits of sand, pebbles and shingle; bays, harbours, promontories, headlands; huge dunes, vast estuaries, marshes and tidal flats. We have the second highest tidal range in the world (the Severn rises and falls by more than 14 metres; 10 centimetres is typical on the Mediterranean) and the largest shingle promontory in Europe (Dungeness). On this record-breaking topographical variety, we have created places of human extremes; wealthy villas cheek-by-jowl with wilderness. Seaside communities such as Sandbanks in Dorset boast some of the most expensive real estate in Britain; others, such as Easington Colliery on the overlooked Durham coast, are among the most impoverished. Many of the sprawling resorts we built so quickly have been hollowed out by cheap foreign travel, while older communities have been decimated by the decline of traditional shoreline industries like fishing and shipbuilding. Even where tourism is flourishing again, it is an industry incapable of providing many well-waged, year-round jobs, and the coast is lined with holiday properties that sit empty for much of the year, as locals are priced out of a view of the sea.

These places of development and deprivation crowd against unexpectedly large sections of 'natural' coast. The character of our greenest countryside is almost entirely the result of centuries of human activity but the coast is the last repository of wilderness, in southern England at least. The survival of these untamed shores is often a historical accident but it is also because a handful of local people have fought tenaciously to save their unspoilt character.

Gazing at the faint lines traced on the sea where the currents collided in Cardigan Bay, I considered this spectacular, everyday view. The rough hillside of Dinas Oleu would never be a major tourist attraction. It has a lovely name, which means 'fortress of light', but it contains no rare plants or archaeological treasures or spectacular rock formations. One thing singles out these four-and-a-half acres for attention: in 1895 Dinas Oleu became the first piece of land to be owned by the National Trust.

A humdrum hill above a bucket-and-spade resort that has seen better days seems an unlikely starting point for a charity inaccurately associated with an upper-class urge to preserve stately homes. But Dinas Oleu is precisely in keeping with the National Trust's first principles, and it began a conservation campaign that has shaped the character of our shores in the last 120 years more fundamentally than any other human endeavour. I was surprised when I heard that the National Trust owns 742 miles of the 3,000-mile coastline of England, Wales and Northern Ireland. Like most people, I had no idea it had played, and continues to play, such a vital role in our coast, and our relationship with it.

Fanny Talbot, a moderately wealthy Victorian woman, offered this hill to the putative National Trust because she wanted to ensure the public would always be able to enjoy it by placing it in the hands of 'some society that will never vulgarise it, or prevent wild nature from having its way'. Octavia Hill, one of the four founders of the Trust, which grew out of the successful movement to save the commons of London, spoke of the importance of having 'open air sitting rooms for City dwellers to have a place to breathe'. This small patch of land, a beautiful view five minutes from the busy streets of Barmouth, was exactly that.

We take our coast for granted, in that we casually view the beach as common land, a playground for the enjoyment of everyone. In almost all areas, the water's edge is actually owned by the Crown, and administered by the Crown Estates, which chiefly seeks to exploit things like the seabed – selling licences for gravel extraction and windfarms – for financial gain. The people of Britain don't own any of it, and could be chucked off it at any moment. Lacking any revolutionary fervour to nationalise the shore, to seize it from an aristocratic family whose possession is an accident of their birth, we have instead channelled our desire for an accessible coast into charitable endeavours and, mostly, the National Trust.

The Trust may have been born by the sea but its early years were mostly spent elsewhere. During its first three decades, it only acquired a handful of coastal nature reserves (Barras Nose at Tintagel, Cornwall, Blakeney Point in Norfolk and the Farne Islands in Northumberland), as it focused its activities inland, battling to preserve the Lake District and the Peak District before taking responsibility for saving great stately homes threatened with demolition between the wars. In the spring of 1965, however, the charity turned decisively to our shores. It launched Enterprise Neptune, vowing to raise £2 million (the equivalent of more than £35 million today) to save the most precious portions of coast from rampaging tourism and industry. Envisioned as a temporary campaign, Neptune was so popular it went on and on, to date raising more than £65 million for coastal purchases as well as acquiring many more acres of donated land. The Trust safeguarded 175 miles of coastline in Neptune's first decade, 99 miles in its second and now protects a total of 742 miles.

In effect, the Neptune coast is contemporary common land. Unlike the National Trust's stately homes, which cost so much to run that they require an admission fee, its coastline can be freely visited by anyone. By law, this land is inalienable: the Trust cannot sell it or give it away, but must manage it on behalf of the nation – for everyone, for ever. Perhaps it is significant that Neptune's biggest individual donor lives in Derbyshire, the county furthest from the sea.

Our bookshelves are groaning under the weight of guides to our coast and the National Trust itself has produced many lovely books about its own seaside estate. I hope to provide something slightly different, and tell a story about our relationship with the coast through exploring the places protected by the Trust. There are universal components to the way humans respond to the sea, but the particularity of Britain's relationship with the coast fascinates me. Rather than another geographically arranged guide to the seaside, I want to look at the different ways we relate to our shores as children, as adults and at the end of our lives. I will consider how we grow up by the sea, develop grand passions by it and are inspired to artistic creation on its shores; how the coast can be a theatre of war or a locus of religious pilgrimage; a place of work or an escape from reality.

Although any discussion of the British coast should include Scotland, the National Trust in Scotland is a completely separate organisation. Because I am exploring only the landscapes owned or influenced by the National Trust, I am saved from doing Scotland a disservice and condensing its incomparable shores into a small book. Even so, this book, like any encounter with such a vast coastline, must be deeply subjective. I cannot hope to describe every one of Neptune's 742 miles so I have instead chosen places that have entranced me with their stories. At the end of each chapter, I offer some practical information to encourage everyone to discover these magical places for themselves.

As I stood on the sunny hillside of Dinas Oleu, I wondered what the pioneering coastal conservationists would have made of our relationship with the seaside today. The Victorians Fanny Talbot and Octavia Hill would be aghast at the scale and ugliness of many coastal developments – the industrial container ports, the immense oil and gas depots, the sprawling seaside resorts – but they would be amazed by the achievements of the conservation movement they began as well. The founders of Enterprise Neptune would also be surprised: the coast has not been swamped by caravans and 'shack' development, as they feared in 1965, and many stretches they judged to be ruined by industry have been reclaimed and recovered. Our impulse to conserve the coast has shaped our shoreline more profoundly than any destructive endeavour over the last half-century.

The four-and-a-half acres of Dinas Oleu may be one of the less distinctive pieces of the Neptune coast but it perfectly represents our shores as they are today, for better and for worse. It would be easy to bash Barmouth as a seaside town in decline. But Dinas Oleu has not been spoiled by the Arousal Cafe or Vegas Amusements. The noise and the aesthetic carelessness of the early twenty-first century would horrify eminent Victorians but here, in Barmouth, human activity was low-key enough to be held in balance by the residual beauty of the place and the generosity of the sea, the beach and the sky.

It was only a short climb but we don't need much to gain a liberating sense of perspective. I descended 'the Fortress of Light' completely refreshed by half-an-hour there, exactly as Octavia Hill had intended. One gift the coast will never fail to provide is a sense that we are small and the world is wide; that it is unchanging while we scurry about; that our time is short but the waves and the rocks have all the time in the world. This should leave us diminished and scared, but somehow it doesn't. We are put in our place, and can view our hopes, triumphs, failures and anxieties as the ephemeral things they truly are.

## Explorations of Neptune

The short, steep walk up to **Dinas Oleu** exemplifies Octavia Hill's vision of outdoor sitting rooms – green spaces, accessible to everyone, close to towns. Many people would not give Barmouth a second glance but it has plenty of charm, a gorgeous beach and a stunning position overlooking Cardigan Bay. Park by the beach (or take the scenic Cambrian Coast railway), cross the railway line by the station and walk up Beach Road. Turn right onto the High Street and look for a tiny lane on your left. Follow it up the hill and five minutes' exertion earns a glorious, almost aerial view of the coast from the first piece of land ever protected by the National Trust. Take a maze of little paths through the gorse, and you will find a rock engraved with a typically Victorian poem by Canon Rawnsley, one of the Trust's founders, celebrating the 'ocean's wild infinitude'. The hillside is also home to 'The Frenchman's Grave', the resting place of Auguste Guyard, a visionary philosopher who was given a home in a model community in Barmouth established by the social reformer John Ruskin.

### OS Map

Explorer OL18 Harlech, Porthmadog & Y Bala

### Nearest railway station

Barmouth, 1/4 mile

## Further Reading

Nicholas Crane, *Coast: Our Island Story*, BBC Books, 2010

Sophia Kingshill and Jennifer Westwood, *The Fabled Coast*, Random House, 2012

Jonathan Raban, *Coasting*, Collins Harvill, 1986

Paul Theroux, *The Kingdom by the Sea*, Penguin, 1983

# 1

# Childhood

*Crackington Haven / Stackpole / Scolt Head Island*

Scolt Head Island

Stackpole
(Broadhaven South)

Crackington Haven

My first memory of the sea is sitting on a varnished wooden bench in an orange life jacket that was far too big for me and listening to a medley of unfamiliar noises: shrieks of wading birds and the *chink-chink-slap* of the rigging on the sailing boats clustered in the small creek. The exotic tang of oilskins, salt and muddy marsh was overpowered by the blue-smoked stench of the boat's engine and then we were on our way: my family, in a small boat, with a big, swaggering sort of man, curly haired and deeply tanned, at the helm.

I was two, although in truth I could've been three, four or five, because for four successive May half-terms at the end of the 1970s we holidayed on Scolt Head Island. A remote and rarely visited hump of dune on the Norfolk coast, Scolt is separated from the mainland at low tide by a modest, albeit treacherous creek; at high tide, it appears truly adrift from the coast; from the air, its four miles of sand dunes and salt marsh can sometimes look like a human embryo.

The only island on the east coast between the Farne Islands and Essex, Scolt's value was quickly recognised by geologists and early naturalists as a sanctuary for birds and a breeding ground for terns, those swallows of the sea. It was one of the first pieces of coast acquired by the National Trust, in 1923, for £500.

Population: one; amenities: a wooden shack called the Hut which eschews electricity, toilets and running water – it may be the finest example of an offshore barrier island in Britain but a bleak, treeless place is not an obvious choice for a seaside holiday except for lovers of bracing solitude, as my parents were. Plenty of us covet wilderness today, and places such as Scolt are cherished as rare wild corners of crowded southern England, but it's hard to imagine that the island would instil in a young child an unbreakable attachment to the beach.

I was certainly alarmed by our choppy little trip in the boat manned by Scolt's sole summer inhabitant, its wind-bronzed warden, Bob Chestney, and discombobulated by life on the island. The wide horizons of the Norfolk coast are an uncomfortable fit for the low horizons of a child. And so my early memories of the coast are not snapshots of a picture-postcard idyll but epic struggles up mountainous dunes, sand blowing in my eyes, marram grass whipping my legs. The beach was a wind-blasted horror and the salt marsh was where Daddy dug big holes in which to deposit our smelly buckets of poo. Children are conservative adherents to routine and security and my one happy memory is of playing with my Matchbox cars on the cobbled area outside the Hut, which faced south and was mercifully sheltered from the north wind.

These recollections were fresh in my mind when I met Tony Flux, a coastal adviser for the National Trust. 'If you put a young child on a beach, aged four, five, ten, they will amuse themselves all day,' he said. 'The most they'll need is an ice cream or a bucket and spade, and they won't feel the cold. Just playing on the sand or in the water must have a quasi-religious, deep-seated connection for us.' Increasingly, he said, the most inspiring part of his job on the Dorset coast, England's only natural World Heritage Site, was facilitating school groups' rare excursions into 'nature'.

We can ascribe our love of the coast to the fact it is the most dramatic arena for showcasing natural things, from waves and whales to seahorses and cormorants, or to nature in another sense: we came out of the sea, evolving from aquatic creatures, and we are 66 per cent, or thereabouts, water (and children are even more watery – we become desiccated as we grow older). There is obviously something universal about our attraction to the sea. But our bond with the coast is not explained in any meaningful way by vague theories about our ocean-dwelling ancestors. Perhaps, in Britain at least, our sense of connection derives more strongly from our formative experiences. Although my own first introduction to the coast was far from idyllic, it established an enduring hold over my imagination. And, as my exploration of our relationship with the seaside coincided with my young twins' first forays onto the beach, I wondered if I would observe the same bond being forged in my children too. When she was tiny, my daughter Esme offered her precious dummy to the moon, a relic, it seemed to me, of our moon-worshipping selves. Her first trip to the beach as a walking person was to the shingle ridge of Blakeney Point, Norfolk, in winter. Here, she met unattractive mud-brown North Sea waves for the first time and hurled herself at them. Was this some primeval vestige of our sea-being selves?

Just as I had experienced as a child, Esme and her twin sister, Milly, were taken on a boat trip in uncertain weather from Morston Creek to Blakeney Point in North Norfolk, where grey and common seals haul themselves onto the sandbanks like sunbathing tourists. Even months after the trip, both girls referred to it. Milly remembered the boat, in which she had leapt about, looking excitedly at the banana-shaped seals. Esme's memory, however, was simply that she had 'wanted Mummy' – and she had. Usually a bold extrovert, she had spent the whole trip huddled in my arms, head down and asking for her mum, who had waved us off from the muddy creek.

*

The twins' first proper holiday by the sea came during a June forsaken by summer, when Lisa and I took Esme and Milly to Crackington Haven on the north coast of Cornwall, part of a four-mile stretch of mighty granite cliffs owned by the National Trust. 'Haggard cliffs, of every ugly altitude, are as common as sea-fowl along the line of coast between Exmoor and Land's End,' wrote Thomas Hardy in 1873. Between Crackington Haven and High Cliff (at 732ft, the highest in Cornwall) dramatic rocks are folded into zigzags. Crackington gave its name to an ancient geological phenomenon, the Crackington formation, a sequence of sandstone and dark-grey shale contorted by the movement of the earth millions of years ago. In the eye-blink of more recent human history, this coast had been steadily gentrified – tidied up and emptied out – after decades of being overshadowed by the easy-on-the-eye coves of South Cornwall. My best friend from university had grown up in nearby Treknow. In the 1980s his school bus used to pick up dozens of children from beach-side villages. Now, when the bus pulled up by the pub in Crackington Haven, a single child got on. Almost every house with a sea view was a second home for someone of wealth and taste, and Thom Yorke from the band Radiohead currently owned the beachside house next to our holiday cottage.

At high tide, Crackington Haven was a small ridge of flat grey stones but, after two hours or so, the departing tide exposed a bay of shiny, purple-grey sand, encircled by rough, rockpool-rich granite edges. This sheltered beach was a long way from the desolation of Scolt Head Island and I assumed it would be paradise for the twins. Milly loved climbing and exploring – so she would adore clambering into the rock pools. At home, Esme's favourite occupation was eating soil and plunging through the long grass of the cemetery behind our house – on the beach, she could run wild and scoff as much sand as she desired. Plenty of their picture books featured sandcastles and buckets and spades, so their seaside schooling had already begun. Like most other over-protective modern parents, we also bought them lurid little wetsuits to help them keep warm when wet, and plastic jelly-shoes to ease their passage over the rocks.

So it was a bit of a shock when we plonked the girls on the wet sand where miniature streams drained towards the retreating ocean, and they clung to our legs, unimpressed by the cold water, damp sand and unforgiving westerlies. The streams were perfect for my favourite childhood beach activity, building dams, so I sat down and created one, expecting the twins to quickly forget their fears and follow my enthusiasm for messing about on the beach. But they didn't. Esme clung and cried whenever we tried to stand her on her own two feet. Reluctantly, Milly eventually collaborated in some sandcastle play by destroying whatever I constructed.

During five days of chilly coastal indoctrination, Milly became enthusiastic about finding rockpool snails (perhaps because they were familiar from books: snails star in children's literature surprisingly often) and Esme learned to shout 'Sea!' from the comfort of our arms while she watched Atlantic breakers worry the stones. Although she devoured mouthfuls of wet sand on every beach trip, this was not nearly as moreish as soil. On our final day, after I'd spent an hour gently lowering her towards various objects of fascination – strutting herring gulls, slobby pink-and-beige-spotted anemones and strings of seaweed with watery pods you could pop – finally, she was off, on her own legs, futilely chasing gulls like a puppy. But still, there were no tantrums when we headed home and she remained far happier careering around the living room of the holiday cottage.

I am not sure that we are born to love the coast. The beach and the sea beyond it are too big and frightening, too wet and cold. Young children seem to have instinctively suburban tastes: they appreciate people, shelter and small things. If Milly and Esme carry any of their own memories of Crackington into adulthood, they would probably be of the first ever ice creams they demolished from the comfort of the cottage living room or the lurid pattern on their bedroom curtains.

But, of course, whatever hazy memories they hold will be augmented by what Lisa and I tell them about that first beach holiday and our own adult conceptions of how children experience the coast.

Over the past two centuries, the beach has become the nation's favourite holiday destination; more recently, it has become the last place in the country where children can roam free, the ultimate sand (or shingle) pit, soft-play zone and water park. Whether or not the coast was our first love as children, it is no wonder we spend much of our spare time seeking it out as adults.

Young children can be conduits for parents back to their own childhoods and a way of retrieving or rewriting memories to find delight in things that were scary and fun in things that were dull. A child may also occasionally represent an older, unvarnished personhood – a human as we might have been before the complicated accumulations of social rules, adult responsibilities and modern technology. Every small child we'd seen on Crackington Haven beach was being taught sandcastle construction by grown-ups seeking to recapture the lost idyll of early childhood. 'History is a child building a sandcastle by the sea,' said Heraclitus, 'and that child is the whole majesty of man's power in the world.' But is our love of the beach solely prescribed by older generations' nostalgia for a nebulous past? Not completely. The coast might be a hostile environment for toddlers but, for older children, it can become an unequivocal pleasure. When we are big enough, the sea's meeting with the land seems to start to speak to us directly, and independently of the joy adults instruct us to find in it.

I had an opportunity to learn more about older children's feelings for the coast when I met Phoebe, Hannah, Mark and Kyle, who were ten, and Isobel, nine, on the Pembrokeshire coast of Wales. These Year 5 pupils from Bloxham Primary, Oxfordshire, were spending their Easter holiday at Stackpole, an outdoor activity centre run by the

National Trust in the grounds of a stately home that the charity had been unable to save from demolition. Despite living about as far from the sea as possible in Britain, their love of the coast was unequivocal, and global. Mark talked about his time on Pacific Beach in California; Kyle the warm sea on holiday in his granddad's villa in Turkey ('You get in the sea and you don't realise you're in it sometimes – apart from the fact it's wet'); Hannah her holiday in Lanzarote. But there was no beach snobbery going on. Phoebe was equally impressed by her pebbly beach near Southsea, and Isobel was fond of the beach huts of Frinton-on-Sea. Ten is an interesting age: children simultaneously hold sophisticated views and yet still love uncomplicated play. These were the things they said they liked doing on the beach: playing with friends, jumping over the waves, burying people in the sand, paddling, messing about with a ball in the sea, body-boarding, long walks, beach volleyball, bicycle kicks in the sea, and chucking pebbles in the water for the dogs and then standing nearby to get a shower when they shook their coats.

The previous day, the children had visited Broad Haven South, a sandy, dune-backed cove of perfection between two headlands, one of the Neptune coast's many jewels. The blue water was adorned by a jutting rock in the bay which Isobel likened to 'a gorilla looking out to sea', and lent a pleasing sense of perspective to the scene. The children were very taken by the fact that this remote cove had once been a private beach belonging to Stackpole's aristocratic owners, the Cawdors. Isobel wondered if living there would be 'a bit boring sometimes because you'd just have the same people on that beach – you'd not meet new people', but Phoebe was convinced 'it would be kind of cool' because 'you could play and go out whenever you like'.

The issue of a private beach touched on perhaps the two most important qualities of the coast for children: a social space for meeting new people and a place where children could be free. Hannah's holiday in Lanzarote encapsulated both. 'I met this new girl and we went everywhere together,' she said, 'and we went onto the beaches on our own.'

Anxiety about children no longer running free is a middle-class cliché today but it reflects a contemporary truth that a combination of rational fears about traffic, irrational fears about stranger-danger and a mixture of rational and irrational health and safety concerns has made it much harder for young children to hang about outdoors as they did just a generation ago. The beach may be the last public place where children are truly let off the leash.

'You can do anything,' nodded Phoebe. 'You can just be free. You can just run around and everything. You don't have to stay in the house every day.'

'I like it because there's not many rules,' said Isobel. 'You can be yourself around other people, and not be somebody who is stuck in a cage.'

'We're all on the beach and we've got no limits,' added Hannah.

'Because there's no one you know,' said Mark, 'you don't feel embarrassed about being babyish.' This was unexpected but I knew what he meant: there were no pretensions, he could play on the sand; the coast was where children could be children.

I wondered whether part of the coast's pleasure was universal to any holiday: if parents are relaxed and having fun then it is nicer for the children. But the ten-year-olds were more interested in discussing their dogs' enjoyment of the beach, and barely mentioned the grown-ups. 'They just let us run off,' said Isobel. 'We get freedom from our parents, which is quite nice.' The beach is exciting for older children precisely because parents dissolve into the background.

Given that children's right to roam has been radically curtailed in most of our country, it will be a challenge to keep the beach as a place of freedom for the young in the future. The Bloxham Primary pupils said they would prefer a quiet beach with lots of wildlife to a coast crammed with people and shops, but I wondered whether these answers were the recent legacy of some healthy brainwashing at Stackpole: they had seen otters, a pike, a heron, swans, a blue tit (really close) and millions of baby elvers on this magnificent estate. Eventually, some gentle dissent emerged. 'Sometimes you like a bit of fun, when it's a bit noisier,' said Isobel. 'Sometimes you're not allowed to do many things when there's wildlife around,' added Phoebe. 'On other beaches you're more free because there's less wildlife.'

In those ten words, Phoebe encapsulated the dilemma for the Neptune coast in years to come. Conservation invariably means rules, and rules constrain freedom. It is currently fashionable for conservationists to pretend there is no tension between people enjoying a natural area and wildlife, but of course there always will be. How we manage this will define how much freedom we give our children and how well we protect our coast.

Before they left Stackpole for further explorations of the stunning Pembrokeshire coast, the children described their ideal beach. It was sandy, warm and backed by classic cliffs and sand dunes. Isobel thought there should be some barbecues and 'some quiet music with the wildlife there, and people sunbathing and playing on the sand, and lots of waves to play in'. And the colour of the sea?

'The lightest of light blues,' said Isobel.

'See-through,' suggested Phoebe.

'Greeny-blueish,' added Isobel.

'Turquoise,' finished Kyle, and they all nodded in agreement.

If children open a door into forgotten memories, so do places. Scolt Head Island was a visible memorial of a time in my life that had almost vanished from view. I realised now that one of the reasons why our holidays there remained so hazy in my memory was because my parents had erased the island from our family's mental map of Norfolk. Something happened on Scolt in the Whitsun holiday of 1980 and we never stayed in the Hut again. Mum and Dad seemed almost traumatised by this loss, and occasionally spoke of Scolt wistfully, as one might of a lost love. Our exit from this Arcadia was painful, and I had never properly understood why. What caused us to leave and why had we never gone back?

By returning, I hoped to understand why I adored the seaside, despite rather unpromising beginnings. And, if I was going in search of childhood feelings, it seemed that Scolt was the perfect place to recapture it. In a brilliant essay about his visit to the island, Caspar Henderson described it as a place for something better than dreaming – hypnagogia, the transitional state between sleep and wakefulness. 'Psychologists suggest that this state of mind is typical of very young children, who have little sense of the past and future but live intensely in the present and thereby experience it in a way that adults seldom do,' wrote Henderson. 'But hypnagogia, or something like it, can be important for adults too, allowing us to differently imagine the past and future as well the dimensions of the present moment.'

Not long after our Crackington vacation, I headed to Scolt, alone. Although it was owned by the National Trust, Scolt was leased to Natural England, the government body responsible for conservation, and Scolt's only residence was still the Hut where we had stayed those four half-terms. The Hut was barred to holidaymakers these days, and the only people permitted to stay on the island were bona fide academics such as the Cambridge don who was a world leading expert in mud snails. Luckily, Scolt's warden agreed that this book might qualify as a form of coastal research, and I was kindly granted a week in the Hut. This time, there was no Bob Chestney, the old warden, to take me to Scolt in his boat. So I walked across the maze of marshes and creeks at low tide. Parking at Burnham Deepdale, I set out early one morning in July, following footprints in the mud to the edge of Norton Creek, which made Scolt an island. I had waded across similar tidal creeks at nearby Wells-next-the-Sea and Thornham and they could be surprisingly intimidating. The water was brown, the bottom not visible and the tidal currents felt like they could take you off your feet if they chose. Norton Creek was barely 50 metres wide at low tide but my heart still beat a little faster as I sank into the mud and stubbed a toe on a mussel bed that showed up as a dark line in the water. Although the waves barely covered my knees on this crossing, I still stopped on far bank and looked back to the mainland with a sense of exhilaration. I had made it back to my childhood island.

In geological terms, Scolt was a babe in arms, perhaps only 800 years old, constantly growing and dissolving, and made of sand and shingle. Originally a ridge of stones lying in the shallow North Sea, it was pushed landwards by north winds and westwards by longshore drift. The sea's ceaseless workings were constantly adding shingle ridges to the end of the island, which reached out westwards and were then pushed south, inland. Sand dunes formed on these ridges and the accretion of mud and small channels in between became salt marsh, an intricate web of capillaries that inhaled and exhaled sea water at high and low tide. Each ridge and marsh bore a name: Wire Hills, Long Hills, Plantago Marsh, Plover Marsh. A 1954 map showed the island ending at Bight Hills but there was now a kilometre of new vegetated land to the west: Scolt was still growing with the vigour of a child.

The North Sea could be many things – including a surprising cobalt blue – but it could never be turquoise, and my childhood beach, Scolt Head Island, was an enormous contrast to our Crackington holiday: instead of the monumental black cliffs of North Cornwall and the vivid rolling Atlantic I found a muddy smudge of marsh and a flimsy sea washed with a muted palette of olives, duns and pewters. For the first couple of hours trudging across Scolt, I was underwhelmed. This empty island of tawny sand dunes and flat grey-green marsh seemed bereft of anything alive or arresting. Why would people come here if they could visit Cornwall? But North Norfolk has a subtle charm that seeps into you like the trickle of the incoming tide, less bombastic than awesome cliffs but both soothing and strangely uncompromising.

'Our landscape is seven-eighths sky,' wrote the children's author Kevin Crossley-Holland, who lives on the North Norfolk coast, 'a vast inverted arena, a sky-dome in which there are often several simultaneous theatres of action. It's a landscape of horizontals – skyline, ribbed fields, decaying ribs of boats – in which verticals, including human beings, often look arresting.'

I climbed Scolt's steepest dune, Norfolk's highest, its sheltered hollows filled with the delicate pink triangles of pyramidal orchids, and down onto the beach. Scuttering footsteps like a skipping child sounded on the sand behind me – an empty case of whelk eggs scudding on the breeze. Ruby-red-eyed oystercatchers and brilliantly camouflaged ringed plovers, known locally as stone-runners, sidled away from their nests above the strandline.

The ringed plover is a squat, timid and extremely personable bird with its white breast, black neck and bright yellow legs and beak. We may spend childhoods on the beach but we are rarely born there. Nesting on a beach is a hazardous lifestyle choice and the ringed plover has an impressive array of defences against predators such as gulls and stoats. Its colouring makes it virtually invisible when it is sitting among Norfolk's flint pebbles; its eggs are even more so, a dainty speckled grey and almost impossible for a novice to find for they resemble small stones; its long-legged young can scoot along the beach as soon as they are born; and, most cunning of all, the female will hold a wing limply in the air, drag it on the ground or collapse as if fatally wounded to convince predators to stop searching for her nest and pursue her instead. None of these wiles, however, was any use against the egg thieves.

*

The early naturalists persuaded the National Trust to buy Scolt because of its colonies of terns, the chalk-winged creatures that nest in their thousands on the island's sandbanks, and a warden has protected these birds – from foxes, and human thieves – ever since. Emma

Turner, the nature reserve's first 'Watcher', caused a sensation in 1924 when she took up residence in the newly built Hut. A gentleman of Fleet Street visited and dubbed the spinster ornithologist 'The Loneliest Woman in England' for her solitary vocation to protect the island's tern colonies. Other journalists 'followed in a bewildering stream', recalled Miss Turner in her memoirs, 'till in desperation I said to the ferry-man, "Drown the next."' Whatever the ferry-man did, it worked, for the unwelcome visits ceased.

It was an unusual job for a woman and Miss Turner was a singular person. Alfred Steers, a Cambridge professor who studied Scolt for sixty-five years and wrote the authoritative account of its natural riches, once found Miss Turner in the sand dunes, engaged in pistol practice, apparently so she could protect herself from unsavoury characters. Egg collecting was pursued with a mania by the Victorians but became frowned upon as birds became rarer. Collecting tern eggs had been made illegal in 1924, the year Miss Turner arrived on Scolt, with later laws strengthening the protection for nesting birds, but collectors continued to slip onto the island and seek out the eggs of its seabirds. They particularly coveted the eggs of Sandwich terns because of their intricate markings; like clouds, their eggs sketched butterflies, ducks, even an elephant, and could fetch £20 each in the 1950s, the equivalent of more than £450 today.

I walked towards the Hut, Miss Turner's former home and the place I most vividly remembered on the island. Constructed from dark oak shingles with a tall tiled roof and round stone chimney, it looked like a fairytale house, set on a south-facing plateau on the island's biggest dune. Turner's successors lived in a smaller shed closer to the ternery and the Hut was given over to academics to study Scolt's geology and ecology (and the occasional holiday jolly such as that enjoyed by my parents).

Most things that loom large in childhood are diminished by the present but the Hut was unexpectedly substantial as I drew closer, its dark boards bleached grey by salt and sun. I climbed up the sand dune steps – one fashioned from an old fish crate – and onto the cobbled patio where I once played with my toy cars. It triggered another discomforting coastal memory: one year, I'd lost my toy VW Kombi in the sand and, despite the whole family combing the area, this precious orange vehicle was swallowed by mysterious seaside forces, never to be seen again. Every summer when I returned to the beach, I would look for it again, always in vain.

The Hut's door opened with a creak and I saw that, oddly, my memory of its interior was like a mirror, the wrong way round. Two lamps were suspended from the high ceiling of the living room. The ceiling and walls were of the same black-brown oak timbers as outside and a large brick fireplace dominated the left-hand wall. There was a gas cooker and a worktop and a plank of wood for a desk beneath the window, which faced south over the marshes, towards the mainland. It was like the insides of an old ship, creaking and groaning in the wind, rapidly warming in the sun and quickly cooling at night.

The logistics that had dissuaded me from bringing the twins with me were unaltered from thirty-five years before: I'd arrived with all the food I'd need for my stay and would have to take home all my rubbish, use a bucket filled with chemicals in an outdoor shed and dig a hole in the marshes to bury my excrement. There was still no heating or running water, just an outside tap gushing rainwater from a tank frequented by drowned voles. I could boil this water on the one luxury: a gas stove. Actually, there was now another: a plug socket, courtesy of a tiny solar panel connected to a car battery to charge a phone or laptop. Disappointingly, there was also an excellent mobile signal. When I stayed there as a child, if we needed help we would have had to hoist a ship's emergency cone on the flagpole behind the Hut and someone on the mainland would allegedly notice and send out a boat.

The Hut was the spiritual home of all who loved the island and its dark walls were hung with old photographs of various gatherings. In July 1928, the Hut was surrounded by the aristocratic Committee of the National Trust: six men in tweeds, ties and hats, with the humble Watcher, Charles Chestney, peering from the window. An unnamed photograph of another celebratory gathering from the 1970s featured twenty-seven adults and four children in flares and anoraks. It was a birthday party for Professor Alfred Steers and there were three people I recognised: at the front, beaming and girlish, was my mum; in the middle, at the back, dark and extremely bearded, was my dad. And to the left stood the tanned, self-assured boatman from my memory: Bob Chestney, the legendary warden of Scolt. The photograph was taken in 1979, the year before our final visit to the island.

Reassuringly for my sense of my childhood, Bob Chestney was exactly as I remembered. The description of his father, Charles, by Jacquetta Hawkes, the archaeologist and wife of J. B. Priestley, one of many literary visitors to Scolt, could equally have applied to his son: 'Chestney, a Brancaster man, had a large quiet body and a magnificent head, set with a formal pattern of curls, now white. He, more than any other man I have known, seems to draw strength and repose from his countryside, that coast of tidal creeks, wide saltmarshes and dunes.'

On the wooden bookshelves of the Hut, between guides to wild flowers and thrillers left behind by visiting academics, was a faded copy of Bob Chestney's autobiography dating from 1993. After a pasta supper in profound silence, I settled down to read it in the tiny west-facing back bedroom, a mouse pattering in the walls.

Bob Chestney had left school at fifteen, was badly injured in the war, and became a brilliant self-taught ornithologist who was employed as Scolt's third Watcher after his father, Charles, for thirty-six years from 1950. He was a successful and highly respected warden. In the 1960s, he realised that bird-loving visitors who enjoyed the spectacle of striding through the tern colony as thousands of screaming birds rose up around them were inadvertently causing breeding pairs to abandon their eggs, so he closed the area to tourists. This was a controversial step at the time but he won over disappointed visitors by personally conducting popular tours of the island and its terns, from a distance. Thanks to these restrictions and his eighty-hour-week vigils during nesting season to protect the birds from predators, breeding numbers soared. From the 1930s to the '60s, there were 1,300 pairs of Sandwich terns breeding at Scolt and Blakeney Point, Norfolk's other significant tern colony, which was also owned by the National Trust. Chestney's control of visitors on Scolt helped numbers increase to 4,850 pairs in 1975. At its peak, Chestney – who enjoyed a fierce rivalry with the warden of Blakeney over tern numbers – claimed his island was home to 22,000 Sandwich terns including fledged young, and 3,000 common terns.

Nothing moved on Scolt without Chestney knowing about it, and that included egg thieves. The professionals were easy to spot, he recounted in his memoirs: they arrived in pairs, carrying rucksacks and binoculars they seldom actually used. 'I rarely prosecuted, preferring to discuss the ethics of the hobby,' wrote Chestney who appeared to enjoy his role as policeman. He was lenient if he caught egg-stealing boys, to whom this hobby might prove an introduction to a passion for wildlife, but on at least one occasion he called in the police when he rumbled 'privileged' egg thieves: two Leeds University students were fined £25 for stealing eggs.

Chestney excelled at his job but he was also patronised, and it gave him a chip on his shoulder. Social divisions were evaporating but there was still a gulf between this self-taught local man and the visiting academics who flocked to Scolt with their learning and high-handed ways. 'My father had taught me the "tricks of the trade" while discussing the many awkward customers he had encountered,' he wrote in his memoirs, which can be self-aggrandising but are always entertaining. 'One should never appear too clever with know-alls. It was often an advantage to appear "thick"; with a Norfolk accent it was possible to achieve the impossible! My father and I considered ourselves to be showmen – we had the greatest show on earth.'

I read on and eventually fell asleep, waking in the night to find black ants marching over me. That morning, as I washed myself under the tap on the dunes above the wiggly brown creeks that turned the salt marsh into a jigsaw puzzle, the first presence in the sky was not a tern or a lark but an RAF jet, a familiar sound from childhood when Cold War manoeuvres made daily incursions into East Anglia's air space. Seconds later, I spotted a hobby, all sharp angles like a 1980s supercar, dashing over the roof of the Hut in mad pursuit of a swallow. It was a relief to find the pair of swallows that nested under the eaves were still feeding their young the following day. I heard a *chh-tee-tee-tee-tee* as a whimbrel flew over; a large wading bird whose migration was said to presage the approach of autumn. Coming a week after the longest day of a late summer, this seemed cruelly premature but it was a gorgeous sound on the still air. I realised that one of the loveliest things about Scolt was the lack of human noise. Some people found it eerie and asked if the Hut was haunted. Wandering the empty island, I often felt as if I was being watched; I kept expecting someone – the warden, or a daytripper – to appear over the dunes. Gazing down onto the beach that evening, I was startled to see a figure swimming in the warm North Sea. I looked again: it was a big bull seal.

Scolt turns every visitor into a watcher, and the jolt of seeing the man/seal reminded me of the moment from childhood when I spotted two vertical lines on the beach. These lines strutted along the top of the beach and turned horizontal every so often. Dad trained his binoculars on them and two men came into focus. They were bending down over the nests of oystercatchers and ringed plovers and were picking up their beautiful eggs.

This picture was my only memory of our last family holiday on Scolt, so I separately asked my parents what they remembered of the

Whitsun bank holiday of 1980. Dad told me about the 'Expeditions': it was our name for little walks we conducted to collect shells or have birds or flowers pointed out to us. We were returning from an Expedition to a ridge of dunes called House Hills when we saw the eggs thieves on the beach. The tern colonies were found at the western end of Scolt and this was where the warden concentrated his efforts but these men had chosen to plunder the quieter eastern end.

Mum hurried us home while Dad stalked the men. Through his binoculars, he watched them post an old margarine container into a rabbit hole. When they had gone, he found the container full of tissue paper and stolen eggs. They had stashed some of their loot to collect later. There were no telephones on the island and the emergency cone on the Hut's flagpole might take hours to be spotted. Dad feared the men would simply walk off the island at low tide.

Luckily, because it was the nesting season, Bob Chestney was installed in his shack at the western end of Scolt so Dad picked up the container of eggs – the proof – and carefully ran three miles down the deserted beach to the warden's HQ. Breathless, he told Chestney about the men, and the direction they were headed. Chestney, Dad recalled, told him he should've left the eggs where they were and then the men could be caught when they collected their incriminating loot. And then he shrugged his shoulders. The men, disappearing across the salt marsh towards the mainland, were going to be allowed to escape. Chestney appeared to be too busy to act, or not bothered about the loss of a few eggs from the eastern end of the island.

Dad walked away feeling helpless and crestfallen. 'I was completely confused,' he told me. 'Here's this hero who was held to be responsible for the ternery and all good things on Scolt and this was going on behind his back and he wasn't strongly concerned. I was shocked.' When he got back to the Hut, Mum said he'd looked shattered: the incident had destroyed his sense of Scolt as a watery Arcadia, a small wilderness that people could not exploit or despoil. It could no longer be a holiday for Dad, or a place of retreat, if bad things happened and good men did nothing about them. As a member of the group of naturalists and academics who oversaw the running of Scolt, Dad also felt conflicted. He should report Chestney for this, and yet he felt that would be traducing someone who worked hard for the island and was deserving of his good reputation. So, as he often did when embroiled in conflict, Dad retreated. We never took the boat to Scolt for a holiday again and my earliest recollections of my childhood by the coast are cast in shadow. Philip Larkin's famous poem about parental inheritance describes how misery is handed on, deepening 'like a coastal shelf'. The seaside may be mostly the opposite, a place for the accumulation of happy memories, but we are complicated creatures and there will always be shade as well as sunshine on our shoreline.

I wondered about the reasons for Chestney's inaction as I explored the eastern end of Scolt, waist-high seablite or *Suaeda vera*, an indestructible matt-grey-brown-green bush, tearing at my legs. These marshes gave the impression of being open and simple but, like the past, they were full of unexpected secrets. Perhaps Bob Chestney had grown tired of confrontation, and weary of pursuing egg thieves when it was difficult to get a conviction. Maybe he thought Dad had accidentally sabotaged any chance of proving they were thieves by moving their stash of eggs and pursuit was pointless. I remembered something that Richard Barnes, a Cambridge professor who has visited Scolt every year since 1971 to study its mud snails, told me about Chestney. 'I liked him but he didn't like academics,' he said. 'If you started to tell him things, he'd go right off you. He liked to trip you up into showing how little you know.'

My dad has always been the humblest of men but I wonder if Chestney saw Dad's breathless intervention as another know-all academic telling him what to do.

I would never know the truth about why Chestney chose not to pursue those particular men but his guardianship of Scolt brought about the highest tern population in its recorded history. After Chestney retired in 1986, tern numbers suddenly plummeted. Some people blamed his successor, an outsider who put local people's backs up and didn't last long, but Scolt's current resident warden, an affable, hugely knowledgeable man called Neil Lawton, pointed out the real culprit. 'When Bob retired, the fox population exploded,' said Lawton. In October 1986 a vixen arrived on Scolt. A dog fox followed and they produced four cubs in the spring. These were killed but the adults survived. 'Thus began a vulpine takeover of the island,' wrote Chestney. In 1989 just 10 common tern chicks fledged, alongside 12 little terns; 1,052 Sandwich tern pairs nested but none fledged at all. 'To watch the most thriving tern colony in Europe virtually disappear in just four seasons, after sixty-one years of Chestney effort, has not been merely disappointing – it has been heartbreaking,' wrote Chestney in 1993. That year, the tern breeding colony was re-established on Scolt after the wardens waged war on the foxes and Chestney, who passed away in 2001, at least lived to see the terns thriving on the island once again. Today, thanks to the labours of wardens Michael Rooney and Neil Lawton, Scolt is one of the most important places for ground-nesting seabirds in the country. In 2013, the island hosted the UK's largest colony of little terns; it also guards more pairs of breeding ringed plovers than anywhere else in England. In 2014, 1,050 pairs of Sandwich tern nested on Scolt and fledged 625 young.

Before I left Scolt, I took a swim off its empty beach, accompanied by little terns that suddenly plunged into the water around me, as the bigger, shaggier-headed Sandwich terns cruised overhead with wings of aluminium. It was exactly as it had been described seventy years before by Henry Williamson, the author of *Tarka the Otter* who moved from Devon to the Norfolk coast for several years: 'In a warm current flowing into the harbour from beyond the point of sand-hills, where white-winged and distant terns were screaming, we bathed ourselves, while the gentle flow bore us along the ribbed sands.'

I had wondered whether the discomfort I'd experienced on Scolt as a child would linger for me as an adult, but all I experienced here now, drifting about in its waters, was a deep dreamy comfort. The island's first Watcher, Emma Turner, grew up in inland Kent but immediately found tranquillity on Scolt. It was 'not an indolent peace, but rather that of rest in motion', she wrote. 'That first day of solitude has bitten deep into my memory; it filled me with wild joy to think that for months I should possess the island with all its mystery and loveliness.'

As I floated in the North Sea, I considered Caspar Henderson's idea that Scolt was a site for hypnagogia. I guess it is obvious that we can reach such a fluid and imaginative state of consciousness in a liminal landscape like Scolt, a small coastal island that flexes like a living thing and grows like a child. It becomes easier to see how we might be affected more than we realise by our surroundings if we are lucky enough to spend time in one of the last wildernesses of southern Britain. Here it is possible to return to a childlike state, alone with the sea and sand and silence, completely absorbed in the present moment.

## Explorations of Neptune

**Scolt Head Island** is one of the best nature reserves in southern Britain because so few people visit. The most popular way to reach it is by (private) boat from Burnham Overy Staithe – the eastern end of Scolt is an excellent spot for a beach picnic – and one or two local people offer limited private tours. Personally, I wouldn't recommend visiting the island between April and July because it is the bird nesting season and Scolt is only so good for ground-nesting birds because they are left in peace. I walked onto Scolt at low tide but Natural England's wardens discourage this because each year they have to rescue visitors who become stranded on an uninhabited tidal island with no accommodation. If you are determined to walk over, you need to obtain an up-to-date tide table and check with locals: there is no sure-fire rule about a safe time to cross either side of low tide. Camping is prohibited, the Hut is not open to the public and there are no toilet facilities.

### *Walk*

If you do make it onto the eastern end of Scolt, there is a lovely walk west along the deserted beach until you reach the highest dune system on your left, at which point several small paths meander up to the most vertiginous point on Scolt, above the Hut, which offers a surprisingly excellent view along the North Norfolk coastline. The far western end of the island is where the terns nest, and this is out of bounds to visitors. There are a few paths along the back of the dunes through the salt marsh but these are rough and it is surprisingly easy to get lost. Scolt is wonderful. I'm sure you won't spoil it but please go quietly, tread carefully, do not disturb nesting birds, take all your rubbish home and don't pick anything – it is a criminal offence to remove *anything* from a National Nature Reserve such as Scolt. Most importantly of all, don't bring a dog. And if you find a small orange toy car in the sand, please get in touch!

### OS Maps
Explorer 251, Norfolk Coast Central
Explorer 250, Norfolk Coast West
### Nearest railway station
King's Lynn, 22 miles; the scenic Coasthopper bus service runs from King's Lynn bus station to Brancaster Staithe (see www.coasthopper. co.uk/ for details).
### Websites
National Nature Reserve
www.naturalengland.org.uk/ourwork/conservation/designations/ nnr/1006129.aspx

**Crackington Haven** is a rare sliver of sandy beach in North Cornwall, and a bustling and increasingly affluent little resort in summer. The coast path all along North Cornwall is uniformly sensational but it is still hard to beat the stretch from Crackington south to High Cliff, which was frequently shrouded in low cloud when I visited. I walked a little circuit south from Crackington, turning right up the small lane just past the harbour and following it for a mile-and-a-half, turning right at Trevigue (a National Trust farm offering holiday accommodation) to join the South West Coast Path at Strangles Beach, with High Cliff rising to the south. The walk back to Crackington is splendid and the rough grassland at Cambeak is full of flowers and butterflies.
### OS Map
Explorer 111, Bude, Boscastle & Tintagel
### Nearest railway station
Bodmin Parkway, 29 miles
### Website
www.nationaltrust.org.uk/boscastle/things-to-see-and-do/view-page/ item938668/

**Stackpole Court** has disappeared but its ambitious landscaped gardens have endured, becoming a unique nature reserve and a quirky backdrop to the perfect – and rather inaccessible – beach of Broad-haven South (not to be confused with Wales' other Broad Haven, which is more easily reached in a car). I watched an otter swimming in Bosherston Lakes, and the ruined gardens are a lovely place to explore before reaching the beach. The Stackpole Outdoor Learning Centre offers eco-educational tourism and activities including kayaking, coasteering, geocaching, bushcraft and surf camps. Another piece of Neptune coast, Freshwater West, three miles west, is one of the best surf beaches in Wales.

*Stackpole Centre*
Old Home Farm Yard
Stackpole
Pembrokeshire SA71 5DQ
*OS Map*
Explorer 36, South Pembrokeshire
*Nearest railway station*
Pembroke, 5 miles
*Websites*
www.nationaltrust.org.uk/stackpole/visitor-information/
www.nationaltrust.org.uk/stackpole-centre/

### Further Reading

Bob Chestney, *Island of Terns*, Quiller Press, 1993

Caspar Henderson, 'Hypnagogia', *Archipelago* Magazine, Issue 5, Spring 2011

# 2

# Passion

*The Undercliffs of Lyme Regis / The Menai Straits*

Plas Newydd

The Undercliffs
of Lyme Regis

Midsummer had arrived like an explosion when I reached Lyme Regis. It was hot; the light dazzled and the shade was black. Hogweed thrust floral flying saucers high in the hedgerows and the air was thick with hoverflies. Suburban Lyme was drenched in the sickly perfume of privet and roared with lawnmowers like a kind of delirium. I needed to escape into the countryside but nowhere was the heat more oppressive than in the six-mile-long, half-a-mile-wide thicket which engulfed the seashore west of Lyme Regis.

The Undercliff is the strangest stretch of coastline in Britain. It is a sign of the restless earth, a natural disaster in slow motion, a constantly slumping section of cliff and rock which makes human habitation impossible. Tilted south, the plants and animals that find home on the Undercliff are fed by sunshine and dozens of trickly springs which produce an intense temperate rainforest.

At first, Ware Commons, a cluster of meadows and thickets that is the portal into the deep Undercliff, gave the impression of being almost normal. There was open pasture and a magpie hopping around, jabbing at a tiny baby adder which coiled against its mortal enemy. Mature ashes parted to reveal the milky blue sweep of Lyme Bay, which has been described as the largest bite from the underside of England's outstretched south-west leg. Golden Cap, the tallest cliff on the south coast, was a pyramid with a flat top to the east; closer was Black Ven, a vast collapsing cliff with the restless, messy look of an open-cast mine.

Before long, the clover meadows gave way to a saggy field of horsetails as high as a man. There was something unruly about this ancient, primitive plant, which loves disturbed ground. It looked like it belonged to the era of the dinosaurs, and it did, heralding the unsettling landscape to come. Past a ruined farm, swamped by trees and catastrophic fissures, the track became a tiny rough path and I was swallowed by a botanical weirdness of Brazilian proportions: turbocharged sycamores were splattered with lichen and laden with liana, preposterous hair extensions of wild clematis, ivy and honeysuckle. In the gloom below grew frondy and high-gloss ferns. Gorse clung to odd pinnacles of rock. Spongy hollows where trees had crashed down were filled with pillowy growth: nettle, bramble, sloe and three-year-old ash saplings, shooting up to fill any void in the canopy. It was a bewildering jumble of native and out-of-place invaders: sallow, holly, bindweed, buddleia, ilex trees and then, oddest of all, a meadow of pampas grass.

In the absence of human life, dancing leaf shadows acquired the form of people. A sleek, disorientated chocolate-coloured shrew, the size of a 50p piece, crossed my path. An ash creaked in the breeze, as distinct as a door in a horror movie. A stream plopped into a pool of grey water where nothing grew and a grey fish accelerated away from my shadow. Dapples on the water showed purple and beige. High above, the leaves of a beech hissed in the light breeze. Somewhere, out there, it was a breezy sunny day. In the Undercliff, it was dark and humid. I was on the coast path but there was no coast. I had walked almost two miles when the whisper of the sea wafted up some obscure fissure and I realised this was an alien sound, so far unheard on my walk.

This unnerving place was suggestive of dark, possibly dangerous desires and perhaps it was these qualities that led John Fowles, one of the great novelists of the twentieth century, to make it his home. Having moved into the Undercliff with his wife, Elizabeth, in 1965, Fowles saw a kind of eroticism in its pinnacles, bluffs and clefts and made it the setting for *The French Lieutenant's Woman*, his masterpiece, a period and post-modern romance telling of the Victorian love affair between Charles Smithson and Sarah Woodruff. Like his own relationship, Fowles's fictional entanglement was complicated, ambiguous and without the guarantee of a happy ending.

Although we have long associated the seaside with young love, in fiction it is more frequently a place of more perilous passion. In *Frenchman's Creek*, Daphne du Maurier perfectly portrays the dangerously febrile intimacy of the creeks of South Cornwall, while Thomas Hardy chose the fearsome black rock of High Cliff, the mightiest drop on the Cornish coast, for the pivotal scene in *A Pair of Blue Eyes* which, coincidentally, Fowles himself was reading, on 10 October 1964, when he and Elizabeth stopped for the night in Lyme Regis and decided to make it their home. The Undercliff combined both the vertiginous qualities of High Cliff with the fecundity of Frenchman's Creek. Powerful, mysterious, unnerving, unpredictable, duplicitous, treacherous, the coast is the ultimate place on which to project all the unknowable wonders, horrors and complexities of the human heart.

The Romans created the first seaside villas by the Mediterranean. For centuries, Baiae was known for its expensive homes and licentious spirit. It was said that everyone who bathed in the sea fell in love but this hedonism was eventually quashed by a combination of Muslim invaders, malaria and volcanic activity. The cooler seas around Britain were never so hospitable and fears of the coast were promulgated by Christianity. There was no ocean in the Garden of Eden. The sea was a 'great abyss' in Genesis, a vestige without form, and its presence on earth was evidence that Creation remained unfinished. Leviathan established that fish were sea monsters; the story of Noah's Ark saw the ocean as an instrument of divine punishment. The sea was a flood, a spiritual void, a chaotic place of madness and diabolical power, and so, for centuries, its shores were avoided by almost everyone but demon-fighting monks and lowly fishermen.

'Cultivated men were not unaware that the seashores, abandoned and thought repulsive for so long, had once been places of meditation, rest, collective pleasure, and unbridled voluptuousness,' wrote the French thinker Alain Corbin in his excellent history of how we came to discover the sea in the modern age. Seaside historian J. K. Walton has found evidence that ordinary people took to the seas off Lancashire for ritualistic 'quasi-magical' bathing before the upper classes rediscovered the sea, but Corbin believes we returned to the coast in the early eighteenth century when the nascent science of oceanography began mapping the mysterious sea, English aristocrats took grand tours to the Bay of Naples and Holland (so artful in its exploitation and defence of the sea), and the first Romantic poets began paying 'ephemeral attention' to 'marine enchantment'.

'A troubled ocean, to a man who sails upon it . . . gives his Imagination one of the highest kinds of Pleasure that can arise from greatness,' opined a writer in *The Spectator* in 1712. Corbin found that a delight in the seashore insinuated itself into English literature in the early eighteenth century. The Romantics did not discover the sea but they were, he suggested, 'the first to propound a coherent discourse' about it. The wildness of the coastline made it an ideal locus for self-knowledge, contemplation and artistic creation.

This Romantic view is one of two entwined historical discourses through which we have sought, found or expressed our innermost desires by the sea. In contrast to the coast giving rise to a rather elevated Romantic state of mind, the second way in which romance has blossomed by the sea derives from a more bodily tradition – the eighteenth-century health craze for the coast, which segued into a keen sense of sexual possibility, and smut.

This physical side of seaside romance emerged during that century when the fashion for inland spas such as Bath evolved into a new coastal health regimen as doctors advocated drinking and bathing in sea water as a cure for everything from nervous disorders to gout and worms. This quackery fuelled the construction of health resorts – Weymouth, Scarborough and the impecunious fishing village of Brighthelmstone. Under the tutelage of the good doctor Richard Russell, and the Prince Regent, later King George IV, Brighthelmstone became fashionable Brighton, the first seaside resort to be linked to a city by train.

Dr Russell's tomb is engraved with a quote from Euripides: 'The sea washes away and cleanses every stain.' For early aristocratic visitors, coastal bathing was a moral quest as well as a health kick, a renunciation of the hedonism of the city. Sea bathing was a cold, salty shock, and required nervous aristocrats to confront their fear of the turbulent ocean. But, as Corbin wrote, it remained a sensory pleasure: 'The soothing embrace of the element evokes both sexual union and a mother's rocking. Sea water suggests the aquatic image of beneficent femininity, insidiously accentuated by the proximity of shells.' A 1796 guide to Brighton found men leering at women bathers 'as they kick and sprawl and flounder about its muddy margins, like so many mad Naiads in flannel smocks'. Despite the Victorian reputation for prudery, men bathed naked in the sea until the late nineteenth century: it was considered manly and practitioners believed that salt water needed to penetrate naked skin to give health. A letter to *The Times* in 1841 complained that women stood on Scarborough beach not as 'single spies, but in battalions' only 20ft from fifty naked men frolicking in the waves. So began the seaside's association with sexual freedom, celebrated in a late Victorian music-hall song which claimed: 'You can do all sorts of things at the seaside that you cannot do at home.' An overnight stay in Brighton could be used as evidence of adultery in divorce proceedings until the 1960s. When a French writer, Francis Wey, visited Brighton a century earlier, he made an observation familiar to us today. 'When English people are not icicles, they are apt to become shameless,' he wrote. 'So decency is a mere convention.'

All classes have made the seaside a zone of sexual liberation and self-discovery. In what she called her only truly romantic novel, *Frenchman's Creek*, Daphne du Maurier turned the Cornish estuaries into a place of erotic danger and enchantment, where her heroine, Dona, could be freed from the shackles of high society. Du Maurier wrote the novel during the Second World War when her war hero husband, a Major-General, became a virtual stranger to her and their three children and, like her heroine, du Maurier permitted herself to 'wander for a bit'. When her husband briefly visited home, he ranted about the war; with a gentleman farmer called Christopher Puxley, however, she could talk of 'music and birds and islands and things'. Christopher, who was already married as well, fell in love with Daphne, and she rented a remote former coastguard's hut, a mile from any road on the south Cornish coast between Polruan and Polperro. Here they would take a picnic and spend days lying together in the hut, door open, listening to the waves crash into Watch House Cove below.

As a place of sexual adventure, the seaside could be furtive and disreputable but over the last two centuries it has also played Cupid to publicly celebrated romance. In the Victorian era, the new resort of Ilfracombe was marketed as 'the Mecca of Honeymooners' and, until the arrival of cheap air travel in more recent decades, our shores remained the honeymoon destination of choice – typified by Florence and Edward's ill-fated, early 1960s Dorset coast honeymoon in Ian McEwan's *On Chesil Beach*. According to a contemporary survey for the National Trust, 7 per cent of us still propose marriage on the coast. Its Neptune holdings must get more than their fair share. On the graffitied wooden walls of a tiny hut built into the cliffs of North Cornwall by the eccentric Victorian vicar Robert Hawker I found scrawled: 'Struth We're Engaged 17.09.09'. Below, an update: 'Struth we're married! 11.09.10'. So I won no prizes for originality a few years ago when I wrote a proposal on the golden sands of Wells-next-the-Sea in Norfolk. (My first attempt to lure Lisa, my girlfriend, to read my beach script was typically foiled by rain but the next day I redrew the words, got her to the top of the sand dune and, dear reader, she said yes.)

I would bet there were rather fewer marriage proposals among the creeper and chasms of the Undercliff despite it providing a vision, from the sea at least, of 'an apparent sub-tropical paradise, a Robinson Crusoe landscape', as John Fowles put it. I did not realise until I got chatting to a well-informed local on the coast path that the tumbledown house I had passed earlier was Underhill Farm, which Fowles had purchased in 1965 so he could break off his increasingly reluctant engagement with London. Having retreated as far as he could from the fashionable world of film and publishing, Fowles wrote *The French Lieutenant's Woman* in a green shed in his garden. This, miraculously, was still standing although it looked like it might topple at any moment, doors and windows open onto a still-tended garden, a 'private' notice halting curious passers-by.

In the late 1960s Fowles described his hazardously sited new home as 'a Circe, a dangerous temptress'. He had fallen in love with this untamed coast. 'We haven't as yet got used to living with half our horizon the sea,' he wrote in a letter to a friend. 'It roars, pounds, hisses, mumbles on the reefs below our fields all day long, and then all night and gives a sort of voice to all those powers of nature that are exterminated almost everywhere else in England.'

Taking a pair of secateurs to cut his way through the undergrowth,

Fowles would disappear into the Undercliff for a whole day, immersing himself in it and coming to know it intimately. He explained its foundations perfectly in *The French Lieutenant's Woman*. The old fishing town and Victorian resort of Lyme Regis sits at the centre of an unusual outcrop of Jurassic blue lias. This is not an attractive stone but 'exceedingly gloomy grey in colour, a petrified mud in texture . . . a good deal more forbidding than it is picturesque'. Neither the blue lias nor another layer of hard, black clay, gault, will absorb the water from the many springs in the area. Instead, these rocks become like a slippery table for other Cretaceous layers, including golden-coloured upper greensand, called 'foxmould', which then become saturated and slump into the sea. 'All this land, 'tis in love with the sea,' a local farmer told Fowles. It wants to tumble down, and join it in a fatal attraction, and the seabed between Lyme and Axmouth is a shallow shelf of previously subsided coast. This instability determines the Undercliff's strange mix of plants and its untouched wilderness: it is the largest active coastal landslide in Western Europe and a rare section of our coast where the land is wilder than the sea. In this swiftly shifting landscape, things are swallowed up but they are also exposed. Lias is highly fossiliferous and the slips constantly reveal its Jurassic treasures. Lyme Regis has been a mecca for palaeontologists and amateur fossil hunters since the turn of the nineteenth century when Mary Anning, a local woman without formal education who possessed a genius for discovering unusual fossils, was the first person to see the bones of *Ichthyosaurus platyodon*.

On Christmas Day 1839, Anning's scientific colleagues had to reassure the government that England was not about to sink into the Channel after an enormous section of cliff west of Lyme Regis slid downhill. Part of a sown wheat field was detached from the 'mainland' and became an island in the middle of the great slip. This field was reaped in August 1840, watched by 10,000 spectators. The Undercliff is more overgrown today than it was in the Victorian era when the slip became a tourist attraction and Mrs Gapper's Cottage, now a fragment of ivy-covered wall, did a brisk trade in cream teas. Other cottages housed woodcutters, pigmen and shepherds. The ruins of one of the largest sheep dips in southern England can still be found in the Undercliff. Still, even at the peak of its tourist industry, the place was wild enough to inspire creativity and represent love and freedom. In 1867 three poets, Francis Palgrave, William Allingham and the poet laureate, Alfred Lord Tennyson (personally inspired by Jane Austen's *Persuasion*, the first novel to make the Lyme Regis coast a place of romance), rambled through this wilderness; it was no coincidence that John Fowles chose 1867 as the year of his great love story.

I studied *The French Lieutenant's Woman* for A-level English and its tragic passion chimed with me as a teenager. As I ventured into the Undercliff, I carried the novel in my rucksack to reread after twenty-one years. I couldn't remember how it ended although I realised that Fowles used his story to explore both historical elements of our passion for the coast – the cerebral Romantic celebration of the shore and the seaside as a place of physical coming together. The book begins with an image which came to Fowles one morning when he woke at Underhill Farm: a mysterious woman, standing alone, at the stormy end of the Cobb, the sinuous stone sea-wall that he calls 'the most beautiful sea-rampart on the south coast of England' and 'as full of subtle curves and volumes as a Henry Moore or a Michelangelo'. Here stands 'the French Lieutenant's Woman', and Charles Smithson and Ernestina Freeman catch her eye as they perambulate along the Cobb, which was also the setting for a pivotal moment in *Persuasion* when silly Louisa Musgrove falls down the Cobb steps and Austen's heroine, Anne Elliot, demonstrates her calm sagacity to Captain Wentworth. In *The French Lieutenant's Woman*, Charles is a Victorian scientist with a passion for fossils, although in truth he is something of a dilettante, knowing that he will inherit a fortune from his uncle. Well-travelled and world-weary, he is a little troubled by the conventions of his era and the fact that his lovely fiancée, Ernestina, is so unquestioning of them. During their walk, the couple, who are visiting Ernestina's aunt in Lyme, muse on the problem with provincial life. 'Everyone knows everyone and there is no mystery,' murmurs Charles. 'No romance.' Of course, he is terribly, tragically wrong.

Charles first meets the French Lieutenant's Woman properly by chance in the Undercliff and it only takes four further encounters in this potent parallel world – and a couple of unfortunate twists of fate – for his whole existence to unravel. His stay in Lyme allows for a little leisurely fossil hunting, and he fights through vegetation to reach a little green plateau. Here, on a ledge below, he sees a figure. A corpse? No, it is a woman in a deep sleep in the sunshine, loose hair half-covering her cheek. He recognises her from the Cobb, has heard the local tittle-tattle of how she got her name – she is a governess called Sarah Woodruff who was wooed and abandoned by a shipwrecked French sailor who promised marriage but disappeared – and as he cranes over to stare, she wakes up. Embarrassed, he apologises and walks away. 'It is a most fascinating wilderness, the Undercliff. I had no idea such places existed in England,' he declares to Ernestina that evening but doesn't mention Sarah. 'Why, the man is tranced,' cries Ernestina. 'Now confess, Charles, you haven't been beheading poor innocent rocks – but dallying with the wood-nymphs.' Already, the respectable fossil hunter is on literal and figurative shaky ground.

Charles is an archetypical Victorian but there is a less conventional man straining to get out, and Sarah's abandon, and the wildness of the Undercliff, awakens his repressed human nature. As I walked along the coast path, the Undercliff, like Charles, tried to maintain a veneer of respectability. Patches of mature beech possessed a deceptive solidity. It felt like these woods were attempting to be ordinary and ordered but then, oh, they just couldn't, and a few yards further on they exploded, spewing rock and soil and a jackstraw of trees in every direction. Beneath the mock Tudor Victorian mansion at Rousdon that had been a boarding school, I left the coast path and followed the route once frequented by naughty schoolboys past doomy modern-day warning signs absolving the authorities of any responsibility for my well-being. It looked like this mischievous path headed to the shore via a tunnel of sallow and honeysuckle. After some twists and turns I emerged into the open wound of a fresh landslip with the sea in sight for virtually the first time on my walk. This new slump had smashed up not one but two paths, splintered several ladders only built last summer into firewood and bequeathed a vertiginous, acrid grey desert of unprepossessing lias on which brambles and feral oilseed rape were the first colonists. Luckily, a path fairy had replaced the ladders with a thin blue nylon rope, which burned my hands as I slid down the lias. At the bottom were two busted steel staircases and then a stony shore: Charton Bay, a former smuggling hotspot which I didn't realise was actually a private beach. No trace of humanity was visible from this curve of pale-grey stones a mile long, fronted by milky turquoise water and backed by tangled green Undercliff, apart from one other beachgoer who kept himself to himself by the upturned roots of a slipped tree. The water was warm and became dove grey where small waves crunched the stony shore. I swam and then read *The French Lieutenant's Woman* in the midday sun, a buzzard crying in the silence that lay over the slumping cliffs.

Charles gives nothing away of their previous meeting when he is formally introduced to Sarah Woodruff at the home of Miss Poulteney, a ferocious do-gooder who takes in the disgraced governess against her better judgement. Soon after, he is traipsing through the Undercliff on another solitary fossil mission and bumps into Sarah on a path too narrow to avoid her. Sarah slips and Charles finds her 'totally like a wild animal, unable to look at him, trembling, dumb'. He suggests Ernestina's aunt might help her; she reveals that she knows the Frenchman will never return because he is married. Their third meeting in the Undercliff is Sarah's doing: she has apparently decided that Charles, as a man of the world who tells her he has 'a long nose for bigots' such as Miss Poulteney, would make a suitable confidant, and finds him in the greenery to give him two particularly fine fossils. 'I live among people the world tells me are kind, pious, Christian people,' Sarah tells him. 'And they seem to me crueller than the cruellest heathens, stupider than the stupidest animals.' She asks for one hour of his time, to confess to him, and collapses on the ground; Charles is afraid of this raw emotion but agrees to listen on the condition that she will then take his advice. 'We know more about the fossils out there on the beach than we do about what takes place in that girl's mind,' warns the wise local doctor, correctly suspecting that Charles is finding some pleasure in his 'humanitarian' mission to save Miss Woodruff.

The Undercliff is a setting for this fatal attraction but it is more than that. It is an agent almost as significant as any human go-between. When Charles arrives for their fourth, and first mutually conspiratorial meeting, Sarah climbs the steep slope ahead of him, affording him a glimpse of 'the white-ribboned bottoms of her pantalettes, which came down to just above her ankles'. She takes him to one of her eyries, 'a kind of minute green amphitheatre' with 'a rustic throne' in the form of a flat-topped block of flint against a stunted thorn. How could this place not bewitch? Here, she explains what happened with the French Lieutenant, Vargueness, while plucking a little spray of milkwort, 'blue flowers like microscopic cherubs' genitals'. Vargueness had wooed her and she followed him to Weymouth and gave herself to him: 'I am nothing, I am hardly human any more. I am the French Lieutenant's Whore,' she tearfully reveals. Charles is 'swept hopelessly away from his safe anchorage' and can't help but picture the scene she described. 'He was at one and the same time Vargueness enjoying her and the man who sprang forward and struck him down,' writes Fowles. Despite standing 'with one foot over the precipice', knowing what a touch would bring, Charles pulls himself away, promising to enlist Ernestina's aunt to help Sarah leave Lyme and telling her they must never meet alone again.

The Undercliff already has a reputation as a lover's lane, and in the end the place itself betrays Charles and Sarah almost as directly as they are betrayed by polite society, and by their own desires. When Sarah Woodruff is spotted emerging from the Undercliff a scandalised Miss Poulteney expels her from the household even though she is innocent of all charges rumour puts against her. Or is she? During their fifth, fatal meeting, Charles retreats to the conventional thinking of his age, suddenly fearing the Undercliff's 'universal chaos, looming behind the fragile structure of human order'. During this encounter, he and Sarah are discovered by Charles' manservant, Sam, who is illicitly courting Ernestina's maid Mary in the tangled undergrowth. Perhaps the Undercliff's role in the exposure of Charles and Sarah is fitting, for Sarah is also betrayed by her own emotions. In its mysteriousness, its destructiveness and the way it is set apart from respectable society, the Undercliff is the French Lieutenant's Woman. Sarah is untamed nature. She says it herself, leaning against the hawthorn in her secret dell: 'I am like this thorn tree, Mr Smithson. No one reproaches it for growing here in this solitude. It is when it walks down Broad Street that it offends society.' The same is true of any wild thing, or wild land: we struggle to accommodate it in human society.

When John Fowles left Hampstead and moved to Underhill Farm on the Undercliffs, he chose well: this coast possesses every symbol that a novelist writing about human desire requires. Its fecundity can represent abandonment and fertility, its dense foliage romantic tangles, and its constantly unstable ground is ideal for lovers faced with uncontrollable feelings and moral quandaries. I think that much of Fowles's writing is preoccupied with the destructiveness of male desire and, allowing for some of his rather dated language, a lot of it still rings true. There is something undeniably sensual about the Undercliff. Its landscape seethes with moral turpitude from its unexpected rocky pinnacles to its wet flushes. Most importantly for Fowles, however, the wildness of the Undercliff represented freedom. Many literary critics describe Fowles's Undercliff as 'Edenic' but prohibition is intrinsic to the Garden of Eden; the Undercliff is more Arcadian in its liberating quality. It is where Sarah and Charles can be true to their own feelings; where they – and by implication, all of us – can begin an emancipation from the straitjacket of social values.

The Undercliff gave John Fowles his liberty too. As a child, growing up in the suburban seaside resort of Leigh-on-Sea, he 'secretly craved everything our own environment did not possess: space, wilderness, hills, woods,' he wrote in *The Tree*, a short essay on nature. Entering woods like the Undercliff, he declared, was 'almost like leaving land to go into water'.

For Fowles, however, this coast extinguished rather than ignited romantic love. Fowles's wife, Elizabeth, detested her new life in Underhill Farm, oppressed by rats, rain and solitude, and succumbed to melancholy and depression. She hated '"the silence, the space, the emptiness," all the things I love, alas', noted Fowles in his journal in 1966. He wrote of her 'terrible bitterness' and determination 'to destroy our life here' and escaped their arguments by roaming the Undercliff alone. The Undercliff was the perfect place for 'self-liberation', he wrote in *The Tree*. In his journal, in 1966, he added: 'The sun shines, the sea glistens, our birds and insects weave their summer world around us. It is beautiful, like being in a glass sphere whose diameter is the sea horizon.'

Fowles was in this entranced frame of mind when he began *The French Lieutenant's Woman* and perhaps the jarring of his rapture with his wife's depression informed the gloomier sexual politics of his novel. While Elizabeth played a crucial role as the first editor of Fowles, his doleful journals make it seem miraculous that their marriage endured until her death from cancer in 1990. It may have helped that the

Undercliff conspired with her against Fowles and ejected him from his own Arcadia. In 1968 the field beyond their garden slipped away, and Underhill Farm became a fissure-ridden liability. Even then, Fowles could not find fault: 'The landslide is strangely beautiful in a chaos creating sort of way: wild tilted tables of turf, naked faces of flint and greensand, like a golden dough, even the fences twisted flat as if the land hates fences and has at last got its revenge.' They had to move, however, and considered everywhere from Cornwall to Gozo before plumping for Belmont House in Lyme Regis. Their new home's wild garden was important but more so was its situation – a five-minute walk from the Undercliff. Fowles could not break off his infatuation with the place.

Elizabeth, however, was far from alone in disliking the Undercliff. 'I hope you like *this*,' said the first walker I met there, gesturing at curtains of dark creeper. It's an interesting landscape, I volunteered. 'I can't see it,' he muttered. 'All I can see is trees.' Further on, I passed the monumental beech where Meryl Streep perched when she played Sarah Woodruff in the acclaimed film of *The French Lieutenant's Woman*. More than thirty years on, this fine tree was a glorified grey stump, two splintered forks stretching towards the sky, undone by the latest slide. During filming, the crew who struggled to shoot in the gloom and heaved heavy equipment over impossibly rough ground got T-shirts printed that read: 'i hate the undercliff.' Fowles pitied such haters. Modern man cannot cope with untamed nature, 'where iron and concrete and plastic are powerless, where it defeats all use except enjoyment on its own terms. That is why we have lost so much, and are now lost ourselves,' he wrote. 'The Undercliff is indeed a lost place; but most profoundly, the lost place is in ourselves.'

As I walked a dragonfly shot overhead, wings whirring like a boy making a machine gun noise with his tongue, and I wondered if this unsettling place was only a place of peace, love or artistic inspiration for rather unusual people. For everyone else, such coast sows terror or discord. As if to confirm my feelings, there rose a high-pitched voice by a stream which I first thought was a child but then realised was a young woman in a furious argument with a young man. 'Why do I have to listen to you when you don't listen to me?' I could only hear the girl's side of the quarrel as she screamed, 'What is *wrong* with you?' A dog began barking. I hurried down the final stretch of the path and with a whoosh the sallow thickets and brambles gave way, and there was the sea, the Cobb, a busy car park, a row of white beach huts, ice creams, beach tents, smooth tarmac, crazy golf, purple kayaks, a pint of prawns (£9.50), vanilla diabetic ice cream and red, white and blue bunting which flapped in a phenomenon alien to the Undercliff – a fresh breeze. This colour and bustle and order appeared completely unreal after a day in a rainforest wilderness. Weirdest of all was the flat, calm, trim bowling green where white figures stooped, turning their backs on the savage Undercliff just behind them. Truly, Britain is a land of bewildering contrasts.

Most people seemed to be made miserable by the Undercliff but the miserable-seeming John Fowles stayed true to it for the rest of his life, treasuring 'its solitudes, its silences, its sheer beauty, its exuberance of growth, its memories of very different pasts and cultures'. He considered it not simply a fascinating zone of geological confusion or a wonderful nature reserve but rather like a poem or piece of music, 'not quite of this world'. In 1989, despite nursing 'an awful feeling of impotence' for being unable to scramble up its crumbling slopes anymore, he stood on a bluff in the Undercliff. 'I felt how lonely, yet how clean, pure, it was – and not just an unmarred, hostile solitude, but one for which I felt an old affection,' he wrote.

As I finished his masterpiece for the second time by deserted Charton Bay, I wondered why Fowles prevented his characters, Charles and Sarah, from finding the peace he had experienced on the Undercliff. Would Charles stay true to his betrothed, Ernestina? Or would he follow his heart – and lust – for Sarah? And would

Sarah, another woman imprisoned by Victorian mores, have any say in the matter? In a postmodern twist his authorial voice had long threatened, Fowles supplied three alternative endings to *The French Lieutenant's Woman* once Charles and Sarah are catapulted from their coastal love nest into the real world. The first is short, conventional and a daydream. For all its sadness, the second, longer denouement is truer, for supporters of Sarah at least, even though Fowles never allows us inside her head. A third is Fowles at his gloomiest, although literary critics feel it is an ending in which both Charles and Sarah are able to find Fowles's much-prized freedom.

Before the coast path plunged into the Undercliff, there was a notice warning of its closure at Culverhole 'because of an ongoing landslide'. This stressed the danger posed by the 'broken ground at this location'. Broken ground. It was an interesting phrase and Fowles used it several times in his journals. 'I am poor, near useless these days, at negotiating scrub, especially when it is on very broken ground,' he wrote in 1989. 'Broken' is too human a word for the earth. We try to mend broken things but the glory of the Undercliff was that it couldn't be fixed and that this permanently unfixed state was what gave it life. Wild things are much tougher than us. Most of the time, the things we break are what we make, hold or possess: hearts, for example.

It may be a truism that broken hearts can inspire great artistic creation but this familiar idea was vividly brought to life when I looked from the four tall windows of the long dining room belonging to the elegant eighteenth-century mansion of Plas Newydd. The capricious waters of the Menai Straits flashed with green from the woods and silver from the sky, dark trees hugged the opposite bank; beyond them, if the weather was benign, rose the mountains of North Wales. 'The Menai Strait is one of the most beautiful stretches of water to be found anywhere around the coast of Britain,' declared the Welsh painter Kyffin Williams, who admired shimmering shoals of mackerel when he lived by the narrow channel that turns Anglesey into an island.

The room was bathed in a greeny light and there was something pulling my eye away from this unmatchable prospect. In 1936 the owner of Plas Newydd, Charles Paget, the 6th Marquess of Anglesey, commissioned a young artist, Rex Whistler, to cover the wall opposite the windows with a painting. The masterpiece that Whistler created is a fantastically detailed mural of an imaginary kingdom by the sea, a watery Arcadia, full of fun, tricks and the tokens of the great love, and heartache, he found here.

I was initially underwhelmed by this epic creation. I know little of art but at first glance this rendition of two Italianate harbour towns seemed an old-fashioned, eighteenth-century pastiche. More informed critics might dismiss it as Rococo or wonder why such an alien scene was plonked in North Wales. Why have a tribute to southern Italy distracting from the real beauty outside? Its ornate quayside also looked slightly wonky, as if Whistler had muddled his perspective. It was my perspective that was wrong though, and the beautiful tale told in thousands of brush strokes on the walls of Plas Newydd showed how the coast could permit passions – love, loss and art – to run wild.

Rex Whistler is less well-known than his namesake, James Abbott McNeill Whistler (no relation), for a number of reasons, including his premature death. Born in 1905, the second son of a builder and a nurse, Rex grew up in suburban south-east London. Completely self-taught, he sketched on the beach during holidays in Southwold and Cromer and when he was just sixteen he became the youngest pupil of Professor Henry Tonks, the most formidable art teacher of his generation, at the Slade.

'It has been said that Rex could not resist a lighted candle. Nor could he resist a lovely face, when lit or lightable for him,' wrote Laurence

Whistler in his sagacious biography of his older brother. Rex was twenty-five when he first set eyes on Lady Caroline Paget, the eldest of five daughters of the 6th Marquess of Anglesey and his artistic wife, Marjorie. Six years later, the Marquess gave Rex the job on the banks of the Menai Straits that was to define his life and love.

Rex found himself by the sea during what Laurence Whistler called the Between Time, 'with the precarious enjoyment of a rigid but more beautiful world dissolving, and a freer but uglier one not yet established'. Rex's generation, the Bright Young People, as gossip columnists called them, tore up social mores and danced while economies collapsed and the stately homes and Empire of the old order disintegrated. They fell in love with dizzying passion, declared it to the world in art, poetry and letters and their florid outrageousness was met with the contempt of many contemporaries. 'Even to want to write about so-called artists who spend on sodomy what they have gained by sponging betrays a kind of spiritual inadequacy,' declared George Orwell in 1936. 'They will have few ideals and illusions to console them when they "get to feeling old,"' predicted Evelyn Waugh, a Bright Young Person himself. 'They will not be a happy generation.'

Rex belonged to this rackety era. One midsummer, Rex and friends including the aristocratic young aesthete Stephen Tennant and the photographer Cecil Beaton drove to Stonehenge, then unfenced, hauled the American poet Elinor Wylie onto one of the stones and mock-worshipped her, let off fireworks and danced to a gramophone. Rex reckoned it was a 'wonderful orgy' although Laurence Whistler dismisses that remark as typical of his brother's playful hyperbole. Laurence believes his brother was too industrious to be decadent but became one of these upper-class pleasure-seekers because of his talent. 'He was destined to be "taken up" for all the good and ill that that portended,' he wrote.

The ill was to set his sights on unattainable love. Many people assumed he was gay. Tennant was gay; their mutual friend Siegfried

Sassoon was bisexual; and Rex partied with a Wiltshire set that included E. M. Forster and Lytton Strachey, who couldn't decide whether he was attracted or repelled by Rex's 'ugly but lust-provoking face'. Like many boarding-school boys of his era, Rex gained his first sexual experiences with fellow pupils and Laurence thought he was shy with women. Free love, wrote Laurence, 'was more a topic than a custom' of the Between Time. When Rex finally fell in love, though, it was with the professional force of an artist.

'Mysterious' was the preferred adjective for Lady Caroline Paget. Her younger sister, Elizabeth, was more conventionally attractive but, dark-haired, pale and slender, Caroline created quite an impression. As 'beautiful as the Milky Way', wrote Lord Lytton, the father of Antony Knebworth, a dashing pilot whom Caroline was intended to marry until he crashed his fighter plane. 'No one can eclipse that moonlike beauty,' said Rex's friend, David Cecil.

Laurence observed that while Rex was 'committed' to Caroline, she 'was sweet in return though quite detached'. Rex's great confidante, the writer Edith Olivier, agreed: 'Rex adores Caroline. She has a *tendresse* for him but at any moment leaves him.' In the autumn of 1935 Rex painted Caroline clutching a red rose. *Girl with a Red Rose* is not a straightforward romantic portrait, however: Caroline's eyes are downcast, aloof, and the long black glove on her right hand caused unfavourable comment – associated with 'decadence, Paris, the demimonde' as Laurence wrote.

When Rex took the night train from Euston with Caroline and entered Plas Newydd for the first time, it must have had a profound effect on him. Gazing from the dining-room windows, the green waters of the Straits are unsettling. At first sight, they could be mistaken for a river. It is only the water's latent energy that tells you it is the sea: it flexes, travels in all directions, and rises up.

Taking in this view, in love with the daughter of the household and accepted into her family to undertake a lavish commission for which he would be paid the princely sum of £1,000, Rex could be forgiven for feeling a moment of social vertigo. He had only stepped onto Anglesey once before, when his family travelled in an open Ford to 'dismal lodgings' for a wet holiday as a teenager. His entrance into an aristocratic family mirrors that of Charles Ryder in *Brideshead Revisited* and some wonder if Evelyn Waugh took inspiration from Rex.

Rex's mission was an ambitious one. He had to paint a 'virgin' wall 58ft long, facing the four windows, because Lord Anglesey wanted a dinnertime conversation piece to start all conversations. This was harder than it sounded. 'Through the windows was a view such as even Turner might find it hard to deflect a casual eye from,' judged Laurence Whistler, 'for in fresh weather lights and shadows feel their way along the whole of Snowdonia, caressing and erasing; while the water of the Straits clucks and silvers just under a steep-down lawn and a battlemented sea-wall.'

Rex resolved to answer the drama of the Welsh coastline with a kind of mirror and place an imaginary kingdom on the bare wall. 'I am going to paint the walls to make it appear as though, when dining, one is sitting on a terrace overlooking a harbour,' said Rex, with 'a little sea girt town on a promontory and a lot of ships and rocks and islands etc.' He had painted epic murals before – the celebrated *Expedition in Pursuit of Rare Meats* adorns the walls of the Tate's basement restaurant in London – but the challenge of this seaside creation saw him hit his artistic stride. Rather than paint directly onto the plaster, he laboured in a studio by the Thames in London on a continuous roll of canvas so large it had to be shipped over from France. 'I've never seen Rex *enjoy* a piece of work so ardently,' wrote Edith Olivier. 'His face lights when he speaks of it.'

During the first year, he travelled to Plas Newydd at weekends and sketched in charcoal on the bare plaster what he was creating in London. It was the perfect excuse to spend time with Lady Caroline. A photograph from 1936 shows him up a ladder, drawing, while

Caroline stands admiring him at work, a dog in her arms. Despite walks through Plas Newydd's formal rose garden and down to the wilder shores of the sea, Rex's romance with Caroline stalled that summer. Plaintive letters became jokily desperate. 'Beautiful Caroline, are you looking forward at all to dining with me tomorrow night or having supper? I do hope you are a little bit as I am so longing to see you again. You are going to come, aren't you? Please please PLEASE darling Caroline, don't chuck me. You know you are such a chucker – in fact an absolute chucker queen.' This was the humorously hysterical style of the day but, over time, Rex became less flippant. Caroline told him that he lacked experience with women and his reply read: 'Well, perhaps not, but I'll have to find ways and means. There are lots of ways, of course but it needs, unfortunately, so much means too.' Finally, Rex became wholly serious: 'I feel rather extra unhappy because things are so wrong between us, aren't they. I suppose I have hoped for more affection from you than I have any right to expect . . . I do realise that this is not a case in which I can say: "I knew at the beginning that it wouldn't last long" because there hasn't really ever been a beginning, has there?'

Rex cast himself as a victim of unrequited love. 'So much of my unhappiness comes from the *accident* of most of my love being attracted to one person . . . who doesn't return it,' he wrote to Edith Olivier. But there are no accidents in love; we are responsible for the beats our hearts skip and Laurence Whistler tersely concluded: 'The "accident" came from his invariable choice of a girl for supreme looks and grace without regard to any deeper quality.'

As 1936 drew to a close, Rex was so pained by love that he broke off contact with Caroline. 'I've been thinking about you young lady,' he wrote, mock-scolding from London, 'and I consider you done me wrong – or rather, you never done me right. So you see, you aren't my girl-friend no longer. You never really were, were you? I've *loved you*, you see, Caroline, while you have never loved me at all, – only liked me.' All his pent-up romantic feelings were poured into the imaginary landscape of his painting.

Finally, in June 1937, Rex's 58ft by 12ft canvas was transported to Plas Newydd for installation. If a picture tells a thousand words, Rex Whistler's mural could fill a book. Beneath great rolls of cloud, an eighteenth-century town stands by the water. It looks like an Italian fantasy but it consists of a fantastic blend of real buildings: St Martin-in-the-Fields and part of Admiralty Arch from London next to Trajan's column from Rome and Florence's cathedral. A row of houses is modelled on Brighton's Regency Square. In the blue hills beyond stands Lord Anglesey's ancestral home, Beaudesert (at that time, tragically, being demolished), alongside Harlech Castle in Wales and Mow Cop Castle in Staffordshire. On the right-hand side is another harbour featuring Amalfi Cathedral, a government building in Bonn, part of Caernarfon Castle, some windows belonging to Plas Newydd and, perhaps most bizarrely, a portion of Totnes high street in Devon, framed by Rex's version of the mountains of Snowdonia.

The harbour wall and quayside look a little wonky but this is a *trompe l'œil,* or fool for the eye, one of many such visual tricks. Rex played with perspective in all kinds of ways. Neptune, the God of the Sea, steps into this world in the form of wet footprints, which come up the quay steps and follow the viewer wherever they stand in the room. A rowing boat featuring a friend of the family at the oars also changes direction in the green ocean, depending on the viewer's position.

So much is open to interpretation, but it is easy to detect heartache in Rex's coastal kingdom. On the right-hand side are two trees with crossed trunks, two lives entwined and yet apart. A pair of boats are drawn up on a distant shore, side by side but empty. A gondola carries Lord and Lady Anglesey and four of their daughters, but Rex put Caroline in a boat of her own: a sleek sailing boat with a red sail. Its chic pilot is reclining, languid but also very much in control, an image of a woman who knows her own mind and is choosing, perhaps, to be alone. Where the picture turns a corner into the left-hand recess, there is a boy gazing up at a girl in a window: Rex's Romeo and Juliet. In the foreground stands a self-portrait, Rex as a gardener, long broom in hand, wearing a red cravat also seen in the Tate mural, which matches Caroline's sailing boat. At his feet is a gardener's basket containing a single red rose, its petals falling onto the paving, a token of love and loss.

Rex spent much of the magical summer of 1937 socialising with the Angleseys as he perfected his picture at Plas Newydd. His time by the sea stoked his romantic hopes. He made up with Caroline and they played tennis in the gardens, walked by the water and swam in the Straits. In June, a few days before Rex's thirty-second birthday, the play *Victoria Regina* opened at the Lyric a hundred years after the Queen's accession. Rex had created its dazzling set. 'Rex in a dream with Caroline, who for the first time seemed a part of his life – as if she shared his triumph,' wrote Edith Olivier of the opening-night party at the Savoy. 'They are a perfect pair – both quite unfit for marriage.'

And their tempestuous attachment remained unpredictable. A month later, they attended one of Cecil Beaton's notorious fancy dress parties in Wiltshire. Caroline wore a dress that Rex had designed for her and yet she was in what Rex's friend David Cecil called 'a detached, elf-maiden mood and would hardly speak to him'. By now, Rex had another admirer, Patricia Douglas, a stunning but troubled eighteen-year-old whose mother had eloped with a wealthy Canadian when she was seven leaving her in the rather disreputable company of her anti-Semitic great-uncle, Lord Alfred Douglas, Oscar Wilde's former lover. In August, Patricia joined Rex and Caroline at Plas Newydd, where the trio became inseparable. Rex was not the only one to find something magical about the Menai Straits. Brimming with romance, Patricia rang Edith Olivier to say she was 'wildly happy' with 'so much to tell'. Edith judged Rex was 'physically in love with Patricia, who is passionately so with him'. But she doubted he would propose marriage to Patricia in front of Caroline. 'It would be like two children in a wild beast's cage,' she wrote.

'I realised that Rex was in love with us both, it was a strange triangle,' Patricia wrote some years later. 'Caroline was bisexual, we were always together, in the daytime walking by the coast and swimming naked on a little island. At night we would all sleep together, kissing and lying in each other's arms.' Patricia said the threesome never made love but later that summer, according to Laurence, Rex consummated his relationship with Patricia, for one night only, cried, apologised and left her 'as bewildered as he was disconsolate'.

Rather like the powerful feelings Charles Smithson and Sarah Woodruff developed in John Fowles's Undercliff, the real life intimacy forged on the banks of the Menai Straits between Rex, Caroline and Patricia could not survive beyond such bewitching surroundings. Despite a jokey petition 'to Beautiful Darling Caroline To beg her to Reconsider her decision to leave Plas Newydd' signed by Rex, Caroline went away that autumn and Rex was left alone in the house to finish the mural. In 1938 he wrote: 'I love you sweet Caroline so much more than I've ever been able to persuade you of. I believe you think I love you less than I used to do . . .' At the end of the year, Rex sent his final bill of £400 to Lord Anglesey, describing it as 'hideously exorbitant'. With characteristic charm, he added: 'Of course there's such a bill you could send in against me as would wipe out any claim of mine. How could I hope ever to repay for all those lovely days of fun and bathing and sunshine, moonlight and luxurious nights and enormous delicious meals . . . rows and rows of champagne cocktails . . . pyramids of potted shrimps and absolutely countless bottles (all told) of heavenly claret.'

For all his heartache, this was a period of exceptional productivity for Rex Whistler: Plas Newydd was one of four epic murals (and the only one so directly connected with the seaside) he painted in the four years before the Second World War. Each shared 'an incomparable lightness of touch, great technical skill, inventiveness, originality and wit,' judged Hugh and Mirabel Cecil in their contemporary appraisal of Whistler's life and work. Ben Pentreath, an architectural designer, wrote of the twentieth-century painter-muralists: 'Whistler surpasses all others understanding at once the capriciousness of the task, the role of allegory, combined with quiet wit, and, above all, the sheer technical brilliance required to create illusions of another world.'

Rex and Lady Caroline were drifting apart before he completed his mural but war was to separate them more permanently. Lord Anglesey offered to write to the War Office and request a posting for Rex as a war artist, painting camouflage well out of harm's way. But Rex was determined to join the front line and became a tank commander in the Welsh Guards. He may have been inspired by the bravery of Lady Caroline, who risked her life to drive Light Rescue teams to Blitz bombings in London.

The final touch on his mural at Plas Newydd was a lit cigarette balanced on the edge of a step. Rex promised the Angleseys he would come back for it after the war. But he never saw the Straits again. His first day of action was to lead his tank troop in the ill-fated Operation Goodwood, which was halted with the loss of more than 400 tanks and 5,000 casualties. Diverted to investigate the French village of Giberville, Rex's tank became tangled in fallen telegraph wires. When he climbed out to seek help, he came under fire, a mortar shell exploded under him and he was instantly killed. In London, Laurence Whistler picked up a midday paper and spotted a familiar-looking drawing on the Diary page: it was one of Rex's last sketches. His brother was dead. Rex's mother and Edith Olivier and his other friends were heartbroken. How Caroline heard the news, and how she took it, is not known.

The war drove plenty of people into each other's arms and yet it did not cause Caroline to fall in love with Rex as he desired. Their romance by the waters of the Menai Straits appeared a classic case of one-sided love until I interviewed Charles Duff, a graceful, white-haired theatre historian who was also the adopted son of Lady Caroline Paget. His mother, thought Charles, was portrayed 'as a stuck-up bitch' in Laurence Whistler's biography. 'She could be selfish and wilful but they were both very complicated and I think he was very difficult too,' he said of Caroline and Rex. Charles had a different understanding of his mother's mysteriousness: she could not fall for Rex because she was not available. In 1934, aged twenty-one, Caroline met Audry Carten, an actress and playwright, and fell in love. 'From that moment onwards, she had a partner so she wasn't really free to be anyone else's,' said Charles. His mother was a lesbian but was unable to live openly in an era where most gay people still sought the cover of heterosexual relationships. According to Laurence Whistler, Caroline told one of her sisters that a woman was far more fulfilling in love. A dedication from Caroline to Audry in a book read: 'To my darling *darling* Audry from *her* C'.

I learned that Rex and Caroline did finally consummate their relationship but happiness still eluded him. In September 1938 Rex, Caroline and her sister, Liz, visited Raimund von Hofmannsthal in Austria. 'By now he was Caroline's lover,' wrote Laurence Whistler, 'but it does not seem to have made a radical difference. His letters never speak of fulfilment.'

Rex's sexuality was complicated as well. 'He liked his women but worshipped them from afar,' thought Charles Duff. During the war, Rex rekindled his romance with Patricia Douglas, who although now married, met him for a week – in bed – at Claridge's. Patricia believed Rex was gay without knowing it and didn't really require physical love. Another of Rex's wartime loves was Ursula Ridley, the unhappily married daughter of the architect Sir Edwin Lutyens who had earlier enjoyed a passionate affair with Laurence Whistler when he was tutor to her two sons. Of Rex she recalled, 'Caroline kept him in an agony of unfulfilled desire – and yet I don't think he could ever have given real happiness to a woman. He was infinitely loving but could neither find nor give the love he longed for with his imagination, which was greater than his emotions, or desires, could ever attain.'

Rex's mural at Plas Newydd may have been stubbornly anachronistic in an era of modernism but the way it expresses his passion for Lady Caroline lifts it beyond a lightweight piece of nostalgia. I did not realise until I left North Wales, however, that it is a much bigger act of love. I'm no art critic but when I crossed the River Dee on the A55 to Chester, and saw the mountains of Wales clustered behind me, with all the majesty and drama of a sharply defined, separate kingdom, I suddenly realised that Rex Whistler's Rococo land by the sea was not ludicrously ignorant of its surroundings but a deeply involved engagement with it.

I had a jolt when I read a story about Daphne du Maurier that made me spot a connection between her coastal passions and those of John Fowles and Rex Whistler. *Frenchman's Creek* is a romance in which Dona takes advantage of the secluded estuaries of South Cornwall to conduct a liberating affair with a French pirate; a crude biographical interpretation – as I suggested earlier – would attribute its plot to du Maurier's wartime dalliance with Christopher Puxley in the coastguard's hut. But on a summer's day ten years before she wrote *Frenchman's Creek*, du Maurier rose early, walked up the steep hill from Pont Bridge to Lanteglos Church and married Major 'Tommy' Browning, the tall, dark and handsome army officer whom she had known for just three months. Together they sailed in his boat, *Ygdrasil*, west out of Fowey along the coast to Frenchman's Creek. Here, hidden away, they spent their first night as husband and wife, the only sounds the lonely cry of wading birds and the slow slapping of water against the side of the boat. Knowing this, we see du Maurier's evocation of the magical secrecy of the Cornish creeks in a different light. They are 'a source of enchantment, a new escape', she writes in *Frenchman's Creek*, 'a place to drowse and sleep, a lotus-land'. In the novel, the creek is the site of Dona's self-liberation rather than merely a convenient place for a rendezvous with a one-dimensional French pirate. In life, this intimate landscape opened up du Maurier's greatest romance – her marriage – and she loyally acknowledged the feelings it stoked in her. Similarly, John Fowles's *The French Lieutenant's Woman* is as much an enraptured love letter to his new sanctuary, the Undercliff, as it is a fable of individual and sexual liberation. And for all the symbols of unrequited love for Lady Caroline in Rex Whistler's mural, it was the coast that helped unlock Rex's passion. His greatest work of art is a hymn to the waters of the Menai Straits and the mountains behind.

It is not simply habit or history or culture that makes us site our romantic lives by the sea or scrawl proposals in the sand. The line of beauty between land and water speaks to the passion inside us not because it is an uncomplicated aesthetic pleasure but because it contains ambivalence. We often liken the sea to consciousness: its surface glitters, its depths are unknowable; its tides ebb and flow like desire; its turbulent currents are as unpredictable and all-consuming as our emotions.

And yet for all our passion, the way we find analogies to the human condition on our shores is only really a relatively recent inclination, inspired by the Romantics. For far longer than it is has been an instrument of love, the sea has been an instrument of war.

## Explorations of Neptune

The National Trust owns Ware Commons, which is the portal to **the Undercliff** and where the unique wilderness begins. If you are visiting by car, park in the Lyme Regis Holmbush long-stay car park (DT7 3LD) and pick up the South West Coast Path down a private road on the western side of the car park. This takes you into the commons, an attractive mix of small open pasture, tangled woods and some sea views. Through a gate on the western side and you leave National Trust land and enter the National Nature Reserve which is managed by Natural England.

A walk along the coast path all through the Undercliff from Lyme Regis to Seaton is a good five-hour hike on a rough, undulating path. There are no tearooms or toilets on the Undercliff these days! An X53 bus can take you back to your starting point. Unfortunately a landslip blocked the coast path at Culverhole in 2014. At the time of writing, the diversion takes you a long way inland and the local council has warned it may take several years to establish a new coast path route. If the path is still blocked, I'd recommend an up-and-back walk to Rousdon or Culverhole, returning again to Lyme. There are no paths 'in' or 'out' of the coast path as it winds through the Undercliff but I took a little path down to the private beach at Charton Bay. This has been rerouted and repaired by the landowner but is only for the intrepid.

### OS Map
Explorer 116, Lyme Regis & Bridport
### Nearest railway station
Axminster, 5 miles
### Websites
South West Coast Path www.southwestcoastpath.com
Undercliff National Nature Reserve
www.naturalengland.org.uk/ourwork/conservation/designations/nnr/1006009.aspx

**Plas Newydd** on the **Isle of Anglesey** is a gorgeous and often over-looked National Trust property. It is worth getting one of the house's stupendously well-informed volunteers to talk you through the Whistler, and look out for the stories of the flamboyant 5th Marquess and the 1st Marquess, a hero of the Battle of Waterloo. The elegant house, redesigned by eighteenth-century architect James Wyatt, has lovely gardens and there is a woodland walk which leads to vistas of the ever-changing Menai Straits.

*Plas Newydd*
Anglesey LL61 6DQ
*OS Map*
Explorer 263, Anglesey East
*Nearest railway station*
Llanfairpwll, 1¾ miles
*Website*
www.nationaltrust.org.uk/plas-newydd/

## Further Reading

Alain Corbin (trans. Jocelyn Phelps), *The Lure of the Sea – The Discovery of the Seaside in the Western World 1750–1840*, Penguin, 1995 (1988)

Daphne du Maurier, *Frenchman's Creek*, Penguin, 1964 (1941)

Margaret Forster, *Daphne du Maurier*, Chatto & Windus, 1993

John Fowles, *A Short History of Lyme Regis*, Dovecote Press, 1991 (1982)

John Fowles, *The French Lieutenant's Woman*, Jonathan Cape, 1969

John Fowles (ed. Charles Drazin), *The Journals: Volume 2*, Jonathan Cape, 2006

Laurence Whistler, *The Laughter and the Urn*, Weidenfeld and Nicolson, 1985

# 3

# War

*Dover / Northumberland / Orford Ness*

Dunstanburgh Castle

Orford Ness

South Foreland
Lighthouse

The White Cliffs

The White Cliffs of Dover is a bit of Britain that we all think we know: a national icon so frequently featured in song, poem and sweeping helicopter shots on television that we no longer really see it. 'Chalk is one of England's emblems,' wrote Nicholas Crane in his book based on *Coast*, the enduringly popular BBC series. It is easy to glance at Kent's fine chalky cliffs, think fleetingly of their stirring, patriotic associations, and switch off, confident they cannot reveal anything else. I was a little perplexed that the National Trust had made such a big song-and-dance about raising £1.2m to add a 0.8-mile stretch of the White Cliffs to its Neptune coast in 2012 and I was surprised it raised the money almost instantly. My expectations were not immediately confounded by the vista from the National Trust's busy Langdon Cliffs visitor centre on a brilliant day in July. Perched on the cliffs above Dover was like peering from a graceful London terrace onto an industrial estate. I couldn't see any of the geological magnificence I stood on, but our recent human history was writ large below: Dover Castle, Dover harbour's eastern docks, mammoth warehouses, an immigration removal centre and, in the far west, the nuclear power stations Dungeness A and B. No wonder there were relatively few British visitors: to judge by the letters on the number-plates in the car park, the tourist throng here was resolutely continental – PL, D,

F, NL, S. Perhaps for them, Britain was an exotic island, just off their shores. To be fair, Langdon Cliffs was not a miserable indictment of modern Britain either. The Trust's visitor centre, a piece of steel-and-wood architecture with a slightly despondent-looking grass roof, was typically well organised, the cake was excellent and if I squinted slightly, the sand of Dover beach glittered like the French Riviera. But rather than seagulls or Vera Lynn, the air only sang with safety announcements from port Tannoys and a metallic clunk-clunk as cars entered the mouths of the waiting ships. These escapees would get the best view of the White Cliffs, from the ferries which resembled detached lumps of chalk – chunky, castellated and bright white in the sunlight – as they crossed the narrow band of water that defines our nation.

And then I discovered the hole. The hole changed everything. The walk east along the White Cliffs crosses a cliff-top territory of fine chalk grassland and arable fields, which the Trust was returning to grassland. These fields were full of red poppies, sow thistles and wild carrot, the first wild species to recolonise after years of ploughing. And a few yards from the footpath at Fan Bay was a patch of elder and blackthorn scrub that concealed a sliver of a hole in the ground, not much bigger than a large letterbox, edged by an old slab of concrete.

I didn't actually discover the hole but was taken to it by Jon Barker, a young archaeologist by training who was now a Trust manager on the cliffs and a great enthusiast for things like holes in the ground, which were the hidden bonus in the Trust's recent purchase. 'I knew there was a hole but I didn't tell anyone about it,' said Jon, his eyes glinting with excitement. Holes usually brought problems.

The hole didn't look big enough to squeeze inside but Jon had fixed a rope to dangle into the blackness and suddenly disappeared. Hanging on to the rope, I followed, twisting my torso and stretching my legs to land on slippery wet chalk. All natural light swiftly disappeared. I didn't have a torch but Jon's showed a shaft sliding downwards, interminably, the first of three staircases of nearly fifty steps each that descended deep into the White Cliffs. Dark, wet, and not very welcoming, this was Fan Bay Deep Shelter: an underground hospital and sleeping quarters for 180 men, part of a great riddle of secret tunnels dug all along Kent's chalk coast where our countrymen hid and waited for war.

There is hardly a mile of the Neptune coast that is not marked by our fear of invasion: ancient promontory forts, castles, towers, gunneries, lookouts, pillboxes, radar stations. These ruins, made picturesque by the passing of time, speak of our anxieties over the conquests that came, and those that didn't. It is no wonder that the sea has been feared for most of our history for it bore our enemies to us: the Romans, the Angles, the Saxons, the Vikings, the Normans, the French, the Spanish, the Germans, waves of violent invaders and peaceful monks bearing nothing more brutal than a bible and a desire to convert us.

Even in West Cornwall, not a place associated with invasion (unless it was the Saxons pushing the Cornish to the land's end), an old miller who lived at Vellan Dreath, near Sennen, in Tudor times once experienced how potential conquest could come at any minute. On a day when the sea was obscured by a thick mist, it was momentarily parted by the sun, and the man, glancing from his mill, spotted the tall mast of a great ship. Then he heard the splashing of oars from a boat containing five or six heavily-armed 'Dons', as the Spanish were known. The Dons approached the first building they saw: the mill. Its door had a hole into which you stuck your finger to lift the latch, and a few swipes of a musket by the miller and his son caused Spanish fingers to quickly retreat. The invaders returned with reinforcements and the miller and his son concluded it was time to run for it. They set fire to a rick of gorse which blew smoke into their pursuers' eyes. When the invaders saw the millers again they were halfway up the hill, each hauling a sack of flour on his back to protect themselves from the guns, which the Dons began firing. Sadly, the old miller was struck by a stray shot and fatally wounded. His son reached safety, however, and threw down his sack, complaining it was much heavier than when he started because of all the lead shot lodged in it.

In the Second World War, the guns got bigger. Kent has always been the front line for most aggressive incursions and when Churchill visited Dover he was said to have been horrified to see enemy ships, in clear view, passing along the Channel. So a series of powerful cross-Channel guns, the Kentish Heavies, were duly placed along the coast and nicknamed Jane, Clem, Winnie and Pooh (Jane was a comic-strip hero, Clem was Churchill's wife, Winnie was Winston and Pooh followed on from that). These monstrous guns could reach the French coast but were aimed at ships. A Trust guide, Trevor Wiltshire, told me that his father had worked on the cliff-top anti-aircraft guns. Every morning, Trevor remembered, his dad used to walk to South Foreland Lighthouse and train his binoculars on Cape Grenay on the far side of the Channel. If he saw the radar-jamming truck turn up, he knew it would be a busy day and would dash back to his gun. Overalls and tin hat on, he would then shoot until 4 p.m. – heavy, noisy, gruelling work. But at least he went home for tea every evening.

It may have been a war of great powers and their mammoth machines but the gloom of Fan Bay Deep Shelter eloquently revealed the human scale of the conflict. The tunnel was constructed with 9ft metal arches used in coal mines, with corrugated metal between each arch. As Jon Barker put it: 'These cliffs were the coal face.'

After the initial, alarming descent, the next staircase still possessed discernible, if rubble-covered stairs. After the third staircase, the tunnel floor became flat. Tunnels branched off and turned corners and quickly became labyrinthine. One led to an opening on the cliff edge, where two sound mirrors had been installed some years before the Second World War. These were part of the world's first early warning system and didn't work very well, although the operational network which communicated its findings proved useful to its successor, radar, which was rather more successful.

It was hard to imagine these cold tunnels of hooped, rusted metal crammed with bunkbeds and humid with fear, but there were still remnants of the old life: by an arch, a piece of wire twisted into a hook made by a soldier who wanted to hang his cap by his bed; a Pools coupon and a needle and thread were also discovered tucked into the tunnel wall; noughts and crosses were chalked on the walls, showing how conflict mostly killed time. On bricks from a barracks' toilet block used to seal off one tunnel, a soldier's writing spoke to us. A few words were missing but you could get the gist:

IN SUCH A CAPER

HAVING SHIT AND GOT NO

PARADE IS DUE

I DARE NOT LINGER

HERE GOES I'LL USE MY FINGERS

Secret holes were vivid time capsules and particularly valuable here on the Kentish coast, where so many of the surface-level wartime buildings were bulldozed as part of a post-war eyesore-clearance programme. The eradication of recent history meant that everyone knew about Dover Castle but the story of the cross-Channel guns was less well remembered.

Nevertheless, people were desperate to access these mysterious holes and wartime graffiti were outnumbered by more contemporary scribbles in Fan Bay Deep Shelter. Everyone who ventured inside seemed compelled to record their presence: a visitors' book scratched onto the walls with lumps of chalk: P Wood '02, Dick '06. The Internet helped popularise the UrbEx scene, where underground obsessives exchanged grid references and recorded their visits to forbidden bunkers rather like elite mountain-climbers, the secretive deeps as glamorous as any heights. On Trust land at nearby St Margaret's, an atmospheric coastal suburb once home to Ian Fleming, there was a steel grille sealing off another underground shelter: it had been dug around by a renegade tunneller. Elsewhere, another subterranean explorer decided to ignore a bunker's original entrance altogether and dug down into it at night from the middle of an adjacent field. The Trust was planning to open Fan Bay Deep Shelter to regular visitors and Jon Barker's vision was not to clean it up but ensure it retained its current grubby, evocative state.

That morning, when I had arrived on the White Cliffs it was deceptively hazy and there was no trace of France, and no sign of Britain's proximity to the Continent. When I emerged from Fan Bay Deep Shelter in late afternoon, sighing with relief in the brightness, the air was clearing and our neighbours shimmied into view. France was so close I could almost see what they were eating in Calais; it looked closer than Lincolnshire appears when viewed from the North Norfolk coast, closer than Wales from Somerset, closer than Devon from Lundy. It looked as close as Dungeness away to the west.

As night fell, Calais became a smudge of sodium on the horizon. The Channel was like a broad, peaceful motorway, and the low throb of aquatic traffic did not cease all evening. When I woke from a night's sleep next to this bustling body of water, my mobile phone had one text: Welcome to France, it said. I could find plenty of French DJs burbling on the radio but no John Humphrys. The White Cliffs might for ever be a piece of England but modern telecommunications unpatriotically decided that this was France.

That morning the Continent was shrouded in low cloud and suddenly I understood how vulnerable past populations must have felt. The land across the water was sometimes visible and sometimes invisible but the motives of the people who lived there may have been pretty opaque to the residents of England. This seemed bizarre.

Barely 8,000 years ago, we were joined at the hip to Europe. Just 320 generations ago, our ancestors could have strolled these chalky downs and across a green plain to the Continent. When the water came in, there were boats. Each ferry crossing must rub away a little more of the difference between us. (There was also now a concrete tunnel filled with trains and cars, which would delight the UrbExers of the future.) How could such a short stretch of water make such a difference, make us talk, eat and think so distinctly? Why didn't the people of Dover and Folkstone and Calais and Dunkirk all speak Franglais when there was such a frenzy of people moving to-and-fro across this narrow body of water? In centuries to come, historians would surely find it unfathomable how human beings estranged themselves so effectively from each other over such a tiny quirk of geography, in such a short space of time.

The previous day, a storm had made the sea wild and tough and joyous. Now it was sullen beneath low cloud, its waves choppy and frustrated as if the water had realised the limits of its power. Foam like sheep's wool was blown from shore across the rolling green pasture above it. On the horizon, to the north, the gothic ruin of Dunstanburgh Castle stretched out its full length as if it were a sleeping dragon.

I was walking from Craster on an October day so filthy that even the cows had turned their backs on it and there was no one around: the perfect conditions to experience the best ruined castle on the English coastline. Set on a rocky headland with nothing but the unspoilt coast of Northumberland unspooling to the north and south, this was the ultimate feral, forsaken rebel building.

From Bamburgh to Alnwick, the coast of Northern England is well populated with fine castles, tokens of the ancient quarrel between the Scots and the English. But what makes Dunstanburgh so interesting has little to do with repelling border raiders or launching a conquest of Scotland. Its brooding presence on the cliffs perfectly reflects its origins as a dark Avalon, a paranoid island of colossal ambition, built in a hurry by a bad man in an era when life was nasty, brutish and short.

Perhaps Thomas, Earl of Lancaster, would have been a decent person had he not been born in 1278. He was the son of Edmund 'Crouchback', the younger brother of warlike Edward I, and it has been suggested that the king preferred his aggressively spirited nephew to his own son, who became Edward II in 1307. Lancaster inherited the earldoms of Lancaster, Leicester and part of Derby from his father, adding the earldoms of Lincoln and Salisbury and further titles through marriage to Alice de Lacy, Countess of Lincoln. He was powerful and vicious. Lancaster 'defouled a greet multitude of gentilwommen and of gentil wenches; yif eny man offended hym a lite, he lete slee hym anon,' according to the fourteenth-century chronicler Ranulf Higden. The historian John Maddicott found that Lancaster's estate records showed 'a rapacious, grasping and cruel landlord, so powerful that he could ride roughshod over the rights of others and defy the law with impunity'. Lancaster's marriage was unhappy – his wife bore him no heirs and left him in 1317 – and perhaps this made his political ambitions even more deranged, as he cloaked himself in Arthurian legend and used the pseudonym 'King Arthur' in various treacherous dealings with the Scots. (*Vita Edwardi Secundi* reported allegations that he accepted £40,000 from Robert the Bruce to abandon a siege of Berwick in 1319.)

In Edward II, Lancaster encountered a weak king beset by debt and the difficulties of consolidating his father's push into Scotland and war of conquest against Wales. The real cause of Lancaster and other powerful earls' contempt for Edward, however, was his habit of courting favourites, especially a Gascon knight called Piers Gaveston. Edward fathered both legitimate and illegitimate children but rumours suggested he also enjoyed a physical relationship with Gaveston. Powerful earls may have forgiven Edward his alleged sodomy had not land and influence quickly accrued to Gaveston and, in 1312, Lancaster led an army against the knight, forcing his surrender at Scarborough Castle. While Gaveston was escorted to London, he was seized by Lancaster's ally, the Earl of Warwick. After a mock trial, attended by Lancaster, a sword was driven through Gaveston's body and his head was cut off and presented to Lancaster.

Edward II held Lancaster personally responsible for Gaveston's death, and from then on regarded him with mortal hatred, according to the *Scalacronica*, a chronicle written in 1355. Fearing reprisals, Lancaster quickly made plans to construct a castle. Coal from Newcastle fired three limekilns; oxen and carthorses were donated by friendly locals (although one carthorse was stolen from Scottish raiders); wood for doors and windows was obtained from Scandinavia; and a mason called Elias was hired for £224, paid in silver, to construct the most magnificent gatehouse ever seen in Britain. The result was Dunstanburgh. Awesome and grandiose, it was place of refuge from his English enemies and a defiant show of strength.

Through the spitty rain, the jagged ruins of Elias's twin-towered gatehouse were still imposing today. The skeletal sandstone remnants of its highest points resembled the heads of Easter Island statues. In the early fourteenth century, this 24m-high structure, situated high on a rocky headland, on the mighty contours of an Iron Age promontory fort, would have seemed even more impressive. In the late thirteenth century, Edward I's new coastal castles – Aberystwyth, Harlech, Beaumaris – were designed to be three storeys high; Lancaster's Dunstanburgh boasted five storeys. This architecture thundered with royal ambition. Other castles in northern England had square towers; Lancaster chose round ones, again echoing the architecture of Edward I.

The great gatehouse still dominated the coast path but in the fourteenth century there was no Craster and no path. Instead, the only route to Dunstanburgh came in from Embleton, to the north. The positioning of the gatehouse facing south-east, into what was then nothingness, was a puzzle until 2003, when archaeologists discovered the foundations of a stone quay on the foreshore. Castle accounts from 1319 also mentioned the earl's oars. Visitors were more likely to arrive by boat than horse, and the gatehouse would create a fearsome impact from the quay. Again, Lancaster was following the trends of the day: VIPs arrived by boat at royal castles in Wales and the Tower of London as well.

The sea's roar was unchallenged when I stood in the great grass bailey of Dunstanburgh, where soldiers were once stationed and locals may have sheltered from the marauding Scots. Nothing called above it until an oystercatcher went up, an uxorious bird, fussing after his mate. Looking inland, there were traces of an old moat, once 101m long and 5.5m deep. An English Heritage survey found it linked three freshwater lakes, forming a continuous stretch of water curving around the castle to its west. Dunstanburgh was once virtually an island. These meres were a larder, supplying fish and wildfowl for the castle, but were also intended to intimidate: if visitors approached via the road from Embleton, the towers reflected in the water would have been a daunting sight. It was also Lancaster's imitation of Avalon, the island where King Arthur was buried, the favourite legend of every unpleasant medieval aristocrat. (Edward I ordered the construction of a round table at Winchester.)

In Dunstanburgh, Lancaster created a monstrous castle out of all proportion to its military value: it was, like most buildings of war, a complete white elephant. It is probable that he stayed in his grand design just once, shortly after its completion in 1319, on his way to the abortive English siege of Berwick-upon-Tweed (which he allegedly kiboshed). He slept, who knows how soundly, in a chamber at the end of a narrow passageway shaped like a dogleg, which was designed to protect his inner sanctum. It was the architecture of paranoia, as all military constructions tend to be, and Lancaster had good cause for concern. His enemies were closing in.

The powerful barons, including Lancaster, forced the banishment of Edward II's next great favourite after Gaveston, Hugh Despenser the younger and his father. But this victory was the beginning of the end. In the manoeuvrings that followed, those keen to fill the space vacated by the Despensers were willing to betray the men they had fought alongside.

Perhaps we should not judge anyone too harshly across the murk of seven centuries. Today we are left with only the wars and reputations traduced in scurrilous medieval chronicles; few acts of gentleness remain. We know that Lancaster gave generously to several monasteries, as was expected of good earls of his era; indeed, judged against other men of his age, Lancaster's savagery might appear rather mild. Sir John de Lilburn, who gave his name to the imposing tower at the north end of Dunstanburgh Castle, was a 'schavaldour' – a word from the local dialect meaning leader of an armed gang. If Lancaster was ruthless and deceitful, Lilburn lived completely above the law. Despite being a knight of the royal household, he ambushed and attempted to murder a royal judge at Alnwick in 1315 to avenge the hanging of alleged traitors at Berwick. A year later, he ransomed Scottish prisoners of another royal knight and kept the money for himself. In 1317 he was suspected of participating in the highway robbery of two cardinals and the bishop-elect of Durham and rounded off the year by seizing Knaresborough Castle in Yorkshire from another knight. Lilburn was recruited by Lancaster but deserted him, rejoining Edward II's household in time to fight against Lancaster at the Battle of Boroughbridge.

It was here in North Yorkshire in 1322 that Lancaster was intercepted. Lilburn had picked the winning side: Lancaster was trounced by the royalist force, captured alive and given a humiliating trial in which he was mockingly saluted as 'O King Arthur, most dreadful'. Edward II arrived in time to witness Lancaster's beheading; Lilburn was rewarded with the post of joint constable of Dunstanburgh Castle.

His tenure of this behemoth of war was short-lived and Lilburn could never renounce his old ways: in 1327, the year he became sheriff of Northumberland, he stole £100 of goods from the parson of Embleton.

Six centuries sitting idle had softened Dunstanburgh into a picturesque ruin; and the forgiving smudge of time made its murderous architects with their beheadings and betrayals almost jolly, questing knights. As I turned away from the castle, and glanced through rain-flecked glasses at the choppy waves beneath glowering cloud, I felt that the only aspect of the scene that could be a portal into our savage past was the sea. Even though we no longer needed to urgently scan the horizon for signs of invasion, it was the only thing that carried a threat, and could reawaken a frisson of the fear and powerlessness that must have haunted almost everyone in earlier times.

My assumption that no coastal ruin could give us an inkling of the anxiety and paranoia that scarred our warlike past, let alone induce real terror today, was short-lived. It was abruptly terminated when I took a boat across a small, brown tidal river to Orford Ness, a sinuous shingle spit which curves down the Suffolk coast like a femur. For eighty years of the last century, the general public was not permitted onto this inaccessible, low-lying peninsula. It was, as W. G. Sebald noted, visible from the small town of Orford but no easier to reach than the Nevada desert or a South Sea atoll. Notices along the riverbank read: 'WARNING: This is a prohibited place within the meaning of the Official Secrets Act. Unauthorised persons entering this area may be arrested and prosecuted.' Orford Ness was home to some of the most secretive, audacious and potentially destructive experiments in the deadliest century of all. This coast was the front line of the Cold War.

Like Scolt Head Island, Orford Ness is as young as geology gets, assuming its current form in the Middle Ages, a constantly changing promontory of marsh, meadow and small rounded flints created by longshore drift pushing south material from rapidly eroding Dunwich. Known locally as 'the Island', the Ness is the largest vegetated shingle spit in Europe, containing an estimated 15 per cent of the world's reserve of coastal vegetated shingle, a fragile, arid ecosystem of pebble-loving, salt-tolerant plants. It is one of the most precious nature reserves in the country and it is scarred by ruined buildings, unexploded bombs and rumours of death rays, lethal experiments and faked invasions.

Orford Ness has always been an aberrant place. In the twelfth century, a bald-headed, long-bearded *thing*, 'a Fish having the shape of a man in all poyntes', according to John Stow's *Chronicles of England* (1580), was caught by local fishermen, who took it to the castle. The Wild Man of Orford was fond of fish and swimming and not fond of church (taken there, he 'shewed no tokens of adoration'). He could not be persuaded to speak, even by torture. When he was permitted a swim in the sea, he tore through a barrier of three nets to escape but, oddly, returned to captivity. Eventually he escaped again and never came back. Unlike other mer people, the Orford manfish had no tail and accomplished no magic; this, according to Sophia Kingshill and Jennifer Westwood in *The Fabled Coast*, makes him one of the most credible aquatic wild men of legend. Perhaps he really lived, untouched by civilisation, on the marshes of the Ness. In later folk tellings, the manfish evolved into a more conventional merman who avenged its imprisonment by blocking off Orford's harbour with the shingle spit of the Ness.

In 1913 the modern horror began. Orford Ness was bought by the War Office to become only its third airbase in the country. In the following decades, pilots, scientists, engineers and spooks arrived to work on secretive experiments to devise better, deadlier bombs. The military left in 1985 and 'the Island' was acquired by the National Trust on 1 April 1993 but, unusually for a Trust site, it is still closed to the public for much of the year. The Ness is a wilderness of hazardous waste, abandoned to the birds, and also contains fifty decaying structures from its Cold War days: sheds, shacks, bunkers, towers and masts. Most alarming of all are the nightmarish ruins of six large concrete laboratories on the beach. Called the pagodas, these are psychotic cathedrals of Mutually Assured Destruction.

Nothing and no one can prepare you for Orford Ness, although Grant Lohoar did his best as we took his small open boat 200m across the water from the homely harbour of gentrified Orford. Lohoar, with 'hands the size of disc brakes', as one of his Trust colleagues had told me, was stocky, a superb storyteller and certainly a reassuring presence. A ranger on the reserve since the Trust's acquisition, he knew the island as well as anyone, and still it kept its secrets. Despite the restrictions, I had wangled two nights, alone, on the Ness, sleeping in a large single-storey building that had once been the secret site's electronics workshop and photographic studio.

Grant was not a fussy man but the Ness, he warned, as we drank tea in his ramshackle office inside an old military stores building, was a tough place. Cold and hostile in the winter; hot and hostile in the summer; the wind blasts all year round. If you aren't swallowed by an intertidal mud creek or disorientated in the fog, you might step on an unexploded bomb. When Grant first arrived, he had to call bomb disposal on an almost daily basis. In the 1990s a team of twelve experts scoured the site every day for eight weeks, and found nearly 800 bombs, which took an enjoyable three days to blow up. These days, the bomb squad is summoned about three times a year. The Trust has been told the site will never be totally cleared. There is asbestos, a chemical dump and concrete cancer. The sea is always revealing new bombs and mysterious, hazardous waste. 'We have found some seriously nasty, unstable stuff out there,' said Grant.

He warned me to stick to marked routes around the derelict

buildings and not stray across the shingle. This wasn't entirely for my own good. 'To us it's not really about you blowing yourself up or falling in a hole and breaking your leg and not being discovered or getting stuck in the mud as the tide comes up,' said Grant. 'We don't care what happens to you. It's about not causing irreparable damage to this valuable coastal habitat.' The shingle plants grow in broad strips formed by the sea throwing small and big pebbles together. Once this delicate arrangement is damaged, it is virtually impossible for it to re-form.

The Ness was divided in two. On the landward side of a big sea bank were grazing marshes, lagoons, reed beds and an unthreatening collection of Second World War-era huts and sheds. The view back to Orford and its castle was bucolic. Over the bank, on the seaward side, the comforting scale of southern Britain was ripped apart. Before the North Sea lay a bewildering landscape, which shattered time, a sense of proportion and any human comfort.

When Grant left the island at the end of the day, I walked slowly towards desolation on the seaward side of the Ness. I had no idea how the aftermath of a nuclear holocaust might appear but I once witnessed the damage caused by a tsunami and it was something like this. The shingle was scattered with fifty-year-old debris. A bit of corrugated metal swung in the wind, creaking. A pit in the shingle was crammed with enormous twists of red rusted metal, like toys chucked aside by a hysterical baby giant. Then there were the ripped buildings, which appeared to have been blown up overnight but had actually been slowly shredded by sea and salt wind over twenty-five years.

Calling the labs 'pagodas' gave them an exotic, far-eastern association. To W. G. Sebald, who wrote a hallucinogenic account of his visit in the mid-1990s, these hefty buildings, each with a large overhanging roof set above the building on concrete posts and piled high with a cap of shingle, resembled prehistoric burial mounds. To me they looked like poisonous fungi. Their 10ft-thick walls of reinforced concrete were further bolstered by abutments of native pebbles, so that the buildings appeared to be sprouting from the shingle spit.

When the War Office acquired Orford Ness, they immediately created a rough grass airstrip on the grazing meadows and the Ness's first scientists began experimenting with high explosives, incendiary bullets to attack Zeppelins and, most fancifully, the production of artificial clouds. Some of the scientists were both Oxford dons and flying aces, who tested their theories themselves – putting planes into terminal spins (just a decade after the first flight) or dropping bombs on the shingle of the Ness. One pilot, Oliver Wills, considered Orford 'a lovely holiday' after the Western Front of 1918. 'I am experimenting on bombs and have dropped eight already, nearly killing as many fishermen,' he wrote. 'But it seems rather absurd wasting perfectly good fishermen when food is so scarce. I must be more careful next time.'

Between the wars, Ness scientists played a crucial role in developing radar. As the Second World War loomed, 500lb bombs were dropped on Ness buildings to learn how to reinforce and protect airfield buildings. In 1940, a lighthouse keeper was killed by an unexploded bomb on the beach – one of several deaths on the Ness – but the biggest sensation was the strange story of Shingle Street. It was rumoured that an attempted German landing took place at a beach just beyond the southern tip of the Ness. It was apparently repelled by soldiers and a boom that set the sea on fire, causing charred bodies to drift into shore along the coast. Historians now believe that this mysterious event was a complete fabrication, a piece of black propaganda designed to discourage the Nazis from attempting to invade.

When the Cold War began to bite, Orford Ness played a significant role in Britain becoming a nuclear state. Its isolation and privacy made it an ideal outstation for the Atomic Weapons Research

Establishment (AWRE), based at Aldermaston, Berkshire. For Britain's nuclear deterrent to be credible, its bombs needed to fall and detonate reliably. So Ness boffins tested the bombs' ballistics when released at 40,000ft and devised trigger mechanisms to ensure these bombs would detonate when required and not before. Nose cones, tail fins and electronic guidance systems were finessed at the Ness for bombs and delivery systems with names like racehorse pedigrees: Black Night, Yellow Sun, Red Beard, Blue Peacock, Green Grass. The first of these British atom bombs was dropped over Suffolk in 1955, a Blue Danube 'dud' containing all the casing and firing mechanisms but with a placebo instead of nuclear material. Orford's labs specialised in what was known as 'shake, rattle and roll' – subjecting the bombs to extreme vibrations and temperatures. When finally the Cold War began to thaw, the AWRE left the site in 1985, taking most of its equipment back to Aldermaston. There followed an intriguing twilight period when the island was still owned by the MoD but was derelict and undefended. The Ness became a lawless state. People held raves, raced 4WDs, coursed hares, smashed every window and looted what remained. 'You name it. If it should not have been happening, it was happening out here,' Grant had said before I struck out alone onto the shingle. 'If it moved, it was shot. It was also a major drug-smuggling hotspot.' Soon after the Trust took over, Grant and a colleague confronted two men who landed a boat on the Ness without permission. A few years later, they turned up in the headlines: drug dealers, murdered in their Range Rover in an Essex lane.

I tiptoed through the windy silence to Lab 1, which conducted its first experiment in 1956, on what happened to be the eleventh anniversary of Hiroshima. Its doors faced north-east, away from prying, vulnerable civilisation and towards the unpopulated North Sea. As I stepped up to the doorway, a wild cacophony of shrieks made me jump: baby jackdaws, nesting in a rusty vent. Rosebay willowherb, nettles, daisies, elder: all the dereliction specialists were here. Dwarf forget-me-nots adorned the concrete roadway.

The inhabitants of this deserted community of death were wary of me. My ears rang with lark tinnitus, the high-flying birds as invisible as a spy plane. A Chinese water deer skulked away, pausing to turn its fangs towards me. A jackdaw heading for its nest hurriedly rerouted when it spotted me. I was as nervy as they were, and kept expecting an official to loom over the horizon, hurrying up to arrest me. This is what it would feel like to be the last person on earth: getting twitchier each day, convinced that someone would appear. And they never would.

Part of the reason I felt like the lone character in a sci-fi about Armageddon was because there was so little in this scene that was familiar. The only comforting thing that gave the Ness a sense of scale and anchored it somewhere in the last three centuries was the sturdy red-striped lighthouse on the beach. Before its light was turned off in 2013, owing partly to its predicted destruction by coastal erosion, it had been the only human intervention in the landscape that made the world safer, not more dangerous.

Peering inside the labs, I realised I was seeking recognisable signs of humanity. They had been stripped of their equipment long ago but the walls were an innocuous pale-green (AWRE had insisted on futuristic lead-free paint, an oddly health-conscious choice for such a hazardous place) and there were corrugated metal doors, pieces of torn piping, Bakelite light switches and the swinging skeletons of old steel lampshades now found in fashionable East End bars. Lab 2 once contained what was reputed to be the largest centrifuge in the world; Lab 3 a thermal chamber. By the door of Lab 5 was a big red emergency stop button like those in Cold War movies. What terrible thing would have happened if it needed pressing? Would anyone still be alive to do it?

Next to Labs 4 and 5 was a control room from where scientists had monitored the experiments in the pagodas. A flat-roofed building with nicotine-coloured bricks and big windows that dropped almost to the ground, it looked exactly like a 1950s primary school after a nuclear disaster. Shattered windows, grass on the caved-in roof, rubble, shards of asbestos and yellow *Danger!* notices everywhere. I stepped inside and a corridor stretched ahead. On the walls were big iron radiators: domestic objects and oddly comforting when you ran your palm over their cold curves. A swallow dipped around the broken eaves. A ginger rabbit appeared and disappeared like a whisper on the gravel. It wouldn't take many days on the Ness for the hallucinations to begin.

An underground tunnel ran from the control room towards the labs. Someone on Orford Quay reckoned their father dug a sub-terranean bunker on the Ness. 'Have you seen where the water table is on Orford Ness?' Grant Lohoar had scoffed. Here I saw he must be right: this tunnel was no more than a metre deep and it carried only cables.

The precise character of the experiments on Orford Ness remained as uncertain as a footing in the shingle. What went on here? What happened on this secret site during the eighty years in which it was ruled by nuclear scientists and American spooks? 'If you ask anyone in a pub round here, they'll say Orford Ness is where they tested atomic triggers,' Grant had told me earlier in the day. 'It's so much more than that.' Later, he turned to me and chuckled. 'Have you worked out what's the truth and what isn't yet?' I hadn't realised that he took such a postmodern approach to the truth. But he was compelled to: even after working for twenty years on the Ness, he saw it accumulate new mysteries like flotsam, shaped and reshaped on the strandline.

'When I arrived, nine out of ten stories about Orford Ness you heard were apocryphal. I'd still say seven or eight of them are,' said Grant. 'That's fundamental to Orford Ness. This is a place of insane secrecy and huge amounts of mis- and disinformation, official or otherwise. Any site that has been closed for more than three-quarters of a century that close to civilisation builds up myth and legend.' Over the past twenty years, he reckoned he had spoken to several hundred former employees, many of whom quietly revealed themselves on his guided walks. The striking feature of each new account of activities here was how little each person knew of anything beyond their own job. Some site workers were taken across the island to their workplace in a bus with blacked-out windows. Everyone kept their heads down and said nothing, not even to their families. Grant Lohoar discovered his father-in-law had worked there and none of the family had ever suspected. Men from the Ministry would pay impromptu visits to the wives and children of Ness employees and quiz them about what they knew. Even with the Cold War all rubble and memories, the authorities refused to give up the peninsula's secrets. Like other contractors on the base, Grant's father-in-law had signed the Official Secrets Act. After the Trust bought the Ness, Grant persuaded him to write down his memories of his job. He dutifully sent eight pages off to the MoD and a couple of lines came back. The rest had been censored.

Secrecy turned simple features of the landscape into sinister riddles.

Take the most obvious visible symbol of Cold War Orford Ness: the roofs of the pagodas. Why were these great concrete boxes topped with mounds of heavy shingle raised on pillars above the labs? One theory was that the shingle was camouflage. Another was that if something went badly wrong, a controller could detonate charges inside the concrete pillars to bring the roof crashing down on the lab, thus containing any radiation. And the truth? The shingle was mass to absorb energy in the event of an explosion. The windows below the heavy roof had been perspex, designed to blow out if there was a blast; the overhanging roof would direct flying debris into the ground. Then again, during one of his tours, Grant was informed by two retired American scientists that the design of Labs 4 and 5 was complete overkill if we believed the official line about what happened on the Ness: it never housed fissile material. 'You pays your money, takes your choice about whether you believe that or not,' Grant Lohoar said with a shrug. The Trust was once contacted by someone claiming to have served as an armed SAS officer tasked with escorting nuclear weapons in unmarked vehicles from Aldermaston and Burfield to the Ness in the 1960s. But Grant met plenty of people offering colourful Ness tales, and many turned out to be untrue. Even if it never housed fully loaded nuclear weapons, however, some experimental bombs would have contained fully operational explosive charges which could have caused major damage if they had accidentally gone off.

A shortage of facts is replaced with endless stories. One of the less exciting pieces of conjecture is that little of any significance actually happened on the Ness. Was it a backwater operation? For all the talk of great secrecy, at times its experiments seemed decidedly haphazard. Old locals delight in recounting stories about lorries passing, tarpaulins flapping to reveal the tail fin of a bomb sticking out. Villagers always took a keen interest in the island's doings. Shortly after the war, the island's chief ballistics officer recounted visiting 'Mrs Brinkley's shop' in Orford at lunchtime on the day they began a series of trials dropping a 10,000lb Blue Danube bomb: 'Having weighed out my tobacco, Mrs Brinkley said: "I see you dropped that old atom bomb this morning." Lifting my jaw back to its normal position, I think I managed to say "Oh!" before going back.' Another local man told me how he was allowed onto the Ness as a boy to fish for cod by the lighthouse and then he'd push his fish-laden bicycle back home, right through the middle of the Atomic Weapons Research Establishment.

Exploring Orford Ness was like watching a thriller where you keep thinking you have encountered the ultimate villain only to find someone bigger and scarier pulling their strings from the shadows beyond. My accommodation in the old barracks-style lab building was, given its situation in the middle of nowhere surrounded by marshland, creepy. The pagodas were, at dusk, somewhat spookier. The most sinister place on the Ness, and the biggest secret of all, however, was Cobra Mist.

From a distance, it was an uncertain size: a large grey steel block at the northern end of the peninsula that looked like a nuclear power station. To its north were masts that appeared to be constantly changing size and number. Finally, after two days on the Ness, I managed to work out that there were twelve, all of the same size. Cobra Mist was built in a hurry in the late 1960s, a joint collaboration between the British and the Americans at a cost of £56m. (The Americans footed the bill.) It closed prematurely, in 1973, and ever since this big grey building had been the repository for the most fantastic stories of all. The best was that it housed the UFO that supposedly landed in Rendlesham Forest in 1980, one of the most vivid extraterrestrial sightings in this country. The oddest thing of all, however, was the truth: when I visited, forty years after its closure, Cobra Mist was still alive. It was still a working building, and still owned by the Foreign and Commonwealth Office.

Mothballed after its closure in 1973, its transmitters were later deployed by the diplomatic radio station, which morphed into the BBC World Service. Since these broadcasts ceased from Orford Ness in 2011, a private company called Babcock International Group used the transmitters periodically to broadcast continental radio stations. Over the years, Cobra Mist's on-site staff dwindled to two part-time caretakers, who travelled from the mainland every Friday to check on the building.

The day after my exploration of the pagodas was a Friday so I approached Cobra Mist to see if anyone was there. At the end of a decaying concrete track, through fencing still hung with faded signs warning of electrification, was a rutted concrete plaza, empty of vehicles. Behind this was the building: a windowless box on stilts, sides smudged with brown mossy stains, the size of a huge warehouse. At the bottom, a small front door was wide open. I walked over, my heart genuinely thudding below the screams of lesser black-backed gulls. I stepped inside. A small carpeted reception area featured a round table on which was thrown a couple of trade magazines. Spooled across the floor, a cable led to an industrial vacuum cleaner. The walls were lined with woodchip and were mouldy.

I called out. 'Hello? Anybody . . . home?' No answer. Doors led off the reception and I opened one: a storeroom. I called. Nothing. I opened another door. A dark stairwell. My 'hello?' echoed into nothingness. I dared not go any further, and stepped back into the brightness outside. At that moment, three men drove up wearing dark glasses. Uh oh.

Suddenly, however, the normal world reasserted itself. It was the weekly caretakers, John and Mark, who had popped to the jetty to collect a visitor, a young man who was to do something inside with a computer.

It would be hard to find a less likely embodiment of sinister Cobra Mist than John Oakes and yet his whole life was bound up with this strange building. I don't know how he had stayed so cheerful.

John was in his fifties and his first job had been as an office boy for the builders of Cobra Mist. The queue of lorries stretched all the way back up to Orford church, boats brought girders up river, ships even pulled on to the beach. The cover story put to the media that Cobra Mist was an experimental radio transmission station caused local anxieties about how it might interfere with people's televisions. On several occasions, if a television blew up, a resident would call the MoD and be quietly given a new one.

Once Cobra Mist was built, Oakes worked on the mainland for a couple of years until he found himself unemployed. He bumped into a villager on Orford Quay who was a driver for Cobra Mist, and John became a driver too. When the station closed in 1973, he became one of three caretakers. All the equipment was stripped from this expensive spying station but it was maintained, at a constant temperature, until the Foreign Office could find another use for it.

Every night, John had slept in one of its dark, empty, windowless rooms. Old Bill, a one-legged caretaker, slept around the corner. One night, John heard the tap-tap-tapping of Old Bill's wooden leg pacing the corridors. Eventually, he got up to see what was going on. It wasn't Old Bill. The tapping continued. John paced the corridors with his torch. Finally, he found the source: a broken fan turning, in a distant room. It must have been spooky work. 'It was,' said John, 'because there were all these wires left everywhere blowing in the draught, making a noise.'

After a bit of persuasion, John agreed to show me around. At the front of the building was a windowless conference room, a time-warp from 1984. Along the corridors were fuse boxes and ventilation shafts but mostly only faint lines on walls and floors where once things were fixed. The paintwork and the floor tiles could belong to a factory from the 1960s. But its whiff of metal, asbestos and glossy paint did not feel like a derelict industrial building from the twentieth century. Despite John's jolly presence, there was something more chilling here.

Further back was a cavernous storeroom, filled with shelves and shelves of grey boxes labelled with codes such as C-980797. In some lay dozens of washers; in others valves. There was no outsourcing or just-in-time-deliveries in the 1970s and a government building like this one had its own supplies, run by a full-time storeman. He would place a hair across the hinged wooden desk that guarded his stores so he could tell if employees raided them in the night. These disused stores included a prodigious quantity of glass cleaner after it was ordered by mistake: Cobra Mist only had one small window.

There were several empty halls the size of a five-a-side football pitch, including a tall room where the radio transmitters once sat.

One of these was a metal box the size of a garage, filled with valves, condensers and piping. Eleven thousand volts once entered it, and the valves were cooled with water: a hazardous mix. Another transmitter was the DRM Orfordness Transmitter, which was supposed to make medium wave sound as good as FM and had been launched with a great hullabaloo in 2003. It was another futuristic failure for Cobra Mist. John raised his eyebrows.

We climbed the stairs to the second floor, to the secret centre of Cobra Mist. The electricity wasn't working up here so I followed the yellow light cast by John's torch as closely as I could. We moved through a maze of black rooms at high speed. Each was a different rectangular size – some the size of a classroom, some the size of a gymnasium, some the size of a broom cupboard. Each was big and bare, with a high ceiling. Each one was empty.

I never realised a featureless room could convey so much. There was nothing here and yet it felt as if layers of security and familiarity and time had been peeled back by some omnipotent, amoral hand. The dark heart of Cobra Mist was quietly terrifying.

John heaved open a door, its edge lined with layers of what looked like copper. I touched it. 'Careful,' said John, 'that's beryllium. If it gets inside your skin it will make you sick.' I quickly pulled my fingers away. Down a corridor and round a corner in the blackness, we came to a small room, a guard's compartment before the main chamber. The ceiling tiles around its edge were clear glass, so guards could look through the top of the ceiling and along the ventilation shafts to ensure there were no wires, bugs or spies. Further on were the remnants of an airlock. The walls were stuffed with metal and wire wool. A radio still wouldn't work beyond these divides. Then, the chamber, a sealed metal unit which the guards could check above, beside and below. It was a large rectangular room the size of a school hall that once buzzed with computers and secret radar equipment. A raised control area looked over the scene through three big windows.

On the far side were brackets on which would have hung a big screen or, perhaps, one of those illuminated maps you saw in Cold War thrillers. The metal lampshades still held blue bulbs to bathe the whole area in a cold light. All was dark and silent and yet it still felt deadly: a paranoid, dystopian setting for a secretive group of people paid to obsess over the Enemy and do whatever they could to expose its secrets, and guard their own.

We moved through the blackness, past more tiny sealed rooms. John kicked at a door that promised to be an emergency exit but couldn't open it. 'Too much gull shit,' he grunted. We circled around and entered a large room where the young man John had brought to Cobra Mist was on his mobile standing in front of a small laptop, silhouetted by a temporary floodlight. What was he doing? I had no idea but it looked like another scene from a spy thriller.

John nodded cheerily, not remotely discombobulated, and bustled over to another emergency door. With a whoosh, we were out into the brightness, on top of Cobra Mist's roof, looking north over its field of aerials towards Aldeburgh. It was a relief. Here had once stood a fan of masts linking a spider's web of antenna strings. 'It was so stark white it looked fantastic in the sun,' said John of the old aerial field. 'But you won't find any photographs of it because everyone was too scared – they were under the Official Secrets Act.'

This parabola faced north-east: to Russia. Here, the purpose of Cobra Mist was revealed. It was an experimental, 'over the horizon' radar system designed to spy on air and missile activity in the USSR. But mystery still surrounds what, exactly, it did and why it closed so abruptly in 1973, at the behest of the Americans. By that time, Cobra Mist had attracted the attentions of investigative journalists who argued it could destabilise fragile relations with the Soviet Union. When it closed, Cobra Mist's local workforce went on strike in protest. Redundancy payments were eventually agreed but it was claimed that disgruntled employees snatched valuable equipment from the secret station. More than a thousand shrubs and bushes decorating the site also disappeared overnight.

According to the historian Paddy Heazell, Cobra Mist was summarily shut by the Americans because it never worked. Pentagon papers claimed the station's radar transmitters reached the required power but the computers of the day were not powerful enough to decipher meaningful signals from all the noise they harvested. The favourite local rumour is that its radar was jammed by two Russian trawlers bobbing in the North Sea. Cobra Mist was, like Dunstanburgh, an expensive white elephant but John disapproved of that cliché. 'It was an experimental station,' he pointed out, arguing that it may have led to other innovations even if it wasn't one itself. But Heazell believes there is more information still to be revealed that may better explain its sudden closure and, possibly, secret activities that continued to be conducted there. The National Trust owned almost all of Orford Ness but not Cobra Mist. Why was this monumental property still held by the Foreign and Commonwealth Office? The USSR was clearly concerned about Cobra Mist long after it shut and it was mentioned in arms limitation talks as the Cold War drew to a close in the 1980s.

There was another mystery: John Oakes loved his job. This initially baffled me but it quickly became an attractive characteristic. 'There's no job like it,' he said. In the past, it was better because there was more to do: stripping out old fittings and equipment, helping build the new radio transmitters. Protecting the building was a grave responsibility – these humble caretakers were members of the British Diplomatic Service in the 1970s – but they had fun too. Secrecy conferred a certain freedom on the workers of the Ness: they worked in virtual isolation and any boss was a spectral presence. In one dark room there was a symmetrical pattern of white gaffer tape on the dusty floor. 'We used to play badminton in here,' said John. The guards had marked out a court with the tape.

We headed downstairs. 'All this space, just crying out for somebody to be doing little secret jobs,' sighed John. He loved the place. The Foreign Office was still involved with the building, he believed, so he hoped it wouldn't be left to rot. What will become of it? 'Who knows? Someone said storage but it's so hard to get to. They keep having reviews and meetings, and they say, "You'll be all right for a little while yet," and I'll be retired soon so I will be all right.'

Orford Ness faced an uncertain future, in all senses of the word. The Ness is unlikely to remain an 'untrue island,' as Robert Macfarlane calls it, for much longer because it is growing longer and slimmer and at some point soon the rising sea will detach it from the mainland. Grant Lohoar hoped we would never know all its human mysteries. 'The day you know everything about Orford Ness will be the end of Orford Ness as we know it. What good is a riddle if you know the answer?'

Unlike at Dunstanburgh, where the sea had been the only thing that bore a genuine sense of menace, here I cleaved to the soft grey waves as the most comforting thing on the island. Sitting by the water's conversational meeting with the shingle, I did not need to turn many degrees to take in Sizewell nuclear power station and Slaughden's Martello Tower to the north and then Cobra Mist, a building called the Black Beacon erected as part of an early radio navigation system, the bombing range and the labs. To the south were the cranes of the industrial port of Felixstowe, which a century ago had been a fashionable resort. All alarming human themes were here: energy, greed, commerce, paranoia, mistrust and violence. And civilisation? The lighthouse or perhaps the small town of Orford looked like its best representative although Orford Castle was another symbol of our long attachment to war. I chided myself for judging the Cold War relics of the Ness when equally sinister experiments were still taking place around the globe. Our current and future destructiveness would not be written so physically in buildings like those at Orford Ness because computers don't say much when they are not switched on.

The ruins of the Ness spoke eloquently of human energy, but perhaps even more about the power of nature. Although most of our recent wartime constructions endure beyond their exceptionally short relevance as a working building, they speedily age and disappear from the coastline. If we stop frantically fixing, painting, tending to our theatres of war, they soon fall apart. Even buildings constructed to contain explosions are quickly ruined, not by a nuclear bomb but by the North Sea's northerlies, easterlies and salty spray. If the world ended, said Orford Ness, our creations would soon be smoothed over by the sea, human concrete pulverised into shingle once again.

## Explorations of Neptune

Brits tend to float past the **White Cliffs of Dover** on ferries but the National Trust's recent purchase has enhanced a splendid clifftop stroll. This is a real tea-room trail because you can eat at the start, middle and end of this walk. If you begin at Dover, there is an excellent cafe with panoramic views at the Trust's Langdon Cliffs car park. It's a simple two-mile stroll to South Foreland Lighthouse, where one of the old lighthouse cottages has been converted into Mrs Knott's Tea-room, with lovely old teapots and cups. Apart from the flowers and butterflies – look out for the chalkhill blue in July and August – the highlight of this clifftop walk is **Fan Bay Deep Shelter**, which the Trust opens to guided tours in 2015. There is no parking at South Foreland Lighthouse but in summer there is a bus between Langdon Cliffs and South Foreland. If you want a longer walk, it is well worth continuing east, through the interesting seaside suburb of St Margaret's At Cliffe (where Ian Fleming once lived) and on to more National Trust coastline by the war memorial at Bockell Hill. The footpath here is part of the Saxon Shore Way.

*Langdon Cliffs*

Upper Road

Dover

Kent, CT16 1HJ

*OS Map*

Explorer 138, Dover, Folkestone & Hythe

*Nearest railway station*

Dover Priory, 2.5 miles

*Websites*

www.nationaltrust.org.uk/white-cliffs-dover/visitor-information/

South Foreland Lighthouse

The Front, St Margaret's Bay, Dover, Kent CT15 6HP

www.nationaltrust.org.uk/south-foreland-lighthouse/

Fan Bay Deep Shelter
www.nationaltrust.org.uk/white-cliffs-dover/our-work/projects/

One of the best and simplest Neptune coast walks is the mile-and-a-half stroll from **Craster** to the sublime dereliction of **Dunstanburgh Castle**. Craster is heaving in the summer and you need to park in the car park (NE66 3TW) before you descend into the picturesque little fishing village. To the north of the harbour is the coast path which follows the gently rolling green fields north, with Dunstanburgh dominating the horizon in front of you. This stretch of National Trust coast feels like a well-populated park in summer but in the winter it can be desolate. The ruin of Dunstanburgh is owned by English Heritage but National Trust members get in free. Admission is worth it for the view from one of the ruined towers. The path continues north around the sandy sweep of stunning Embleton Bay and up to **Low Newton**, a model village built for fishermen in the nineteenth century and restored by the National Trust. Refresh yourself at the Ship Inn and then head home!

### *Dunstanburgh Castle*
(Open weekends only, November–February)
### *OS Maps*
Explorer 332, Alnwick & Amble
Explorer 340, Holy Island & Bamburgh
### *Nearest railway station*
Alnmouth, 7 miles
### *Websites*
Dunstanburgh Castle
www.english-heritage.org.uk/daysout/properties/dunstanburgh-castle/
Low Newton
www.nationaltrust.org.uk/embleton-and-newton-links/visitor-information/

Littered with unexploded ordnance and toxic waste, **Orford Ness** is one of the least accessible National Trust properties, which is part of its magic. Access is permitted only via the NT ferry at Orford Quay on open days, departing 10 a.m. until 2 p.m., with the last boat from the Ness at 5 p.m. There are a limited number of tickets each day and the Ness is closed between November and March, and open only on Saturdays during the bird nesting season. A guided walk will enable you to get into some of the pagodas, and if you are lucky enough to be guided by Grant Lohoar, you are in for a treat. You'll need to book ahead for guided walks. You can wander the Ness unaccompanied but the presence of unexploded bombs makes it sensible to stick to the marked trails. A red route takes you over marshes and dunes and across the shingle, and you can wander out to the lighthouse and follow the red markers on a loop around some of the mysterious, crumbling military installations. Other marked routes are open depending on the bird nesting season.

### OS Map
Explorer 212, Woodbridge & Saxmundham
### Nearest railway station
Wickham Market: 8 miles
### Website
www.nationaltrust.org.uk/orford-ness/

## Further Reading
Paddy Heazell, *Most Secret: The Hidden History of Orford Ness*, The History Press, 2010
W. G. Sebald, *The Rings of Saturn*, Vintage, 2002

# 4

# Work

*The Goodwin Sands / The Isle of Wight / Durham / Strangford Lough*

The Durham Beaches

Strangford Lough

The Goodwin Sa

South Foreland
Lighthouse

The Back of the Wight
(South West Isle of Wight)

Waging war was one of two ancient ways in which we have engaged with our coast. The other is through our work. Fishing has shaped the human character of our shores more than any other endeavour, and for centuries was the primary way we related to the sea. More recently, the Industrial Revolution demanded the exploitation of the mineral riches found near our cliffs and many mining operations left warlike scars on our shores long after their labourers disappeared like a retreating army. But some of the most intriguing old ways of seeking profit from the coast are the disreputable diversifications once practised by fishermen and other seaside inhabitants. The morality of making money from the sea is sometimes pretty murky.

One indisputably noble shoreline occupation is the lighthouse keeper. South Foreland Lighthouse is a squat white building whose castellated stonework gives it the look of a miniature fort. Its beam, like that of many other lighthouses, is now extinguished, and it sits on the White Cliffs east of Dover as a monument to more hazardous times. In its day, it was the most important lighthouse in the country, its brilliant eye winking vessels safely through the busiest shipping channel in the world.

When I arrived at South Foreland, it was a gloriously sunny July day and it was difficult to imagine any menace in the sapphire-coloured

English Channel. Standing on the balcony hugging the gigantic closed eye at the top of the lighthouse, all I could hear was the wind and the larks. To the west was Dover Castle; to the east, an obelisk commemorating First World War veterans above St Margaret's at Cliffe. To the south-east, surprisingly large in the Channel, were the Goodwin Sands. From this angle, it appeared possible to walk across the Channel on these orange flats. As dusk fell, I looked again. Where the Goodwins had been there was just a sliver of silver spray on the horizon. It was like a conjurer's trick. I shivered.

There are the wrecks of 55,000 ships recorded around the coasts of Britain and Ireland and there is no more naturally baleful place than the Goodwins, banks of sand inconveniently placed in the English Channel which come and go with the tides. 'A most dreadfull gulfe, and ship swalower' was the verdict of William Lambarde in 1570 and his description of the Goodwin Sands as 'either sea, or land, or neither of both' is perfectly fitting today. On large low tides, the sands become firm enough for games and picnics. When the tide rises, however, the sand turns into a treacherous bog. If run aground, a ship cannot simply wait for the next big tide to float off because the sand can suck it down and swallow it. If the sand doesn't snatch a stranded ship, the currents probably will, sweeping sand away from its underneath and breaking it apart.

In *The Merchant of Venice*, Antonio's ship was said to have foundered 'on the narrow seas; the Goodwins, I think they call the place; a very dangerous flat and fatal, where the carcasses of many a tall ship lie buried'. Shakespeare wrote these lines not long after a burning Spanish galleon, part of the 1588 Armada, had crashed onto the Goodwins. The Great Storm of 1703 caused four Royal Navy battleships to be wrecked on the sands, with 1,200 fatalities. Traumatised survivors reported the apparent reappearance of the Spanish ship, 'a great warship of Drake's day, her sails tattered, burning from fore to aft and her guns firing'. Another ghost ship of the Goodwins, *Lady Lovibond*, is reputed to reappear every fifty years since her destruction in the eighteenth century but has been delayed in modern times: her last appearance was in 1934 when a lifeboat was dispatched to a burning ship on the Goodwins that did not exist.

This legend is a nice illustration of one of the most notorious coastal lines of work: wrecking. The term is confusing for it describes a continuum of lawless labour ranging from looting to premeditated murder. In medieval days, the sea and everything in it was annexed by royalty until protests by shipowners led to a charter granted by Henry III that permitted the owner of wrecked goods to reclaim his property within three months of the loss of a ship. The ruling contained a crucial clause that shows the law of unintended consequences: if a man or beast escaped alive, the ship could not be considered a wreck. This unfortunate law, which was not repealed until 1771, encouraged wreckers to murder survivors. In *The Wreckers*, an entertaining history of the practice, Bella Bathurst suggests there were two types: active and passive wrecking but, in truth, the consequences of human actions are uncertain in storms. Morality turns opaque. An example of passive wrecking is the scavenging of motorbikes and nappies from the stricken *MSC Napoli* washed up below the spectacular (National Trust-owned) cliffs at Branscombe, Devon, in 2007. Police called this opportunism 'despicable', but throughout history the unofficial law of finders keepers has always trumped the formal law that calls it theft. 'For a fully-laden general cargo vessel to run aground in an accessible position on an island in winter is more or less like having Selfridges crash land in your back garden – a Selfridges with all the prices removed,' as Bathurst put it. Wreckage has long been regarded as a right by seaside dwellers who saw no shame in picking the fruits of great storms. On his journey around the Norfolk coast, Daniel Defoe noted scarcely a barn, shed, stable or hogstye not 'built of old planks, beams, wales and timbers etc, the wrecks of ships and ruins of mariners' and merchants' fortunes'. Everyone loves a floating tub of brandy – Excisemen found four hogsheads of brandy hidden in the cellar of the local parson after a ship was wrecked off Porthleven, Cornwall, in 1939 – but wrecking could also be rather wholesome. A ship with a cargo of oranges sank off Cromer, Norfolk, during the Second World War when exotic fruit was in short supply. Women and children biked to harvest oranges from the beach, and men took them by the van-load to sell at Norwich market.

Passive wrecking might be a victimless crime but active wrecking is not. The Cornish, in particular, are fabled as professional wreckers. Local people were reputed to display 'false lights' to deliberately lure ships onto the rocks, biting fingers or ears of dead passengers to obtain their jewellery and even murdering survivors to ensure they could claim all of a ship's bounty. The myth-making of Daphne du Maurier's *Jamaica Inn*, a splendid gothic-horror romp about a gang of wreckers who terrorise the coast of North Cornwall, has enhanced the idea that the Cornish are leaders in this industry but, as Nicholas Crane points out in *Coast*, this reputation may be unfairly caused by our tendency to attribute its people with the same characteristics as its 'cruel' and 'merciless' clifftops.

There are twenty-six wrecks per mile of coastline recorded in Cornwall, according to the *Shipwreck Index of the British Isles* produced by Lloyd's Register; on the Goodwin Sands, however, there are thirty-two wrecks per mile. Like the hazards of Cornwall, the Goodwin Sands were a business opportunity: local people could profit from others' misfortune. In the stuffy-sounding Lloyd's Salvage Association Reports 1866–68, I read one of the most vivid accounts of real wrecking, written by J. A. W. Harper, the secretary of Lloyd's. At 1.30 a.m. on 30 August 1866, the *North*, a 1,238-ton cargo ship, ran aground on the Goodwin Sands. The captain and crew launched lifeboats. Some were picked up by a Dutch lifeboat; others by a German brig. The history of British lifeboats is a laudable one but in many places is derived from local sailors, 'beachmen' or 'luggers', who would race each other in their nimble boats to reach a wreck and salvage its treasures. Saving lives was somewhat incidental to the bounty. After the *North* went aground, the keeper of a Goodwin lightship reported 'the boats were swarming' as soon as daylight came. The Deal boatmen had turned up. Despite locals giving reassurances to the *North*'s captain that the crew's belongings would be rescued, seven chests were delivered to the Receiver of Wrecks (the official responsible for reuniting wreckage with its owners) containing precisely nothing. 'Who emptied those chests?' wrote Harper in his acerbic report. 'Was it the sea? Did the water break open the locks, clear out the contents, and deposit the chests, after the operation, on the ship's deck from which they were taken? Did the cockroaches do it?' Thousands of pounds of goods – rigging, sails, provisions, compasses, tools, copper – were missing: the ship had been stripped.

Six miles from the Goodwins, Deal was ideal for wrecking in the nineteenth century. Its 800 fishermen and their fleet of boats could quickly disperse goods via the town's secretive alleyways and the close-knit local community tended to maintain a protective silence. A Kent MP quoted a local magistrate who said how rarely cases of larceny were brought against Deal boatmen but Harper argued that was because the whole community was complicit. A marine dealer was charged with possessing goods stolen from the *North* and tried at Canterbury but was acquitted. In an unusually forgiving tone, the local paper reported: 'Although Foster's acquittal gives the greatest satisfaction to our inhabitants ... they all agree that he has had a most extraordinary escape.' Wrecking was blamed on the occasional 'black sheep', but Harper estimated it would have taken at least 100 men to strip the *North* so quickly. 'That is a tolerably large proportion of black sheep,' he wrote.

The Deal beachmen were notorious, but their community's defence of them was not simply a dastardly collusion. They were fishermen, a hazardous occupation which did not provide a regular income and risked their lives to save people from the wrecks. Why should they not receive some compensation from the ship's chattels, which would lie at the bottom of the Channel without them? 'The Deal beachmen are a bold, daring race of men,' Harper acknowledged, but he argued that public sympathy for them was misplaced: landsmen often believed their feats more heroic than they really were and the fishermen were wealthier than they claimed.

Harper's report depicted a 'full blown system of illegal wrecking on the Kentish coast' and called for the government to act against a situation where the courts offered shipowners 'no remedy'. He may have been a lone voice in Kent, but others had noted the criminal character of the English coast. In 1863 a French official observed that the English 'trade of salvage comes to border on piracy'. Three years later, a statement by French marine underwriters described the 'trade of salvage' on English coasts as 'little worthy of a civilised nation, and for which we can scarcely find a parallel, unless among the wreckers of the Bahamas'. Even in the twentieth century, passing sailors were amazed by local attitudes. 'I have been wrecked in different parts of the globe, even in the Fiji islands,' wrote the Dutch captain of *Voorspoed*, a cargo vessel wrecked in Perran Bay, Cornwall, in 1901, 'but never among such savages as those of Perranporth.'

Despite such terror, prosecutions for wrecking have been vanishingly rare. The only known case where 'false lights' were mentioned was on Anglesey where Chaptain Chilcote brought charges against three 'opulent inhabitants' of the island in 1773 for plundering rum and brandy from Chilcote's ship, *Charming Jenny*, said to have been lured by false lights onto the rocks. Three of the crew died although Chilcote and wife reached the Welsh shore on a makeshift raft. He lay there, drifting in and out of consciousness, while 'savages' rushed to the scene and by the time he staggered up and found his wife she was dead, 'half-naked and plundered'. He could not be certain she had been killed by the looters but two of the accused were sentenced to death by hanging.

Just as nefarious a coastal profession is smuggling. Because coastal people are such good storytellers, the historical figure of the smuggler is usually romanticised and remembered with affection. We know they break the law, and yet somehow it seems forgivable – perhaps betraying our sneaking admiration for the underdogs who get one over on the taxman. Typical is the tale of Granny Grylls, who lived on the Cornish coast. When she was a young woman, she would often be seen walking to the beach and back carrying a baby that was never heard to cry. One day she was stopped by a customs officer who said, 'Well, Mrs Grylls, that baby of yours is very quiet.'

'Quiet her may be,' she replied. 'But I reckon her's got a deal o' spirit in her.'

And so she had: Mrs Grylls's baby was actually a jar of brandy.

Smuggling is a perpetual feature of the working coast. The Magna Carta of 1215 records wine illicitly brought into England, and wool taken out. Reputable trade was plied through established ports; disreputable trade via the secretive coves, cliff paths and coastal hideaways of our less-developed edges and so the Neptune coast has more than its fair share of lying, cheating and Excisemen-evading local legends, particularly in North Yorkshire, Cornwall and the Isle of Wight.

I have always sensed something vaguely disreputable about the Isle of Wight, and not merely because this splendidly curmudgeonly island once housed three prisons. (One closed in 2013, causing local anguish about job losses.) One of the last parts of England to be converted to Christianity, the Isle of Wight enjoyed a fashionable boom after Queen Victoria built a holiday home there in the 1840s, and Alfred Lord Tennyson, the poet laureate, followed. Every visitor knows about the Needles, which attract fog, peregrines and scenic television shots, but the National Trust also protects a great swath of the south-west coast, from Tennyson Down to St Catherine's Point. This is known locally as the Back of the Wight, an eroding territory of abrupt ravines called chines and isolated villages cut off from the rest of the island by high downs. Here, much of the tideline is hidden from view because the big cliffs are slumping tiered affairs like the Jurassic Coast of Dorset and East Devon.

Rich in fossils, this landscape is also the source of many smugglers' tales. Tennyson Down offered a sweeping, open prospect but things got more promising, from a smuggler's point of view, when I passed Blackgang Chine: Land of Imagination, a theme park built on a former smuggling hotspot which was opened in 1843, making it one of the oldest surviving such attractions in the country. Perhaps it showed there were gainful forms of employment for former smugglers. A few miles on, Watershoot Bay, the elusive heart of the Back of the Wight, was completely different from the slightly tacky attractions on the busier parts of the coast. Below the grandeur of St Catherine's Down, home to a half-built lighthouse that was sited too high to help stricken ships, this rocky little cove was completely untouched by commerce and not easy to find, particularly as the road leading through the woods was temporarily inaccessible to vehicles after a land slip. It was a summer's day but apart from three body-boarders, there was no one around. It could have been Western Scotland. The beach was all awkward boulders and beach rubbish. A magpie harried a young raven over blackthorn that was sculpted like weed in a stream by the incessant south-westerly wind. A collapsed pinnacle of dirty grey clay looked like a slag heap and the whole scene resembled a recently cleared industrial site because the land was so disturbed, not by humans but by the interminable erosion of greensand and clay. As on the Dorset Undercliff, greensand lay on top of gault clay or 'blue slipper' as it was known here and the lubrication of rainwater created slips. The rage of the sea did its best too.

The Back of the Wight's remoteness was perfect for the smuggling during the eighteenth and nineteenth centuries which, as depicted by local man Fred Mew, was a communal conspiracy against the authorities when agricultural wages were intolerably low. Smuggling was organised during the fishing season, between May and September, when a few absent fishermen would not be noticed. They sailed across the Channel to collect the 'tubs', usually of brandy from Barfleur or Cherbourg, which would then be brought ashore in multifarious creative ways. After several fishermen disappeared, a letter would arrive stating that a load of 'faggots' would be delivered at a certain time. The 'shore gang' arranged to be at a landing place and find out when and where the Excisemen would be on patrol. 'This information was usually obtained from one of the coastguards who was not averse to some extra pocket money,' wrote Mew.

Sometimes tubs would be concealed in false bottoms of boats. On other occasions, they would be weighted and hung over the side of the boat. If the smugglers were approached by the Excisemen, they could simply cut them loose; they knew every rock on the coastline and would retrieve the cargo at a later date. The shore gang would clamber down the cliffs and haul in the 'crop' with ropes, hiding it in ricks, pigsties, cellars or churchyards. If the Excisemen spotted signs of suspicious activity, they would search properties the following morning. On one occasion, tubs had been buried near a hive of bees in a garden at Chale. When Excisemen searched the garden, the owner 'accidentally' knocked over a hive and the angry swarm prevented further excavations. Another time, dawn broke before a crop of tubs could be carried away so they were hidden in the stacks of corn. When the farmer came to open the stacks to dry them, he caught sight of the tubs and told his labourers that the corn was not so wet as he thought and he would leave the stacks: in other words, the farmer wanted a slice of the loot. Frequently, claimed Mew, local gentry and even vicars were in on the game.

Viewed from this century, it seems a jolly ruse but the economics were similar to drug smuggling today – everyone took a cut and the drug was adulterated to augment the profit. Farm workers like Mew's father, veteran of numerous smuggling runs, typically earned thirteen shillings for their weekly labour so would go into partnership with friends to put up the money for a four-gallon tub of brandy, which cost fourteen shillings. Fishermen received three shillings each for transporting it and shore-hands received three shillings for each tub safely landed. Farm labourers might work fourteen hour days in the summer before walking twenty miles to work all night hauling tubs ashore. The tubs were diluted with the same quantity of water and colouring and eight gallons were sold for £2 10s. Mew claims that the Back of the Wight's smuggling days ended with a major seizure in 1874, when hundreds of pounds of fines for local people 'made dear drinks of it', but broader economic changes contributed to the decline of smuggling. Earning a living on our shores has historically been fraught and unpredictable but new ways of making a profit from the coast were emerging. Growing prosperity heralded by the Victorian tourist boom eased the Back of the Wight's passage to respectability, and the island became the treasured landscape it is today.

The Industrial Revolution may have had its most dramatic impact upon our cities, but it also transformed our shores. For coastal communities once dependent upon smuggling or fishing, there were suddenly lucrative new job opportunities – though they came at a price. The beach at Easington Colliery was once a vision of hell. 'I could see dozens of men bent on the task of retrieving the sea coal,' wrote the journalist Robert Chesshyre. 'A fire, around which those drying out their sodden clothes had gathered, burned beneath the conveyor, and, immediately below where I stood, two ancient lorries were backed into the waves, each surrounded by men armed with shovels, who dug energetically in the shallow water. Further out the fierce wind whipped up venomous, coal-stained waves . . . The beach was as black as a coal tip, which is literally what it was.'

He wrote this account not in the Thirties nor even the Sixties but in 1986, when the mines on Durham's coastline were still spewing mountains of waste to be scavenged on the beach. The shore was a free dumping ground for mines tunnelled below the bed of the North Sea. For J. B. Priestley, who visited this hidden corner of industrial England in 1933, the ruined landscape and poverty-stricken people were 'a symbol of greedy, careless, cynical, barbaric industrialism'. He was scandalised by what he saw and concluded of one Durham mining community, Shotton: 'No doubt it was fortunate for England that you could dig down at Shotton and find coal. But it did not seem to have been very fortunate for Shotton. The Cotswolds were to be congratulated, it seems, on their lack of coal deposits.' At its peak, 2.5 million tonnes of waste were tipped on Durham's beaches each year: 40 million tonnes in total. As Chesshyre put it, fifty years after Priestley's lament: 'No industry would have been allowed to despoil the beaches of Sussex as the coal industry has been allowed to despoil these Durham beaches.' Both writers discovered that the working coast can be a shock, a traducing of nature. A colliery town by the sea looks, as Priestley said, 'as weird as a cart-horse with scales and fins'. I had never before visited this part of England and was keen to see if it was still as polluted and desperate as it had been in 1988, when the National Trust took the brave and unusual decision to buy a mile of this ruined seashore from British Coal for the princely sum of £1.

Built to service its mine, the town of Easington Colliery was a sprawl of red-brick architecture that couldn't care less about the sea. Its main street, Seaside Lane, sloped down towards the coast before veering away, unconcernedly, for neighbouring Horden. The terraced streets faced in on each other, backs to the water, and halted, abruptly, before the best piece of real estate, the fields by the clifftops. The mine owners who hurriedly erected the town for their workforce were oblivious to coastal vistas.

The town bore a certain amount of baggage, being one of the poorest communities in Britain. It was the sort of place that only ever featured on news bulletins as a representation of problems of unemployment, welfare or obesity. Seaside Lane boasted News+Booze, a sign for the 'Coast' club night and two large, handsome Edwardian schools that would elsewhere have been quickly converted into chi-chi apartments, but here were derelict and awaiting demolition. For all this, Easington Colliery was not as bad as I had been led to expect. In 1993 the mine had become the last of the Durham pits to shut and, in the years since, the town had been tidied up by regeneration money; it looked like a community that was pulling itself back up. But it was still a curiously blank place. There was an open field and a mound where the colliery once was; in fact, there were grassy mounds everywhere – soil pulled over a demolished industrial landscape like a freshly dug grave. There was a memorial at Easington Colliery but on most old pit sites were new business parks, which lay clean and virtually vacant. The death of work was writ large on the landscape.

The Romans knew that coal could be found in Durham and for centuries shallow seams were excavated via bell pits, a bell-shaped hole in the ground, worked by the city's monks. Mining arrived on the east coast in the 1840s but gargantuan industrial mines did not operate until the turn of the twentieth century. The Easington Coal Company started the first of three shafts in 1899; neighbouring Horden opened its mine in 1900. Pitmen came from all over the country: West Durham, Staffordshire, Ireland and the Cornish mines, which were already then in terminal decline. Easington Colliery and Horden grew like gold-rush settlements. Pursuing seams far under the North Sea, by 1920 Horden was producing one million tons a year. By 1930 it employed 4,428 people and mined 6,758 tons of coal in a single day, a European record that stood for thirty years.

Urban myths of the 1930s featured miners who could afford to buy two pianos and only drank champagne, but working conditions for miners were actually grim. In the five years to 1931, more than five thousand people were killed in the coal mining industry. In 1951 an explosion underground caused the death of eighty-three men at Easington. 'In these unhappy districts there is a war on,' wrote Priestley, 'and the allied enemies are poverty, idleness, ignorance, hopelessness and misery.'

The environment was quickly impoverished too. At first, the sea washed away small amounts of dumped coal. Horden's beach was still sandy in the 1930s. Billy Butlin contemplated building his new holiday resorts at nearby Crimdon and Castle Eden but wisely changed his mind. Priestley recorded that the dingy Durham sea of 1935 'had somehow lost its usual adventurous escaping quality'. The surge in output led by mechanisation in the 1940s caused spoil to wash back onto the beaches in ten-metre drifts.

After the war, scavengers known as 'beach men' bought ex-Army vehicles and used them to transport waste coal they gathered from the shore. During the miners' strike of 1984/85, many more local people scoured the beach for coal. Mines closed, unemployment rose and Chesshyre was an early user of the term 'underclass' to describe those who once inherited a job from their father and now only inherited joblessness. Coal production ended at Horden in 1986 and Easington closed seven years later. 'The miners' legacy is back-to-back colliery houses, a closed Co-op store and the worst health in Britain,' wrote Chesshyre. 'The brass went elsewhere and the muck remained behind.'

Beyond Easington Colliery and Horden was the beach. On a dirty Saturday in October, dominated by a chilling drizzle the locals called a sea fret, I parked in a lane and entered a characteristically characterless grassy clifftop field where mine-workings once were. Across the field was a path along all twelve miles of the Durham coast, five of which were now owned by the National Trust. The land was managed for conservation and public access. But the public did not appear to want to access it. In the town, the colliery club had been absolutely bustling, but here it was just me and a single dog-walker.

Sycamore leaves were mottled with black blobs like liver spots on elderly people's hands and a hawthorn hedge was burnt brown by the closing of the season. The bracken was a mix of going-green and coming-brown, with none of the bright ginger seen on sunny fells. A nice sculpture of a tern in metal attempted to brighten the scene, as did a pair of recently discarded zebra-print knickers with a purple bow. At least someone had some fun down here in the years since the colliery closed.

Below crumbly, slumping limestone cliffs was an impressive beach, empty in both directions. It was no longer black with coal but the sand was red-brown and dotted with arrestingly coloured stones: umber, clay and most commonly, a spectacular sulphurous yellow. These were not natural hues: they had been stained with iron oxide and then washed and rewashed by the sea and made the beach appear an eerie abandoned planet, which was useful to film-makers: Durham's beaches starred in *Get Carter* and *Alien 3*.

Scrambling down the cliff, I realised the sands were divided in two. A red-brown sand led into the waves but all along the middle of the beach ran a miniature cliff, a metre tall, where the sea had cut into a wedge of compacted grey sludge. This was 'minestone', all that remained of the liquid waste from coal washeries and coal tailings that had defined this coast so recently. Two decades on, it didn't look or feel disgusting; in fact, it could easily be mistaken for an ancient geological deposit. Close-up, this little cliff's stripy cross section revealed beautiful strata of colours that could have been coal, rust, tin, iron and rubble, the alluvial deposits of industrial Britain.

If it was a natural cliff it might represent 200 million years of natural history but human affairs were so supercharged that this deposit was a snapshot of just eighty-three years of mining. We have changed our environment with frightening speed. In 1995 Christopher Somerville described the waste as 5ft high, 250 yards deep and a mile long and noted estimates that the waves would scythe through it to reach the cliffs in fifty years. But the sea was proving far more efficient than that (assisted by a five-year, lottery-funded project at the turn of the century to remove spoil from the coastline). We may be vandals but the natural world relentlessly repairs our damage. Nature certainly recovers from industrial trauma more quickly than we do.

I met Gareth Wilson and Wayne Appleton, two National Trust rangers, for a walk along the cliffs overlooking the magnificent Blast Beach, which two decades ago had been another scene of industrial ruination. Now the landscape was austerely grey but only tainted, rather than dominated, by the old pollution. Wayne got out his phone and showed me photos of the coast he'd taken that summer: the sea was a brilliant blue, the limestone clifftops decorated with wild flowers: rock rose, bloody crane's bill, fairy flax, yellow wort. The Durham coast encompassed 92 per cent of Britain's para-maritime Magnesian limestone grassland.

Even during Priestley's day, the areas around the mine had pockets of beauty. 'The country itself was very queer,' wrote Priestley on his 1935 tour. 'Running across it, like great cracks, were the narrow valleys called "denes", where there was usually a rushing stream, and perhaps some trees.' As we walked, these steep valleys emerged like surprises on the coast path, tree-filled time capsules from the pre-industrial era. We followed the path through Hawthorne Dene, an overgrown garden belonging to a ruined gothic mansion that had been set on fire by vandals and then demolished in 1979: it was now an oasis of mature sycamores and old fruit trees. It was magical.

At the bottom of the valley, we gazed up at the fine brick-built arch of a bridge that took the railway across the dene high above our heads.

'That was my school project,' nodded Wayne. 'Everybody did football and I did the bridge.' He smiled. 'I was a bit sad at school.' Wayne, who was in his thirties but still looked like a teenager, was a lovely man, softly spoken and bearing the kind of engrained understanding of his home environment that it would be impossible to acquire in a couple of years on the job. He was also an interesting example of the changing employment prospects for the young people of East Durham. His father, grandfather and great-grandfather were all pitmen – his granddad's claim to fame was digging underground to join Easington and Horden collieries together – but by the time Wayne left school the mines had closed and the outlook for young people was bleak. Wayne had been among a class of sullen fourteen-year-olds who were taken out one day by Denis Rooney, the first National Trust warden here. 'There's a bow-saw, chop the tree down,' Denis told him, and they got to work. Wayne loved the fact that he'd been given some responsibility and began volunteering for Denis.

Being the Trust's first warden in Easington Colliery was an unusually tough job: Denis Rooney had to become a rubbish collector. British Coal used the beach as its dumping ground and sewage pipes spewed waste into the shallows, so why wouldn't the locals use this abused coast as a tip too? Wayne once had to dive out of the way of a burning Transit van after it was pushed over the cliff. Those not fly-tipping wore balaclavas and roared across the clifftops on trail bikes, cutting fences, churning footpaths, ripping up wild flower meadows.

'When I started, Denis was quite hated because he was strict with the motorbikers,' remembered Wayne. 'He couldn't leave his Land Rover anywhere because he'd get it stoned.' Luckily, however, because Denis once worked in the colliery, he was known and respected and gradually people started to take notice of the work he was doing on the land. He helped establish a space on brownfield land where the bikers could go, and he got tough with fly-tippers. Below him, on the beach, the sea performed its own clean-up operation.

Visitors today who last saw the place twenty-five years ago would struggle to believe the transformation. Robert Chesshyre returned in 2010 and had to pinch himself: 'A carpet of wild flowers lay at my feet; ponies cropped the next field; the nearby North Sea – dotted with white sails – sparkled,' he wrote. On my visit, three years later, the sea was clean and kids on motorbikes no longer buzzed along the clifftop. 'Now they just sit inside and play on Nintendos and Xboxes,' Wayne noted.

Apart from the dog-walker from earlier, I suddenly realised that we hadn't seen another soul: the landscape was bereft of people. There is currently an influential trend within the National Trust to tone down its rules and regulations and make people feel welcome on its land. Its head ranger here, Gareth Wilson, could not countenance motorbikes – they simply do too much damage – but he was keen to encourage more visitors to this fine coastline. Cornwall's beaches were once dominated by the hellfires of metal mining but are now a pilgrimage for five million tourists every year. 'The future for the Durham coast is to get tourists to come and walk the coast and appreciate it, but at the moment people haven't even heard of it,' he said. 'They can picture the Yorkshire coast and the Northumberland coast and there's this black hole in between.' He also hoped to encourage local people to use it. 'It's been avoided for so long that it is taking a while for that change to come,' he said. 'They need to fall in love with their own stretch of coast again.'

I went for a pint at the Easington Colliery Institute, famed for throwing a party when Margaret Thatcher died. Prices appeared to have stopped rising when the mine closed. Tetley's cost £1.58, a third of a London pint. Much else had stopped then too. 'If you ask people if they would prefer jobs or a clean coastline, I think they would say jobs,' Gareth Wilson had predicted. 'But you can't go back to the past.'

The club was a plain 1960s building containing a large windowless bar, snooker table and pictures of the mine on its walls. The over-40s football team came in, red-faced and sweaty, but they were too young to have worked in the pit. The last pitmen were older, and quieter. I felt it was trite to ask them about the seaside, it seemed so irrelevant to the story of their community but, like everyone in County Durham, they were happy to talk.

Anthony Johnson, a trim man with short-cropped grey hair and a neat jumper, worked in the pit for seven years until he joined the army, moved away for twenty years and then returned home again. In his absence, the beach, like the town around it, had undergone an inconceivable transformation. When he was a kid, the water was pitch-dark and tattooed with oil and chemical spillages. 'If you swam in the sea you'd come out dirtier than when you went in, covered in coal dust,' Anthony remembered. The difference today was 'amazing', he said. 'The sands are not golden sands but they *are* brown at least.' Now he was retired, he fished on the beach most days. 'The sea life and the fishing is coming back. There's been a massive difference in water quality within the last ten years and lobsters and crabs are down there now. Fish I'd never catch have come back – bass and mackerel. It's unbelievable.' Something else has returned too: seaweed. 'We're seeing it on the rocks, like we haven't seen for years,' said Brian McGarry, whose grandfather came from Ireland to the pits. 'There's mussels starting to appear on the rocks too. And the lads will go down and get a bag of winkles. On a clear day when the tide is in you can see the rocks under the sea where you never could before. Mother Nature is cleaning up. I'd like to know where all the coal went, though. It mesmerises me. The tide has taken it out, but where's it gone to? There must be a big hole in that sea out there.'

The only people they saw on the coast these days were old men. 'There's not many bairns going down now,' said Tommy Foster. As boys in the 1950s and '60s, their playground was beach and dene. 'As soon as I came out of school, I'd be down there,' said George Parkin, who lost his uncle in the '51 pit disaster. 'My mother never saw me until I was hungry. I'd be out all day, the beach or the dene.' He and his mates would swim and light fires, collect conkers in the denes and coal on the beach. 'Years ago you could have got bagfuls of it,' said Brian. 'If we went down with a carrier bag now we'd be lucky to fill the bottom.' Anthony Johnson had met visitors from Manchester, Scotland, even Devon, walking the Durham coast, but local people weren't often there. 'People don't realise how much they have on their doorstep. I've lived in Shropshire, some of the most beautiful countryside in Britain, but this beats it.'

I asked them how they thought the town was faring. 'They've deserted the north-east. Deserted it,' said Brian of the government. His comment reminded me of a remark by Robert Chesshyre who on his 2010 visit likened the Durham mines to the army: pit communities were like regiments and life depended on teamwork, discipline and structure. 'But people wait for a lead from others – time and again I was told of the lack of self-confidence in Easington – and only a few, often the brightest, rebel against authority,' he wrote. Social regeneration, Chesshyre was told, lagged ten years behind physical regeneration. Brian had served in the army and agreed with the analogy to working down a mine, miles under the sea. 'It was just the same there – comradeship. You had your bad days and your good days,' he explained. 'When the water broke in or the stone came away it used to be a nightmare.' Then there would be a mad dash to put the pipes and pumps in. The risk of death 'was part of the hazards of mining'. It created a tight community because they needed each other. 'We were watching their backs,' George Parkin chipped in, 'and they were watching ours.'

That solidarity was not felt by the rest of the country and cheap foreign coal and Margaret Thatcher's determination to destroy the once-mighty trade unions ensured that mines were shut even when they were still retrieving a million tons each year, with millions more still underground. 'It was the most profitable colliery in the north-east,' said Brian. 'We were going to go into the Harvey seam and the Busty seam. They had never been tapped. The manager said, "That's the future of your colliery," but we never did it. There's millions of pounds' worth of gear down there as well.' Everyone in Easington Colliery liked to speculate about how much coal these abandoned mines still guarded but most people admitted that, flooded with water, they would be too expensive to open up again. 'We'll never see them open, never,' said Brian.

I gathered that there were now some good local jobs for working people – the Nissan factory in nearby Washington, ACTEM UK, in Horden, an engineering firm which supplies Caterpillar – but far fewer than in the days of coal, and the light industrial parks that had been built over the old mining sites were currently somnolent. Easington Colliery Brass Band was still going, the colliery club had a children's birthday party going on upstairs and it seemed to me the friendliest place in England, but it was obviously much quieter than it had been. It was ridiculous to ask if they preferred pits and pollution or no jobs and a clean beach, but I did. 'Most people would rather have the pits open, especially for the youth and apprenticeships, but you've got to balance the two things up,' said Anthony Johnson. 'The pits are shut. They've done their bit.'

Mining isn't the only disappearing industry leaving its scars on the shores. Just as farmers are a vanishing part of our countryside, so fishermen have been lost to their coastal landscape: industrialised and scaled up, a few big boats in a handful of ports replacing fishy activities that were once a feature of every coastal community. But the main reason why fishermen are disappearing from our coast is because fish and shellfish are disappearing from our seas.

From 11,000ft, as the plane descended into Belfast City Airport, Strangford Lough looked like an enormous silver fish out of water, glittering in the green landscape. Strangford is Britain's largest sea lough (as lakes are known in Northern Ireland), and it possesses many marvels, some of which were immediately apparent after I survived the three speeds drivers like to practise on Northern Ireland's country roads – slow tractor speed, fast while holding a mobile phone, and terrifyingly fast, a top speed reserved for school buses – to reach the lough. A shallow silver mirror of water beyond a broad foreshore of tidal mudflats studded with dark stones, to the south Strangford deepened around an array of tiny interesting islands, part of a drowned drumlin field forged by the Ice Age. These drumlins continued on land, creating an intimate countryside of abrupt round green hills that resembled a basket of eggs.

Almost every view of the lough's deeply invaginated 150-mile shoreline contained some land guarded by the National Trust. The Trust owns a number of islands, manages Mount Stewart, one of several imposing grey-stone stately homes on the water's edge and, unusually, it also looks after some of the shallower seabed. For all this conservation, though, the lough was far less fancified than most of the English coast. Modern bungalows sprouted in scenic positions that would turn planning officers in England apoplectic. By the disintegrating harbour of Kircubbin, a wooden shed with a spectacular view over the sea claimed to be Harbour View Car Wash. I pulled over because I thought it was a joke (the Irish!) but it wasn't. There were bollards, piles of old tyres and a car wash run from a place that would be an upmarket fish shack in Cornwall. On the far side of the bay, boys skimmed stones into the still, sunlit water, creating golden sparks that rose off the lake-like sea. Not far around the corner, the lough's neck narrowed and the sea turned turbulent. The huge volume of water squeezed in and out of this slight opening by every tide formed a thrilling race. As I waited to take the pugnacious little ferry from Portaferry to Strangford, the water was writhing, but beneath the swell, I guessed there was far less activity than in recent decades. In Strangford, perhaps more than in any other place in Britain, the disappearance of its sea life starkly exposed our inability to nurture the fishermen who work our coast and the fish they catch.

Britain is positioned on the North West European Continental Shelf, one of the largest areas of shallow sea in the world with a climate, current and nutrients that create a natural abundance of fish, far greater than, say, the Mediterranean. Despite this advantageous position, our unusually long coastline and our abiding love of fish and chips, Britain is not a nation founded upon fishing like Iceland or the Faroes. While the Romans deployed dolphins to drive fish towards the shore and the Chinese fished with tame cormorants wearing neck rings to prevent fish slipping down their gullets, early Britons conservatively stuck to eating mostly freshwater species trapped in weirs right up until medieval times. Even today when we are fish-deficient – consuming more fish than we can catch in our own waters – we still eat only a fraction of the seafood devoured by the French and the Spanish. By the 1500s, however, sea fishing took off in Britain. East coast fishermen had long plundered herring in the North Sea; from western ports, boats would embark on six-month cod runs to the far side of the North Atlantic, packing their catch in salt for the journey home. Although the Dutch pioneered the processing of fish at sea, the English devised steam-powered trawling and by the mid-nineteenth century our pursuit of 'silver darlings' had turned the ports of Caithness into the largest herring fishery in Europe. The British became known for their aggressive propagation of the idea of the sea as a free larder, a global commons that anyone could plunder.

Over the last two hundred years, fishing has followed an inexorable pattern. A certain fish – herring, cod, mackerel – is harvested with such passion and ever-growing efficiency that it becomes virtually extinct, at which point the industry turns to another species and does the same. British fishing is regulated by the Common Fisheries Policy of the EU, 'the worst news for fish since the invention of the hook', according to Richard Girling in *Sea Change*. The EU set member states' fishing limits at 200 nautical miles in 1977 and decided that everyone should fish in a shared European pond. Six years later, it established a system of national quotas in an attempt to limit catches. Politicians repeat the mantra of creating a prosperous and sustainable fishing industry but this has proved a chimera. Quotas have been consistently set far above limits advised by scientists for fish populations to survive and every graph – catches, incomes, number of boats, number of fishermen – points downwards. In 1938 there were 47,824 part- and full-time fishermen in Britain; by 2000 there were 11,559. Despite this decline, globally there has been a terrifying increase in fish catches from 17 million tonnes in 1950 to 91 million tonnes in 1995. For all the advances of industrialisation, fishing remains a form of hunting. As Girling points out, increases in productivity are not like other industries: 'You are not building an asset. Hitting the stock is raiding the savings.'

If Strangford Lough was a bank, it would be bust. It is famed for its 80,000 water birds, and it offers prime feeding ground for light-bellied Brent geese, curlew, eider duck, greater black-backed gulls, knot, redshank and terns. But its truly stupendous treasures lie below its surface: porpoises, seals and fish; millions of brittle starfish, meadows of anemones, sinister-looking dead man's fingers, and sea squirts swaying in the current, in vivid orange, blues and creams. More than 2,000 types of marine animal have been found in the lough, about 70 per cent of all species recorded on the coast of Northern Ireland. Best of all, Strangford Lough was once known for its populations of northern horse mussels, *Modiolus modiolus*, a purpleish mussel which can live for more than half-a-century. These venerable, slow-growing and slow-breeding shellfish stick together in dense matted clumps like a temperate coral reef. Scallops, snails, sponges, sea squirts, worms and half-a-dozen crab species – more than 100 species in total – make their homes within these mussel reefs. One scientist has described this as the richest animal community in the North East Atlantic.

Unsurprisingly, these natural bounties have supported local fishermen for hundreds of years, as demonstrated by the lines of stones on the tidal mudflats at Greyabbey which are the remains of twelfth-century fish traps. Like any high achiever, Strangford has been showered with awards: it is the most designated conservation site in Northern Ireland; an Area of Outstanding Natural Beauty; an Area of Special Scientific Interest; a Natura 2000 site (an EU-wide network of nature protection areas); and a Ramsar site (a wetland of international importance); and (alongside Lundy and Skomer) one of Britain's first Marine Nature Reserves. Conservationists joke it is 'a body of water surrounded by committees'. This is black humour. Despite all those committees, all that protection and all its riches, Strangford's seabed now lies in ruins, its fishing industry all but obliterated.

From my conversations around the coast, I had already realised there was no such thing as a typical fishermen. A career like no other made for an unusual life. While farmers are stereotypically dour, fishermen have always been romantics, adventurers and storytellers. It may be the source of much of our understanding about the sea, but it is also a profession for pub braggarts and the source of umpteen superstitions and tall tales.

'Ask him if it's really true that he was friends with Elvis,' said local people when I mentioned I was meeting Norrie Dougan at his home on the shores of the lough.

Norrie lived in the small, ungentrified town of Killyleagh on a street called Net Walk, where the fishermen used to dry their nets. A stately-looking man with swept-back hair, grey-green eyes and a grey-green jumper, Norrie had fished on Strangford for sixty years and, aged seventy-seven, continued to do so. Salt water flowed through his veins, he declared as we sat in the front room of his bungalow with a handsome view east towards the mouth of Strangford Lough.

He was born a hundred yards from Killyleagh's small harbour and joined the merchant navy at eighteen. His uncle and aunt coaxed him to try his luck in America, where he drove a forklift truck – a machine then unknown in Northern Ireland – and met his wife, who hailed from Comber, just up the road from Norrie's childhood home. The couple returned to Killyleagh when Norrie was thirty and he worked in the local linen mill until the call of the coast could no longer be ignored. Norrie became a full-time fisherman in 1969, in the summer catching lobsters and scallops – large king scallops and then smaller queen's scallops, known as queenies. In those days, basking sharks arrived every summer too, and if he took his little dingy out a porpoise would meet him every morning, lie on its side and look up at him. 'I'd put my hand down and rub along its back.' He liked being able to work a long day if he wanted, or all night, or not at all. 'You make your own hours,' he said, and hours sounded like 'oars', which seemed appropriate. 'It's a good open-air life, so it is.'

In the 1970s big trawlers arrived in Strangford Lough from Scotland, the Isle of Man and Portavogie on the east coast of Northern Ireland. Norrie counted thirteen one day, crammed into the narrow lough, tracing figures of eight in the water. Ernie Dunbar was one of those who came from Portavogie. 'He bought a brand new boat and he had the price of it within a few months. He made a fortune on Strangford Lough.' When other Portavogie fishermen saw Ernie's success, said Norrie, they followed him in. 'Ernie was part of it,' said Norrie. 'He was a good fisherman, so he was.' What made a good fisherman? I asked. 'Looking after things. Keeping things going. To have feelings about the place and feelings for what you are fishing for.'

If Ernie Dunbar did make a fortune, he showed no visible signs of wealth at his semi in Ballywalter. Like Norrie, Ernie was supposed to be enjoying his retirement, but still he fished. I found him in his back yard, fixing up *Boy Will*, a well-worn eighteen-footer in which he still put out a few dozen lobster pots. He had given his trawler, *Boy Jonathan*, to his son, but his son struggled to make a living, sold up and discovered that driving trucks for Tesco was better money than fishing. 'The fishing's the way to the devil. The fishing's the way to the dogs,' declared Ernie. 'The fishermen are getting food handouts in Portavogie now.' A sturdy, cheerful man, Ernie did not seem prone to nostalgia, but he was these days a keen watercolourist and the best of his scenes were his paintings of *Boy Jonathan*. They radiated love for his boat.

'I was glad,' he insisted, when I asked how he felt when his son sold the boat. 'The harder he worked – it didn't seem to be any benefit. I was getting as much money for my lobsters and crabs twenty years ago as I do today but the price of diesel has trebled.' His lobsters fetched £3.80 per pound, the price he received two decades ago when diesel was 50p a gallon, not the £3.50 it was in 2014. The fall in the real price of lobster was partly because of all the middlemen between fishermen and the market – in Spain. Ernie could sell direct to a local restaurant and make more money but there wasn't enough local demand. 'We don't eat fish in Northern Ireland,' he said. 'My father told me that fifty years ago.'

Ernie started fishing alongside his dad when he left school in 1964. Industry experts told fishermen, like farmers, that they must diversify. They always had. In bad times, Ernie laid tarmac and built houses but he always returned to the sea. As well as fishing, his father painted the red lightships and South Rock lighthouse off the east coast.

The scallops, said Ernie, started up in the 1950s and the season ran for six months from November. If a strong easterly blew, east coast fishermen like Ernie ducked into Strangford Lough for more sheltered conditions. 'We did all right too. We always got a good enough wage,' he said. In the early days, engines were 18 horsepower at best. Norrie's scallop dredgers were so small that he brought them up by hand, one on each side. When Ernie bought a boat with a 33hp diesel which could tow two scallop dredgers, it seemed massive. Over the years, the motors and dredgers kept on getting bigger and the scallop season got smaller. Ernie had *Boy Jonathan* built in Portavogie in 1986 for when his son left school. It was their future. By now, locals deployed three dredgers on each side of the lough; the big boats from Scotland and the Isle of Man had six or seven. Strangford was being fished in two main ways. Dredgers possessed short tines like those on the bucket of a JCB, which scraped the seabed. Trawlers featured a net held open by two metal doors with a weighted bottom which was supposed to tickle the queenies which then swam (scallops are surprisingly nimble, moving through the water like a set of false teeth) into the net. In fact, the trawler's doors and the net's weighted bottom both gouged the seabed as they bounced along. 'The kill rate was too good,' said Ernie. 'We found the scallop season getting shorter and shorter. We were running out of scallops at the end of January and then we went to prawn fishing,' said Ernie. 'This part of the County Down coast was overfished.'

Like Norrie Dougan, Bob Brown still puts a boat on Strangford Lough but it is a modest yacht he uses for pleasure, not fishing. Brown, who advises the British government on marine conservation, first visited the lough as a student in 1970, studied its horse mussels for his PhD and became the National Trust's warden there for most of the 1980s. In those days, he enjoyed taking groups out on the water to show them the wonderful life of the seabed with the help of a small scientific dredge. One day in the mid-1980s, he hauled up the little dredger and found it empty. Assuming it had landed upside down on the bottom, he tried a second time. Once again, it brought up nothing. Alarmed, Bob arranged a dive with a colleague. 'We were shocked,' he remembered. 'Aside from a couple of crabs arguing over the interior of a coke can, there really wasn't much to see. The whole bottom was smashed and scarred.' The horse mussels and most other marine life had disappeared.

Bob began to acquire scientific evidence that dredging and trawling were decimating Strangford's seabed. Despite collecting an impressive array of proof, including an underwater film of the damage which Bob showed sceptical officials in 1989, when he appealed to the authorities, Northern Ireland's fisheries department refused to act. 'Their response was completely unacceptable. They said there was no impact,' recalled Bob. A decade of denial and prevarication followed. The fisheries' department in Northern Ireland had a reputation for protecting its fishermen from marine conservation. Fisheries' officials assessed the damage in Strangford using a form of sonar which recorded plenty of mussels. Unfortunately, this equipment could not distinguish between a live mussel and a dead shell: the 'undamaged' mussel beds were actually dead. 'If it wasn't tragic, it would be funny,' said Bob. 'They cast around for every single explanation as to why it was not trawling and dredging – they claimed it was climate change or a toxic bloom.'

But the scientific consensus was clear: fishing had destroyed the horse-mussel beds. During our conversation, Norrie had remarked that the beds were 'good for nothing', because they were inedible. In fact, as Bob Brown explained, they performed a vital service for the fishermen. The mussel reefs sustained the 'useful' edible sea life, including the queen scallops, and these disappeared along with the horse-mussel reef. Only when the Ulster Wildlife Trust reported the Northern Ireland authorities to the European Union for failing to safeguard the protected site of Strangford Lough did the authorities act. Facing hefty fines from the EU, the government finally banned trawling and dredging in the lough in 2003. It was too late. According to Bob Brown, if action had been taken more quickly, it might have saved the local scallop industry. Instead, eleven years later, there is still no scallop fishing on Strangford.

Local fishermen have struggled to accept this drastic curtailment of their shrinking livelihood. Northern Ireland's Minister of Agriculture told the fishermen of the ban and, according to the fishermen, refused to negotiate or discuss compensation (which was never given). 'There were no ifs and buts,' said Ernie. 'The scallop fishery was closed, full-stop. That's a wee bit hard to take.' The fishermen have also questioned the causes of the damage. 'They said we were destroying the horse mussels but we were miles from them.' Ernie said. To say the horse-mussel beds were destroyed by dredging was 'not the whole truth', he maintained. 'I'm not saying the dredger boards had not pulled through the mussel beds: that would leave a bit of a track. But the recovery rate would've been instantaneous.' Ernie believed the main cause of the destruction of both the horse mussels and the queenies was a toxic bloom which spread through the waters one summer. 'Even now, the mussel beds are just dust. They never recovered. It wasn't the case that someone went over them with a dredge. But no hard feelings, nothing lasts for ever.'

More than a decade after the ban, the seabed of Strangford Lough has irrevocably changed. Bob Brown estimates that there are barely 5 per cent of the original horse mussels, and what remains is of a 'dubious' quality. The horse mussels are naturally very slow to reproduce and there are some recent signs they are clumping together with the 'recruitment' of young mussels, but it's a very limited recovery. In most places, the underwater ecosystem has been dismantled. 'The seabed is broken shells, the mussel population structure has broken down completely and as the basic structure of the mussel reefs has been destroyed, getting it back is going to be very difficult,' predicted Bob Brown. 'The nooks and crannies that once protected young mussels have gone.' Northern Ireland is obliged by European law to restore the habitat of Strangford and scientists planned to reseed the mussels but it proved too difficult to rear them in a lab. It may be possible to reintroduce horse mussels from other populations, 'but I don't want to see us damaging pristine mussel reefs to repair a ruined one,' said Brown. Restoration is far more challenging, and expensive, than conservation.

A relic fishing industry continues on Strangford today. Locals put out pots for lobsters, prawns and crabs around a no-take zone in the centre of the lough where all fishing is banned. The fishermen don't like this: Ernie believed conservation organisations such as the National Trust wanted to ban fishing on the lough altogether and wished they were more honest and said so; Norrie was convinced that pot fishing for lobsters or crabs would not harm any recovering mussel beds. Bob Brown believed that pot fishing was still physically and ecologically damaging because it was removing 'key players' from the ecosystem But Norrie was more optimistic that that there were still horse mussels on the seabed, despite the dredging, and that the scallops had also recovered. 'There are plenty there now,' he said. He could catch king prawns the size of – he gave a fisherman's measurement with his hands: almost a foot long. Mostly, however, he potted for velvet crabs, which 'were taboo years ago. Now they're the main catch.'

But Norrie surprised me when I asked him whether this highly restricted pot fishing was sustainable on Strangford. He shook his head. 'My dad used to fish single pots – a pot here, a pot there. Now there's pots on a long line.' According to Ernie, a fisherman can make a living from 100 pots and Norrie belonged to a local fishing co-operative which proposed to limit pots to 100 per fisherman. 'Some of the boys say, "I could not make money on 100 pots," and they are fishing 200, 300 pots out there, aye, destroying the lough,' he said. 'There's a lot of greedy fishermen. They'd take anything' – including egg-laying crabs and lobsters which should be returned to the water. Norrie told me that there were more part-timers now: these 'summertime men' were permitted to catch five pots – enough for themselves. Except they would set five for themselves and five for their granny. The authorities agree that a new pot-fishing permit scheme is required for Strangford, and this is imminent at the time of writing. The lough is lightly patrolled by fisheries officials. 'There's a new RIB [rigid-inflatable boat] on the lough with a girl on it and she's supposed to be checking everything,' said Norrie lugubriously. 'We'll see how she gets on this summer.' It sounded like he did not expect anything to change. The lough, he said, had 'been abused since my young days'.

It appears to be human nature to empty the seas of fish. Many conservationists wonder why fishermen have been protected in such a self-defeating way, but western societies are still in thrall to the last of the hunter-gatherers. People like fish, ports, boats and they also like the idea of fishermen and, in particular, their bravery. Governments follow this popular view: fisheries are listed as a ministerial priority by the British government despite the total value of fish caught barely exceeding that of their takeaway partner, the potato.

The 'tragedy of the commons' was coined in 1968 by Garrett Hardin, an ecologist at the University of California. His theory is that any gain from a commonly held pasture is individual but any loss is shared, and so the benefit a herdsman accrues from putting an extra cow on the common will always outweigh the cost of overgrazing the pasture. And so the greed of individuals will ultimately destroy their communal resource. Revising his theory, Hardin acknowledged that this mutually assured destruction was not the fate of commons in medieval England because commoners organised themselves: they were limited in number, their herd sizes were limited too, and their rights were enshrined by law. Unfortunately, the sea has proved an unmanaged commons, and attempts to manage it have been woeful.

Bob Brown felt that Britain's failure to manage its fishing industry was partly a consequence of 'the old hunter-gatherer philosophy', but also because the Common Fisheries Policy had encouraged an unsustainable attitude. A shared European 'pond' is just too large for local fishermen to exercise responsibility for it, Brown believes; better to return to nations regulating their own fishing areas. More radically, suggested Brown, turn the system on its head: instead of protected marine areas, why not have fishing zones? Making fishermen responsible for certain zones would encourage husbandry: they would behave more like farmers, who must maintain their land in a productive condition for their own livelihood.

Norrie Dougan and Ernie Dunbar's vision for future fishing on Strangford Lough was actually similar to that of scientists like Bob Brown. Ernie wanted a co-op where it was in everyone's interest to look after stocks. Norrie wanted fishing restricted to a few licensed local boats, with the 'foreigners' kept out. (By foreigners, he meant men from Portavogie.) It sounded like self-interested protectionism but local people cared about their local fishing grounds because they depended on them. 'These other boats that come in are not worried about Strangford Lough. Once they clean it out, they go back outside again,' said Norrie. 'Locals have more feelings for Strangford Lough.' He slapped his heart. 'This place is unique, so it is, oh aye.'

The next morning, I walked around Gibbs Island, one of Strangford's tidal drumlins protected by the National Trust. It was a perfect spring morning: mist rising, the water like glass. The still air was full of birds of the land and birds of the sea: sparrows chirping atonally, great tits seesawing, rooks cawing, curlews bubbling. A heron headed into the Scots pines on the domed peak of this little island, carrying a small branch in its beak. Every animal seemed poised to reproduce. I could not see beneath the mirror of the lough whether any horse mussels were doing the same. Bob Brown was a naturally cheerful person but occasionally he reflected on Strangford Lough's unseen losses and felt sad. 'There are no seabed areas that can truly be described as pristine anymore,' he said. 'I'm sixty-three and know I will never see that rich horse mussel community in Strangford

Lough ever again. It might happen in our grandchildren's lifetime. Who knows?'

Before I left Norrie Dougan's house, I remembered to ask him about Elvis. Norrie's eyes lit up. He had been conscripted into the US Army and ended up in the same camp as Elvis. 'Elvis and me were walking down the street to the pub and people were standing and looking at us. Finally someone shouted, "Hey, Norrie, who's that with you?"' He chuckled. In truth, he knew Elvis only in passing but it symbolised the glamour of 1950s America. Why did he return to Northern Ireland with its dying fishing industry? Norrie looked out of his window onto the lough, its waters streaked with gold from the sunset. 'I missed this,' he said. 'So I did.'

## Explorations of Neptune

I confess I did more driving than walking along the 'Back' of the **Isle of Wight** but the superbly scenic coast road which swoops over Compton Down should be enjoyed while it lasts – it is threatened with coastal erosion close to **Brook Bay**. The crumbling orangey cliffs are a splendid spot for fossil-hunting and, in May, the cliffs and chines dance with one of my favourite butterflies, the Glanville fritillary, which fell extinct on the mainland and is now found only on the Isle of Wight. The spectacular cliffs, views and fine chalk grassland of the National Trust's **Tennyson Down** is bombastic and inspiring, and well worth a stroll, and if you are seeking solitude then **Watershoot Bay** is an excellent place to explore. Head south through Niton on the A3055, turning right at a sharp left-hand bend. Follow this road to another sharp bend where it is possible to park on the roadside. You can then take the track towards Knowles Farm, where you will find a lighthouse, a quiet stony beach and some spectacular coastal erosion above. There is also parking on the old Blackgang Road on the hill above the farm. Away from smuggling scenes, another lovely place for a quiet walk untouched by tourism is the National Nature Reserve of **Newtown Harbour**, on the north of the island. The National Trust has significant landholdings here, including the historic town hall, which has no town attached. This is an estuary landscape, with an unspoilt patchwork of tiny fields and quiet lanes inland.

### OS Map

Explorer OL29, Isle of Wight

### Public transport

Portsmouth to Fishbourne (Wightlink) and Southampton to East Cowes (Red Funnel) are the major ferry services to the Isle of Wight but my favourite is the Lymington to Yarmouth ferry (Wightlink) which is smaller, offers lovely views and brings you into Yarmouth on the north-west corner of the island, which is convenient for exploring the west coast. Trains run right to the ferry at **Lymington Pier** station.

All ferries take foot passengers and cars.

**Website**

http://www.nationaltrust.org.uk/visit/local-to-you/london-and-south-east/things-to-see-and-do/isle-of-wight/

I began my tour of **the Durham coast** at Nose's Point, which has a large car park just off the A182 at the southern edge of Seaham. Walking south, the coast path follows the railway line, ducking into mysterious Hawthorn Dene before arriving at the open clifftops that were once the site of the huge pit at Easington Colliery. The flower-rich magnesium limestone grassland on the clifftops and deserted beaches compare favourably with the more celebrated shores of North Yorkshire, and for lovers of solitude Durham is perfect. I picked up the path again at Horden but the 12-mile Durham Heritage Coast Path from Seaham south to Crimdon Park, at the edge of Hartlepool, makes for an excellent long day's walk.

**OS Maps**

Explorer 308, Durham & Sunderland
Explorer 306, Middlesbrough & Hartlepool

**Nearest railway station**

Seaham, 1.5 miles

**Websites**

www.nationaltrust.org.uk/durham-coast/
www.durhamheritagecoast.org

Visitors to Northern Ireland tend to visit the birthplace of the *Titanic* in Belfast and zip north to the Giant's Causeway, leaving everything to the south (including the glorious **Murlough Dunes**) to the enjoyment of those in the know. **Strangford Lough** is one such overlooked gem. The spectacular gardens of **Mount Stewart** – all Antipodean blue gums and tree ferns – are at least well known but the perimeter of the lough is uniformly splendid. The countryside in Northern Ireland is not quite as open to the public as in England and Wales which can make exploring on foot difficult. Driving south from Mount Stewart, it is worth detouring to the Upper Ards, which, confusingly, is the lower part of the Ards Peninsula that separates Strangford Lough from the Irish Sea. This is peaceful, virtually unvisited coastline, and the National Trust rebuilt the picturesque fishing community of **Kearney** in the 1960s. Determined to create a viable community, it offered long leases to artists. Potters, painters and weavers still live in this tiny community, enjoying the light, peace and watching the Isle of Man appear and disappear on the horizon. After catching the car ferry at Portaferry across the mouth of the lough to Strangford, I enjoyed a little walk around **Gibbs' Island**, on the south-west corner of Strangford. Characteristic of the drowned drumlins, this island was a perfect tree-topped grassy hump with nothing but birds all around. There is parking for several cars before the causeway at the end of the track or you can walk from Delamont country park, just off the A22 Comber to Downpatrick road on the western side of the lough. The thing I didn't do but wish I'd had time for, is to take the canoe trail around Strangford Lough and camp on Salt Island.

*Mount Stewart*
Portaferry Road
Newtownards
County Down BT22 2AD
*OS Maps*
Discoverer 21, Strangford Lough (1:50,000)
Northern Ireland Activity Map, Strangford Lough (1:25,000)
*Websites*
Mount Stewart
www.nationaltrust.org.uk/mount-stewart/
Canoe Trail
www.canoeni.com/Strangford_Lough.aspx

Strangford Lough
www.nationaltrust.org.uk/strangford-lough/facilities-and-access/

## Further Reading

Bella Bathurst, *The Wreckers*, HarperCollins, 2005

Richard Girling, *Sea Change – Britain's Coastal Catastrophe*, Eden Project Books, 2007

Fred Mew, *Back of The Wight*, The County Press, 1934

J. B. Priestley, *English Journey*, William Heinemann, 1934

# 5

## Art

*Penwith / The Llŷn Peninsula / The Suffolk shingle*

The Llyn
Peninsula

Plas yn Rhiw

Aldeburgh
Orford Ness

Penwith

The ocean was just as magnificent as I had expected. At Botallack, sunlight turned the distant sea into the sliver of another land. At Porthguarnon, white water fizzed into emerald froth around the rocks. At Nanjizal, the shallows were turquoise under the sun. Beyond Sennen Cove, the ocean became a cool, deep cobalt. Every writer and every artist who has visited the Cornish coast has tried to capture its polychromatic drama: Thomas Hardy wrote of 'the opal and the sapphire of that wandering western sea'; D. H. Lawrence of that 'infinite Atlantic, all peacock-mingled colour'. We have a collective folk image of the Cornish coast from writers, painters and poets; from Daphne du Maurier, Virginia Woolf, J. M. W. Turner, Patrick Heron, Sir Terry Frost; from numerous television dramas and travel supplements. And many of us, five million each year, visit and come away with our own vivid impressions of surf, sand and sky. But no matter how well we think we know Cornwall, it can still surprise us.

Walking the coast path around the western tip of Britain for the first time, I was not prepared for the beauty of the rocks. Penwith, the name of Cornwall's final peninsula which lies beyond Penzance and St Ives, is dominated by granite. It pops out everywhere: in ancient standing stones and chamber tombs on the moors; wrapped in gorse and brambles within Cornish hedges; as inconveniently large obstacles in pasture; and in forming gigantic cliffs, bluffs, ledges, gulleys and chasms – called zawns in Cornish – where the land is exposed to the ocean. When the sun shines, the granite becomes golden; when it rains, it is silver. Sometimes it is pink; sometimes green, or orange with lichen. Shadows fall on it, from the clouds or a solitary raven swirling above. It lights up the landscape and is the reason many artists first came here.

A pilgrimage to the land's end has long captivated us. The West Country inexorably funnels us to its furthest tip and two great peninsulas branch off the 100-mile peninsula that is Cornwall: the Lizard becomes its most southerly point; Penwith its most westerly. Penwith was named 'Bolerium' by Ptolemy, which was probably taken from the Celtic sun god Belenos, and in earlier times, our westerly questing is thought to have had a religious purpose. Today it is mostly to seek pleasure: the thrills of its surf or the relaxation of its perfect holiday beaches. The historic link between the old and the more contemporary way of relating to the south-west coast is art. In the late nineteenth and early twentieth century, spiritual questing became bound up in the act of artistic creation. The power and beauty of this uniquely varied landscape and seascape has inspired generations of artists to experimentation and discovery.

My own pilgrimage was modest: I was walking around the coast of Penwith from Newlyn in the south, famed for its fishermen and its artistic community, to St Ives in the north, famed for its artistic community and its fishermen. Cornwall has claims to be a separate country and, within it, Penwith can seem a province of its own. It isn't: it is another world. All but one of the twelve parishes west of St Michael's Mount have boundaries with the sea and yet Penwith still possesses a mysterious middle. This is high moorland, dark with heather and dotted with standing stones and cromlechs, enigmatic tripods of stone built by the ancient Brythonic people of Cornwall. Between the moors and the sea is a patchwork of tiny fields, framed by

Cornish hedges – stone banks swathed in bracken, bramble, heather and gorse. The gorse surrounds the green pasture 'like stupendous ropes of shining golden bloom', wrote W. H. Hudson in 1908, noting the pleasing pairing of yellow with the blue ocean. Farming hamlets of grey stone cluster between tiny fields that date from the Bronze Age. Place names, which bear testimony to Cornwall's divergent past from England, are particularly odd: Grumbla, Ding-Dong, Break My Neck Farm. The tin mining that once dominated this landscape now serves up picturesque ruins – brick chimneys and stone wheel-houses – along Penwith's northern coastline while the softer south coast is divided by fecund, fern-filled gulleys. Every pause and glance and the landscape offers a scene to paint. Like a great beauty, this peninsula cannot take a bad photograph, at any hour, in any light. A third of Cornwall's edge is Neptune coast, protected by the National Trust, probably because it is so inspirational: moving more artists – poets, painters, authors, sculptors, potters – to creation than any other coastline in the country.

After a dank October day when the cloud sulked on the cliffs and spat rain along the south coast from Lamorna to Porthcurno, the skies cleared as my dad and I reached Tol-Pedn-Pennwydh, the holed head of Penwith. The spectacular blowhole dropping from the clifftop to a watery cave below set our hearts racing but what really struck me were the great grouped clusters of granite on the cliffs. Millions of years had softened these once austere and geometric blocks into near-human figures and they stood, facing the western sea, as if they were wives and children, waiting for a fisherman's boat to return home safely. The brilliant, troubled nineteenth-century Cornish writer John Blight called them the 'guardians of the western coast'. Close to Land's End is an outcrop called The Armed Knight: a man's head in profile, with sharply incised panels of rock forming a body of armour plating.

If Penwith still conjures up other-worldly associations when Cornwall is full of tourists, it must have appeared even more alien in the summer of 1811 when its granite caught the eye of J. M. W. Turner. More than any other visual artist, Turner was responsible for the creative gaze falling westwards. Although beach resorts were beginning to take off, few people made the epic, uncomfortable trip to Cornwall via coach-horse on its atrocious roads. Famed for his seascapes, Turner wanted to paint watercolours of little-seen places for a book that would whet patriotic appetites for the grandeur of England when the country was at war with Napoleon. As the art critic Michael Bird explains, Turner found the cliffs and reefs possessed the Romantic quality of 'the sublime' – a form of nature that inspired wonder and fear. Romantic painters eschewed the classical habit of dividing land and sea with a clear line of horizon; instead they combined land and sea in a maelstrom, often placing the spectator at the heart of the scene, at the perilous water's edge. An engraving Turner produced of Land's End is all glowering skies and ominous bare rocks; for his audience, such pictures would have been as exotic as images of a newly discovered planet today.

Assailed by the Industrial Revolution, the Romantic movement idealised wild landscapes whose majesty dwarfed the people within them. If they were expecting an unspoilt wilderness, however, nineteenth-century visitors to Cornwall were in for a shock: the coastline was dominated by the smoking infernos of tin and copper mining. These first Romantic tourists were not dissuaded but, rather than tripping to its coves, they hailed its cliffs. These were the great attractions and pubs – the Logan Rock Inn, the Gurnard's Head – were named after distinctive formations. After a muddy day on the coast path, Dad and I found our way to the Logan Rock, an old stone coaching inn with a real fire, real ales and real local drinkers. Signed pictures of rugby union players adorned the walls alongside old prints that told the story of 'the celebrated Logan Rock' on the cliffs half-a-mile away.

The rock was a large lump of granite reputed to be so delicately balanced that a gust of wind – or a man – could make it wobble. There were dozens of rocking or 'logging' stones in Cornwall but the Logan Rock was the most spectacular. William Borlase, an eighteenth-century geologist famed for his guide to Cornish antiquities, claimed it was impossible for man to unbalance the stone but in 1824 his high-spirited nephew, a naval lieutenant called Hugh Colvill Goldsmith, enlisted lads from HMS *Nimble* to dislodge the rock. They pushed it 3ft down the cliff but local people were outraged, as were the tour guides who made money showing visitors this natural wonder. Naval top brass threatened Goldsmith with the sack if he didn't restore the rock. In an operation considerably more arduous than its displacement, Goldsmith used scaffolding and improvised levers to return the rock to its resting place. For a long time afterwards, the rock was chained and padlocked in place, which rather emasculated it. When its shackles were removed it never logged as well as before.

Earlier that evening, as dusk was falling, Dad and I had clambered down the coast path to Penberth, a tiny stone fishing hamlet where forty boats once worked and fifty men were employed to winch vessels up its steep stone jetty. One house was built virtually on the rocky shore, side on, as if it dare not confront the waves. The front door was open and the television was on, a rare thing in these parts: a permanent home for a local person. (Most of Penberth was owned by the National Trust, which leased such houses to local tenants.) When we climbed the cliff path out of Penberth, we paused for breath and looked down on its beautiful slipway, big sea-smoothed stones stitched tightly together like the most immaculate crazy paving. A woman appeared and was watching the waves run up the slipway, transfixed by the sea. It could have been a scene painted by the first artists who arrived in Newlyn in 1880. The railway reached Penzance in 1852 and Cornwall could now send produce up to London from the fertile, frost-free fields of Penwith, which grew vegetables and flowers earlier than anywhere else in mainland Britain. In return, London sent back artists, and more tourists.

This was the birth of mass tourism in Cornwall. Unable to compete with the sophistication of Brighton or Bournemouth, the county offered something very different from the very beginning – a romantic vision of a foreign land. An early railway poster likened the Cornish peninsula to a map of Italy. In reality, Cornwall offered the nearest thing to a Mediterranean climate combined with Arthurian legend.

Some of the first painters to arrive had lived in Dutch or French provinces where artistic colonies were nostalgic for the innocence of rural life. Their philosophy was to paint *en plein air*, and Stanhope Forbes, who made his mark at the Royal Academy in 1885 with a depiction of a Newlyn fish sale, found Penwith to be an English version of Concarneau in Brittany. At first, the Newlyn school's scandalous realism was attacked as immoral but, ultimately, Victorians were charmed by its melancholy images of local children, women waiting for boats to come home and weather-worn old folk. Although local people might earn a penny or two for posing, Cornish fishermen were often understandably hostile to being ogled by gentlemen artists over a canvas. By the 1890s, as Cornish metal mining began its calamitous collapse and thousands of Cornishmen emigrated to mines all over the world, sail lofts and fishing sheds in Newlyn and St Ives were converted into studios. Laying the foundation stone of the Newlyn Art Gallery in 1895, the press baron and philanthropist John Passmore Edwards, presciently using language that became commonplace a century later, predicted that the mining industry would be superseded by a new one based on Cornwall's 'scenic wealth'.

As the art critic Michael Bird points out, the fashion for the Newlyn school's paintings of grieving fishing widows waned during the First World War when everyone was losing their menfolk but so many artists and intellectuals now poured into West Cornwall that new ways of representing its landscape flourished. A tradition more buoyant than Newlyn emerged in St Ives after James McNeill Whistler, accompanied by younger artists Walter Sickert and Mortimer Mempes, painted there during the winter of 1883. 'Nature,' opined Whistler, 'contains the elements, in colour and form, of all pictures, as the keyboard contains the notes of all music.' It became a cliché that artists were drawn to St Ives for the quality of its light.

The potter Bernard Leach and his Japanese assistant, Shoji Hamada, were the first of an internationally renowned avant-garde to arrive in St Ives. Barbara Hepworth and Ben Nicholson came at the start of the Second World War, some years after Nicholson first visited and had been greatly struck by a chance encounter with the 'naive' work of Alfred Wallis, a local marine salvage dealer who had taken up painting after the death of his wife. With his painting and her sculpture, Nicholson and Hepworth brought abstraction to the increasingly fusty local artistic tradition. The modernists still found shapes, colours and energy in the scenery around them, however. Patrick Heron, the painter who moved to a remote house, Eagle's Nest, near Zennor, from where he campaigned vociferously against post-war development and road widening schemes that would have ruined Penwith, was convinced that the air 'contains more light than in England: light reflected up and off the sea'. The abstract painter Sir Terry Frost recorded how he created his painting, *Blue Movement*, from many evenings watching the water over St Ives, defined by a common emotional mood: 'a state of delight in front of nature'. Nicholson once described the chore of painting his garden gate: 'As soon as my hand touches a brush my imagination begins to work. When I finished I went up to my studio and made a picture. Can you imagine the excitement a line gives you when you draw it across a surface? It is like walking through the country from St Ives to Zennor.'

That northerly stretch of the coast path is particularly strenuous, fizzing with a lucid, westerly light that England's east coast lacks. Perhaps it is partly clifftop vertigo but the western horizon seems drawn sharper, 'the sea's blue light, with points of diamond', as the doctor-turned-artist John Wells put it. Despite these elevated qualities, visual artists are as susceptible to peer pressure and pragmatism as any other creatures – they just disguise it better – and many of the reasons they took to St Ives were convivial. A railway line to the little town opened in 1877 making it more easily accessible from London. Leslie Stephen, the editor and critic, and his children, including Virginia Woolf and Vanessa Bell, made St Ives their summer home and childhood memories of Godrevy lighthouse later informed Woolf's novel, *To the Lighthouse*. Once a critical mass of artists arrived, galleries, patrons and, later, grant-awarding bureaucrats followed; artists could now make a living in Cornwall. In 1938 alone, the St Ives artists had eighty paintings accepted by the Royal Academy and a whole railway carriage was set aside to convey the canvases to the London show.

When I walked Penwith's coast path in October, a three-cornered leek was in flower, usually a token of April; red campion and devil's bit scabious were also in bloom. This far west, Britain's severe seasons are softened; effete intellectuals flourish when it feels a lukewarm 16°C most days and grass grows all year round. In the early twentieth century, the writer W. H. Hudson became a regular visitor to Penwith, lodging with a local matriarch, Granny Griggs, in Zennor. (Granny's formidable guest list included Sir Alfred Munnings, one-time president of the RA, Edward Sackville-West and the alcoholic novelist Roger Gull.) 'W. H. Hudson always seemed to be nursing some ailment and was no doubt much cosseted by Granny,' recalled her granddaughter Alison Symonds in her memoirs. Penwith wasn't simply a place for gentle recuperation, however: the artists played plenty of golf at Lelant; Australian painters Will Ashton and Richard Hayley Lever organised cricket matches and, best of all, before 1914, there was no closing time. The Sloop in St Ives opened at 5 a.m. to serve returning fishermen.

By the 1960s, the international reputation of the artists of Penwith had diminished: Nicholson left St Ives and London galleries were in thrall to pop art. Locally, however, an artistic community continued to thrive. Painters like Frost, Bryan Wynter and Peter Lanyon (a rare Cornish-born artist) 'were a bit like jazz musicians, they had this edge to them . . . a kind of glamour and turbulence,' remembered Matt Hilton, son of the artist Roger Hilton. 'All these artists, in their 20s and 30s, even 40s . . . driving around in jeeps. It was like a movie going on when we went down to Cornwall.' Creative people were absorbed into Penwith and while there may no longer be a distinctively West Cornish movement, there is still an unusual number of resident artists, particularly in the decades since Tate St Ives opened in 1993. 'If you're not going to live in a city in Britain then this is the next best place to be for art scenes,' Anthony Frost, an acclaimed abstract painter and the son of Sir Terry Frost, told me. 'You've still got amazing things coming to the Tate and artists working here and showing all around the place.'

After my walk with Dad around the peninsula, I visited Anthony at his Penzance studio, concealed within an old telephone exchange. The view across Mount's Bay from his window was almost identical to one described by his father when he looked from his Newlyn studio and I suddenly understood how such scenery could inspire abstraction. 'The sun comes up over the Lizard in the morning,' wrote Sir Terry. 'St Michael's Mount starts off like a Japanese woodcut, a triangle of island and castle nudging through a shroud of mist, and then to the right is a red glow, and if you wait and watch the sun comes up, first as a semi-circle and then a circle behind the Mount, there is a red reflection shimmering in the water, and that's my morning treat.'

Anthony Frost grew up with artists racketing around the peninsula, setting off explosions on bonfire night, playing cricket against the farmers and staying up until dawn painting, or drinking. He also saw how the movement of boats on water gave his father 'his shapes, which stayed with him all his life'. But Anthony's own artistic journey was, like any son's, an attempt to move beyond his father – and that meant moving beyond his father's surroundings too. The Penwith coastline was a backdrop to his life, rather than an explicit theme in his work. Anthony designed many of The Fall's record sleeves (he believed he actually qualified as a member of the band because he once sang on stage with them in Hamburg) and felt that music, not landscape, was his primary influence. His studio featured dozens of vibrant, sunny, half-finished abstracts and ten old-fashioned radio cassette players, set on timers to record radio shows. 'We all need music. I can't live without painting but I know some people could. I don't know anyone who could live without music.' His paintings were named after fragments of lyrics or, in one exhibition, after Captain Beefheart songs. Another show was called Magnetic Fields, which people thought referred to the ancient field patterns of Penwith, but was actually named after a rock band.

Early on, Anthony hated people 'looking for landscape elements' in his work because he wanted to escape any idea he was following his father. These days, however, he is quite happy to have, say, his yellow and turquoise works associated with Porthmeor beach. 'I don't deliberately set out to do that but you can refer them to the landscape,' he said. 'You get amazing Venetian-red bracken and the granite that throws the light back at you – it's almost nuclear. Then there's the sea which is ever-changing. I do find the landscape wonderful. I'm not sure my paintings are about the landscape but they are about colour and I'm sure you're influenced subconsciously or consciously by the colours you're walking through all the time.' The salvaged materials he throws into his works are also taken from his environment and so are often nautical – bits of canvas sail and ripped beach tent or windsurfing sails in fluorescent colours. 'It's a mad one really,' conceded Anthony. 'Because of the materials I use, that ties me. It definitely seeps in, in various places.'

Anthony Frost's bouncy works reflected the uplifting side of Penwith but if the peninsula were simply an easygoing British version of California, as Cornwall is often marketed today, its artistic legacy might be considerably smaller. Visual artists may have been attracted by the vivid light but many writers and poets take inspiration from shade, and the peninsula possessed an abundance of dark power.

*This is a hideous and wicked country,*
*Sloping to hateful sunsets and the end of time,*
*Hollow with mine shafts, naked with granite, fanatic*
*With sorrow. Abortions of the past*
*Hop through these bogs; black-faced, the villagers*
*Remember burnings by the hewn stones*

John Heath-Stubbs, the poet who briefly joined the artistic influx of the 1940s, wrote these lines after encountering a mermaid that you can still find carved into a dark wooden bench in St Senara's Church, Zennor. According to local legend, a beautiful lady would occasionally attend the church. No one knew anything about her but she possessed a mellifluous voice and as the years passed she never appeared any less alluring. One day, a young man called Matthew Trewella, the best singer in the parish, was inspired to follow her when she left the service. He was never seen again. Some years later, a ship dropped anchor near Zennor and the captain was hailed by a mermaid, who asked him to move his anchor because it was blocking her front door. The crew were well aware of mermaids' tendency to lure men to their deaths, and sailed away smartly, but the villagers concluded that Matthew had succumbed to her charms. The story was said to have inspired the fifteenth-century carving but folklorists believed it was the other way round.

Heath-Stubbs was part of an Oxford generation including Iris Murdoch and Philip Larkin. His detection of menace in Penwith might be attributed to his own discomfort with anywhere beyond the drinking dens of Soho (he also wrote: 'Sheffield,/With her necklace of razor-blades, Bradford,/Throned upon her tumbled woolsacks, Leeds,/Crouching over her drain'). After his first visit to Cornwall, Walter de la Mare claimed that he did not feel safe until he had crossed the River Tamar back into Devon. Denys Val Baker, the post-war chronicler of West Cornwall's artistic set, identified a 'strange, brooding, compelling quality' in the land. The novelist Ruth Manning-Sanders, who lived at Sennen Cove, described how she walked the cliffs in wintery twilight and heard the voices of drowned sailors. 'It is then,' she wrote, 'that the sense of the primordial, the strange and the savage, the unknown, the very long ago, fills the dusk with something that is akin to dread.'

None of this menace was present when Dad and I rested from our walk outside the Tinners Arms in Zennor, benign sunshine playing over pints of ale, the only sound the *tick-tick-tick* of passing walkers' poles on tarmac. When I have found myself alone on our coastline at dusk, however, I have felt this dread, from the indisputably eerie Orford Ness to the busy channel below the White Cliffs of Dover. Does it come from a collective unconsciousness forged when we had good cause to fear the sea? Or something else? Artists in Penwith sometimes traced it to the human sacrifices supposedly practised by Brythonic religions in these parts, as John Heath-Stubbs suggested in his line about the burnings by the hewn stones. Perhaps his poetry spooked me but I was filled with a sudden unease when Dad and I encountered a white bell tent inexplicably pitched on the cliff-edge as night fell on the coast path near the Logan Rock. Dread materialised again when a moaning noise emanated from the sea at Porthcurno.

After some time listening, Dad concluded it was only a sea buoy, whistling in the wind, but its song transported me far from carefree Californian Cornwall.

Sven Berlin, a rather saturnine-looking sculptor who left the peninsula in 1953, disillusioned by the split between St Ives' modernists and Romantics, wrote more precisely about the strange potency of this landscape than any other visual artist. 'The open coliseum of each little cove of sand or rock may be the theatre for any natural, supernatural or unnatural event,' he suggested: the sea's breathing, the slow flight of seagulls and 'the mind's incessant vertigo at the cliff edge' could all 'act as the charming of magicians and open up the deeper rooms of experience in man, making him aware of his being part of the natural universe, at the head of a great unseen process of gods and devils, spectres and dragons; of being a channel for unknown and undefined forces; of facing the mystery of life, awakening powers of perception which search beyond the frontiers of normal events.'

Time collapses on the cliffs of West Cornwall. The twisting tunnels of the arsenic calcinator at Botallack, constructed in the nineteenth century, appear neolithic; the standing stones are as redolent of the Celtic-inspired rites of hippies as of neolithic burial customs; and the observations of John Blight in 1861 still perfectly describe the cliffs today. There is no clear calibration between past and present in Penwith; all human history is present, jumbled and insubstantial next to the thunder of ocean and the splendour of granite.

As the history of visual art in Penwith showed, artists were attracted to a place that had already attracted artists. These painters, sculptors and potters were mostly a jolly bunch, social creatures, sculpted into scenes and gathered at pubs. Poets, in contrast, styled themselves as solitary animals, seeking escape from convivial society. My next journey in search of how creativity has been forged on our coastline was to learn about an exemplar of that solitary poetic tradition: R. S. Thomas. A defiant loner who came out of the west coast and spent his long life working his way back there, Thomas was popularly portrayed as the Ogre of Wales, white hair wild, eyes ablaze, and an apparent advocate of the burning of holiday cottages owned by the English. He was a man of paradoxes – a Welsh-speaker who could only write poetry in English; a passionate Welsh nationalist who berated his countrymen in the most uncompromising verse; and although he made his name writing about the farmers of mid-Wales, he was also a man of the sea.

There are two lovely words in Welsh describing a state of being for which there is no precise equivalent in English. *Cynefin* is a person's heartland, the place to which they emotionally belong; *hiraeth* is the anguish caused by estrangement from that spiritual home. 'It was Holyhead itself that made me what little of a poet I am, a horrible little town with a glorious expanse of cliff and coastal scenery. I shall never outgrow my hiraeth for it,' wrote Thomas in a letter to a friend in 1952, when he was living in a fine vicarage surrounded by the flowery hay meadows of mid-Wales. A tall, austerely handsome man, Thomas lived for all but thirteen years of the twentieth century, and in its final thirty-three he reconnected with his heartland, the far west of Wales, where the rocks, trees and ocean resonated with memories, connections and inspiration.

If you are never more than seventy miles from the sea in Britain, you cannot stray more than four miles from salt water on Llŷn Peninsula. Pointing westwards for twenty miles into the Irish Sea, a slender promontory of marshes, meadows and small mountains rising towards Snowdonia, it has sixty miles of coast. The National Trust owns some twenty-five miles of it.

I arrived at night, in the fog, guided by sat-nav, and thereby ascertained nothing about Llŷn apart from it being exceptionally dark, cold and quiet. My holiday cottage, Tan y Bwlch, was close to R. S. Thomas's former home: both were traditional single-storey stone dwellings with a low-ceilinged kitchen containing a big hearth and a ladder leading up to a hayloft-style bedroom in the eaves. As Byron Rogers noted in his excellent biography of Thomas, most of these tiny old houses are now like space stations, 'turning in the void, immaculate and empty, but ready at a moment's notice to spring to life with the arrival of the next paying visitors'. Renovated cottages sporadically filled by English holidaymakers was the fate of Llŷn, once *Pura Wallia*, the heartland of Welsh-speaking Wales, where history and culture were supposed to be vibrant and enduring. 'In the Welsh consciousness, it is the Welshest heart of Wales, much as the Italians consider Italy to become more Italian as they journey south,' said Richard Neale of the National Trust, a fascinating and knowledgeable Welsh speaker who accompanied me on my explorations of Llŷn.

The sun rose the next day, showing me my surroundings in daylight for the first time as if a blindfold had been removed. The house was perched on the side of a hill and possessed of an epic view sweeping down to the ocean. The land would've been picturesque anywhere, but set off by the sea, it looked stunning. Below the mountain moorland were tiny strips of pasture, a dozen different greens, divided by stone walls, clinging to the land before it curved into the sea. There were relatively few villages but dozens of individual white cottages were scattered all over, where people had once scratched a living from five sheep they'd graze on the moors and a pig outside their dwelling if they were lucky. Mod cons were added much later, and I liked the old telegraph wires, sagging and bouncing in the wind between wooden poles skewed by their years in the wet ground.

Sea views materialised in unexpected places, in every direction, when I wandered over the Llŷn peninsula. The great sweep of bay below my cottage was called Hell's Mouth. It looked deceptively benign from a distance, but it was named after its ability to trap and wreck sheltering ships: a black dot on the beach was all that remained of the boiler of one unlucky vessel. Across Cardigan Bay, rising out of the water, were the mountains of mid-Wales and, on a clear day, Cader Idris. Looking west, the light on the water was miragey, like it is as you gaze from Penwith, a spirit tempting you westwards. Gazing from the east coast, the North Sea had no such beckoning quality.

Aberdaron was the last halt for pilgrims at the western tip of Llŷn before the sacred island of Barsdsey, the resting place of 20,000 saints. It was at Aberdaron where R. S. Thomas finally returned to the west in 1967 as the parish vicar. Ronald Stuart Thomas was actually born in South Wales in 1913 and spent much of the First World War in Liverpool, the only child of merchant seaman Thomas Thomas (known as Tommy Twice) and Peggy, a formidable woman from whom he inherited a certain forcefulness and coldness. In his autobiography, Thomas remembered: 'One day on the sands at Hoylake my father pointed southward to where some blue-green hills loomed. "That's Wales," he said. Prophetic words.' This is a nice example of RS's self-mythologising, or what Professor M. Wynn Thomas calls the poet's 'Liverpool complex' – his lifelong sense of being internally exiled from his own country. Interestingly, Thomas could get a similar outsider's view of the main body of his country from his cottage on Llŷn, from where the blue mountains of Wales appear to form a separate land.

After the war, Thomas grew up in Holyhead, the busy port on Anglesey where ferries run to Dublin. 'Holyhead was one of a number of British towns that seemed to be dying – blackening like an extremity with gangrene,' wrote Paul Theroux in *The Kingdom by the Sea*, a caustic snapshot of our coast in 1982. Holyhead has also been dismissed as the place where pebbledash goes to die. (The preponderance of pebbledash is a result of the poor-quality local building stone, which mean that its houses require a protective render.) RS's boyhood was shaped by the sea, 'its noise, its smell, its ferocity on windy days', as he wrote. By day, he would play by South

Stack lighthouse, now a nature reserve. At night, flashes from the lighthouse darted into his room like the sails of a windmill.

When he studied at Bangor University, his early poems about the sea were derivative.

'So now in winter hateful is the sea,/Hateful its low and melancholy roar', he wrote, borrowing from Matthew Arnold's 'melancholy, long, withdrawing roar' in *Dover Beach*. Later, however, the sea became a route back to his childhood, and a scathing portrayal of the wounds left by his cold mother in *Ap Huw's Testament*:

*My father was a passionate man,*
*Wrecked after leaving the sea*
*In her love's shallows*

Later, Thomas considered his childhood self in relation to his much older being while standing on the Llŷn Peninsula, looking north to Anglesey. Playing on the double meaning of headland, he wrote: 'One headland looks at another headland. What one sees must depend on where one stands, when one stands.' Looking back, he saw not uncomplicated childhood joy on the beach but pain, and skewered his family's loveless triangle in an incomparably bleak poem about a family outing:

*There was this sea*
*and three people*
*sat by it and said*
*nothing.*

RS's early adulthood was a journey away from the coast. He was ordained in 1937 and his first post was on the border with England, where he met his wife Elsi, a talented English painter who was as idiosyncratic as her husband. Five years later, he became vicar of

Manafon in mid-Wales. The life of a parish priest did not much suit Thomas, 'a true poet not of belonging, but of estrangement', according to the critic Peter J. Conradi.

Thomas was the ultimate outsider: creatively, intellectually, socially and emotionally. He was a poet who longed to write in Welsh but couldn't and had to 'stand outside an adored tradition like a tramp at Christmas', as Byron Rogers put it. To be a rural vicar in the Anglican Church in mid-twentieth-century Wales was to be an outsider because most of the country had embraced nonconformism. Thomas disliked the English ruling classes, but ambition or snobbery – his own or his mother's – gave him the accent and manners of an aristocrat; his countrymen often assumed he was English. It sounds like he rather relished the old idea that a rural vicar was an intellectual black sheep in a field of labourers: he once vaulted the churchyard wall after conducting a funeral to avoid mourners and so disliked small-talk that on another occasion he greeted a parishioner who commented it was a nice day with: 'We can see that.' He was an outsider to his own family, lacking any ability to express his feelings to those he loved, except very occasionally in his writing. As Gwydion, his only child, remembered, he was 'a man incapable of love, and full of love', the most extreme of his many contradictions.

In RS's century, Welshmen travelled east to reinvent themselves as Englishmen. Ever the contrarian, Thomas took the opposite path. 'I think places had an unusual importance in the lives of RS and Elsi,' his son Gwydion has said. Thomas's arrival at the western end of Llŷn, as vicar of Aberdaron and by now a famous poet, was 'the culmination of a lifelong quest for the "true" Wales he had first glimpsed, as an English-speaking boy in Holyhead, when he gazed across Anglesey and the Menai Straits at the magnificent profile of the mountains of Eryri, Snowdonia, in distant Gwynedd,' judged Professor M. Wynn Thomas. 'I think I came here because of the sea,' Thomas said when interviewed by Byron Rogers in 1975. 'I'd written myself out of hill-farmers, and coming here brought me into contact with things just as elemental as them: you know, sea, sky, the wind, those sort of things.' (This dry joke was typical of his unexpected sense of humour.) 'There are rocks out there on the headlands that are 6,000,000 years old. To see the sun casting your shadow on 6,000,000-year-old rocks . . . drives you furiously to think, as they say.'

Before he returned to Llŷn, RS befriended three eccentric English spinsters, Eileen, Lorna and Honora Keating, who had lovingly restored Plas yn Rhiw, a petite manor house, and were frantically purchasing random patches of land to keep the peninsula exactly as it was, which somewhat alarmed many locals. In the library at the back of their house are Thomas first editions. 'To the ladies of Plas-yn-Rhiw, with kind thoughts from RS Thomas' is his dedication in *Poetry for Supper*, published in 1958. By 1971, they had grown closer and a selection of Wordsworth's verse edited by Thomas contained the dedication in pen: 'To Lorna and Honora, with love from Ronald'. RS was at home with the English upper-middle classes and the Keating sisters clearly admired the dashing poet, showering him with gifts of money. As I flicked through this small trove, out fluttered one of RS's thank-you letters to his patrons. 'Dear Lorna and Honora,' he wrote. 'It was very kind of you to remember my birthday which I thought I had managed to KEEP dark – certainly it is no cause for rejoicing any more. I had asked Gwydion to get hold of a rather expensive book for me, so if he succeeds your gift will go a long way towards it.'

The best gift of all, however, was Sarn y Plas. In 1962 the sisters gave RS a lease on a damp little cottage perched on the cliff overlooking Hell's Mouth as a writers' retreat. When Thomas retired in 1978, he and Elsi moved there permanently, building a small extension but living a terrifyingly ascetic existence. There was no central heating, no television and no space for RS's books or Elsi's paintings. One winter, Elsi recorded matter-of-factly that it was 1.8°C in the living room with the fire on. Water seeped down interior walls and Elsi painted with her feet inside a cardboard box containing an electric stove, burning herself severely on one occasion. Gwydion, their son, found mould growing on his father's shoulders.

An impression of this difficult, stubborn man still lingers strongly in his former haunts today. Everyone seemed to remember encountering RS even though he rarely welcomed casual chat. 'He was a tortured soul but that's where his poems came from,' smiled a lady in his fine old church at Aberdaron, which had been abandoned to the incursions of the sea before the villagers changed their mind and shored up its graveyard, spectacularly positioned overlooking the tiny town's sandy beach.

Richard Neale, who had worked for the Trust in North Wales for several decades, was twenty when he first got to know Sarn y Plas. He had moved nearby to begin repairing the ramshackle estate that the Keating sisters had bequeathed to the National Trust after their death, with the stipulation that RS could stay on in his leased cottage. This was the 1980s, at a time of rising fury about the way English visitors casually purchased second homes for their holidays and Richard recalled one night stepping out of his front door: 'Suddenly on the hill I saw a fire and loads of blue lights, and it was a holiday cottage burning down.' R. S. Thomas had famously provoked media outrage when he sympathised with Meibion Glyndwr, the Welsh nationalist group behind the arson campaign – 'What is one death against the death of the whole Welsh nation?' he pondered – but RS didn't trust the nationalists to be well-organised enough to realise that his cottage was not an Englishman's second home and he erected a large sign in Welsh to say so. During a fifteen-year campaign from 1979, more than 200 cottages and several estate agencies were torched.

Richard would meet Thomas on the lanes. If the poet saw the young National Trust warden approach, he would lift his binoculars and pretend to watch a bird to avoid conversation. Richard persisted and one day revealed where he lived. 'Oh, so it's you who cut the beautiful old fuchsia from the front of the house,' retorted RS. Once Richard and some other lads were fishing off the rocks by Aberdaron. RS arrived with a very primitive rod, promptly caught two mackerel and quickly departed again: fish for supper. 'He was extremely taciturn,' said Richard. 'You got the impression his mind was on higher things.' Eventually, Richard played his trump card with RS: his grandfather had taught the poet Welsh. RS was as uncompromising as his verse: 'He didn't teach me much. I didn't get on very well with him,' he told Richard. 'I got a much better teacher afterwards.'

Given these caustic exchanges, it is hardly surprising that those I met on Llŷn had mixed views on Thomas. Many locals disliked his snobbery more than they admired his championing of the Welsh language and nation. Interestingly, however, RS never repeated the harsh portraits of local people in Aberdaron that had characterised the poetry about mid-Wales that made his name. Instead, in his later years, his poetry turned inwards, toward his struggles with religion, as he waited on a God who did not show himself. The poet and vicar came closest to discovering the divine through the landscape of Llŷn, and its coast was an intrinsic part of poems about his doubting faith and his fears for Welsh nationhood. In the mid-twentieth century, English Romantic literature had helped stimulate the Welsh tourist trade 'by conveniently overlooking the country's society and culture in order to reduce "Wales" to a gloriously inviting empty landscape', argues Professor M. Wynn Thomas. RS was part of a generation who, although working in English, used their writing to repopulate and reclaim their nation. And yet there was a strong Romantic strain in Thomas too and his verse is rooted in the ancient interplay of scenery and weather: 'It blows in off the Atlantic,' Thomas wrote, 'accompanied by rapidly passing effects of light and shade that hold the attention and compel aesthetic awe.' RS country

– mainly the hills, of course, but also the west coast – has become as unmistakable as Thomas Hardy country. As Professor Wynn Thomas says, 'His writing has permanently altered perception of the Welsh landscape itself.'

While I was exploring Llŷn, Richard Neale agreed to show me Thomas's cottage. The road had been closed some years ago because of a landslip and the tarmac was encroached by weeds. A dirty white Mercedes parked in the hedge was slowly being reclaimed by ferns and moss too. Footsteps of other hesitant pilgrims had made a slight impression in the long wet grass leading up to the door. Hunched against the hill, turning its side to the only warmth, and view, to the south, was Sarn y Plas.

The low stone cottage still leased by the Trust to RS's son Gwydion lay empty, as damp as ever and at the mercy of the brambles. Ivy clawed at the stone walls, an elder twisted by the door and cobblestones were covered in a slippery layer of ragged turf. Everything was prematurely aged by its proximity to the sea. The garden, once lovingly tended by Elsi, was overrun with wild garlic. Gwydion's parents would've probably approved, Elsi having wittily chronicled RS's craze for garlic-munching. There were still tokens of their life here. Outdoor chairs were scattered on a couple of small patio areas, as if the elderly couple had felt a spot of rain and hurried inside. Another RS obsession was to make a perfect haycock and someone had cut the little hay meadow by his cottage and left neat stooks in the field. It felt as if the poet might appear at any moment, as he would when tourists pitched up seeking directions, and mutter 'No English' with fake incomprehension before stalking off. With a start, I spotted a small hand waving from an attic window. It was a sculpture, and I remembered reading that Elsi once made one of her own hand, and reassembled it after RS accidentally shattered it during a rare frenzy of spring-cleaning.

It might have been damp and run-down but the cottage was still an ideal hermitage from where a poet could contemplate the sky, the rocks and the sea as it thundered into Hell's Mouth below. It had been a place of writing and could now be a place for a small act of worship. I stood underneath the cramped window at the southern end of the house and Richard Neale took a slim volume of R. S. Thomas's poetry from his pocket and began reading.

> In Wales there are jewels
> To gather, but with the eye
> Only. A hill lights up
> Suddenly; a field trembles
> With colour and goes out
> In its turn; in one day
> You can witness the extent
> Of the spectrum and grow rich
> With looking. Have a care;
> The wealth is for the few
> And chosen. Those who crowd
> A small window dirty it
> With their breathing, though sublime
> And inexhaustible the view.

The appeal of the west coast to artists is obvious when it is blessed with mesmerising light and a rich trove of ancient religion and folk-lore while the cliffs of southern England are giddily beautiful. When I climbed High Down on the Isle of Wight, I could see why it was bought by Alfred Lord Tennyson – contemporary poets must fantasise about the days when their superstar predecessors could purchase such a spectacular muse of a landscape. But why would artists flock to a long stretch of shingle beach sculpted by the brown German Ocean?

During the second half of the twentieth century, Aldeburgh became a creative community almost as renowned as St Ives. Benjamin Britten set up home on the Suffolk coast and, in 1948, founded the Aldeburgh Festival with his partner, Peter Pears and the librettist Eric Crozier. The magnetism of Britten, the greatest British classical composer of his age, attracted other creative people, but I wondered what role had been played by the coast itself.

If Aldeburgh had been fortified by concrete promenades and turned over to mass tourism, I doubt such artists would ever have arrived. The town, a struggling, silted-up port until 'discovered' by discerning Victorian visitors, does not flaunt its beach, a plain, unadorned shingle bank that forms a flimsy barrier to Suffolk's marshes and inland waterways. To the north and south of Aldeburgh, the coast is all legendary nature reserve: Minsmere, Dunwich Heath and Orford Ness. But this is not unspoilt coast in the traditional sense. Looming over it, dominating the horizon for miles in either direction, is Sizewell A and B: the first (decommissioned) nuclear power station a dark block, the second, active station a conspicuous white dome. It seems surprising that artists would reside here but they have done and still do, despite this monstrosity and the sinister Cold War installations on the Ness. 'Installation' is a particularly apt word because both these grotesque human developments, like a good artistic installation, are in keeping with the land around them, and commune with it in an unfathomable way. I suspect that the bleak allure of this coast is older and stranger than the nasty buildings we have put on it. Sinister legends cleave to this coastline: predatory black dogs, UFO sightings and weird creatures. Some years before Sizewell materialised at Thorpeness, a young girl called Sybil Armstrong was looking at the sea from the living room of her wooden bungalow when she saw a sea serpent. Running outside with her governess and cook, they watched the creature, five times as long as a fishing boat, crawl over a sandbank and then 'beat on the sea with enormous oyster coloured fins' making a spray of water five or six times the height of a man, *The Times* reported. It reminded Sybil of a swan taking off.

It felt like February but it was May. The wind was cold, the shingle was beige and the sea was brown and then I heard Maggi Hambling, the painter, thundering in my ear. 'Bronze,' she barked. 'When people say brown or "it's all grey", I say, "Go and look again, it's full of colour."' I also required some artistic prompting to realise that the shingle beaches were full of colour too. 'It takes time to realise how floral shingle is, how pale blue and pale grey, how burgeoning – and how local,' noted Ronald Blythe, the author of *Akenfield* and a writer who inhabits the East Anglian landscape more completely than any other.

The shingle was like a strip field, ploughed into gentle ridges by the sea, which put each stone in its proper place. The big ones were rolled to the bottom of each shingle valley; the small were thrown to the top. From a distance, the shingle appeared empty but, close up, plants sowed themselves between pebbles and the sea's haphazard harvest – one pine cone, one orange glove, one grey sandal, one blister sheet of pills (used), one blue plastic lighter (rusted), two plastic bottle caps, seaweed, hosepipe, fishing line, a piece of green twine. Clumps of blue-green sea kale were flowering, its cream blooms wafting sickly-sweetness among the salt. Peppermint sea holly formed miniature sculptures in the shingle. Spreading low over the stones, large mats of sea pea captured dew and spray from the sea, almost indestructible in the hottest conditions. During a sixteenth-century drought, the crops failed and the population of Aldeburgh survived by consuming sea pea. That night, I ate some sea kale, its fleshy leaves turning racing green on contact with hot water. They were juicy and watery with a trace of bitterness, a less memorable spinach, but definitely edible beach food.

The frequently undemonstrative waters of the North Sea combined with the steep shingle beaches of the east coast allow an intimacy with the sea that is impossible on the west. I sat on a little ridge, centimetres from the waves. The noise of water on shingle was a conversation, pebble to pebble but also sea to land; an eloquence a sandy beach can never obtain. Some waves were placatory and quiet and rustled the rounded flints; others rattled in, loudly declaring their intent to move the shingle. This sea music, clinking 'its shingly trinkets at my ear', as Blythe put it, sang to Benjamin Britten throughout his life. Britten was born and raised in Lowestoft, the northern-most point of the Suffolk coast, and it cannot be a coincidence that he lived within earshot of the sea for so much of his life. In his elegiac memoir of 1950s Aldeburgh, *The Time by the Sea*, Blythe wrote: 'Benjamin Britten, Lowestoftian from day one, might be said to have come out of the sea like one of those oceanic beings who blow horns in the cartouches of ancient maps. Unlike me he was oceanic from the start. Tides accompany his pulse . . .' Britten would run across the stones late at night carrying a towel to swim. 'Out of it came his music,' observed Blythe. 'Supposing, like me, he had come from where he could not hear it?'

Britten's patronage and example encouraged other musicians, writers, painters and poets to stay or settle in Aldeburgh but plenty moved here independently. Before Britten in the late 1930s, Cedric Morris and Arthur Lett-Haines established the East Anglian School of Painting and Drawing inland, teaching Lucien Freud; after Britten's death in 1976, contemporary artists have continued to trade London for coastal Suffolk, including Sarah Lucas, who lives in Britten's former farmhouse, and Maggi Hambling, who created the infamous giant steel seashell just north of Aldeburgh. You can crunch round the four-metre-high *Scallop*, shelter from the wind and run your hand over its cold curves. People scratch things on it and it has been seriously vandalised several times since its arrival in 2002. Some people love it;

others hate it, but it remains one of the most striking contemporary works to take such direct inspiration from our coast.

In the drive of a house in a Suffolk village untouched by rumours of the sea stood a muscular two-tone Chrysler with the numberplate H1 0 GAY. Behind it was an old outhouse extended into a large, light white room of double height with canvasses of the sea on one wall, portraits of the deceased Soho wit Sebastian Horsley on the other, and a desk in the middle. Stalking across a floor littered with white cigarette butts was Maggi Hambling: big grey curls, snazzy trainers and a look so alert it was almost predatory. She had started smoking again, she explained in her wonderfully patrician voice, during the installation of *Rearing Wave*, another impressive sea sculpture, because it was so stressful to watch it dangling from a crane.

Art is easy, reckoned Maggi, quoting Constantin Brancusi; the difficulty lies in being in the right state to do it: 'It's the muse, my darling. One spends one's life searching for the muse.' Muses often come in human form, but on 30 November 2002 another kind arrived. Maggi had just finished the maquette for *Scallop* and drove to the shingle of Thorpeness one Sunday morning. 'There was this exciting storm raging. The sea was like a roaring beast, the waves throwing the shingle up in the air. I got back to the studio and I was actually painting a portrait from memory of a London beggar, twelve inches by ten, little canvas, and being very slow – because I come from Suffolk, I'm very slow – it wasn't until three o'clock that afternoon when I looked out across the water meadows and still these huge winds and rain were roaring about and I said, "What the fuck are you doing painting this memory painting of a London beggar when what's inside you is the storm?" So that was the first little sea painting – I painted directly on top of the London beggar.'

This compulsion to paint the sea probably lurked within for many years. Maggi grew up inland but holidayed with her mother at Frinton-on-Sea. 'As a tiny toddler I'd walk into the sea and talk to it all the time. I can't remember what I talked about but I apparently had real conversations, just me talking to the sea, my friend. As I got older I tried to listen to it, too.' When she moved out of London, she was not tempted by Cornwall or Wales or Scotland: she wanted to return to that same stretch of sea. 'Where art begins for you is very important and art obviously began for me in Suffolk, when I was fourteen. It's my bit of sea, the sea I've known all my life.' She didn't talk to it now, though. 'I try to empty myself so it can talk to me. It's my whole thing of trying to be empty so that the subject can come through me into the paint, onto the canvas.'

The beggar obliterated by a wave was the first of Maggi's North Sea paintings: small, vertical and tremendously energetic oils; detonations of British sea power. 'I can't think of anything else that's got the lot. It's got all that primal, organic thing, and it's got God; you can't beat it for a subject.' She developed a routine, driving twenty minutes from her home to Aldeburgh or Thorpeness and contemplating the beach, always early in the morning, 'when the sea was mine'. After a while, she began to draw in a sketchbook, like a pianist performing scales, getting into the rhythm of the waves. She sat on a stool so the water practically touched her feet. 'When I paint the waves I want them to seem as if they are crashing in front of you, right now,' she said in another interview. 'That's the magic of oil paint over any bloody photograph because a photograph is just a single moment, immediately consigned to history, whereas an oil painting is the result of many hours' work, culminating in a single moment.'

I admitted I could not detect the passion of Maggi's waves in the real North Sea. 'Well that's because you're a writer. You don't use your eyes,' she said merrily. Maggi did not dwell much on the interaction of moon and tides but spotted an aesthetic connection between the curve of a wave and the curve of the moon, which I had never thought about. 'That's because you're a writer,' said Maggi again, with twinkly ferocity.

Aeschylus compared breaking waves to endless laughter, or 'unnumberable laughterings', as Maggi put it, and she found that beautiful. Two decades ago, she created a series of paintings about laughter. A crashing wave is the sea's moment of abandon, when its features are in disarray, and it is rather like another human experience: the orgasm. Critics often consider Hambling's waves to be a depiction of sex. 'You spot a wave way out at sea and then it fiddles about a bit as it comes towards you and then there's the great orgasmic crash,' she said. 'That fits.'

Early on, some locals plotted to topple *Scallop* in the night, incensed by its prominence on the beach and disappointed that its inscription, 'I hear those voices that will not be drowned,' a quote from Britten's opera *Peter Grimes*, was not a more obvious tribute to the composer. In spite of the grumbles, the sculpture has survived, and even become a place of pilgrimage, which is apt because a scallop is a symbol of pilgrimage as well as the Roman goddess Venus. 'I conceived it as somewhere for somebody to sit alone, thinking about life and death and looking at the horizon and all these deep things, and unless it's the middle of winter or very early in the morning, it's full of children,' said Maggi, but she wasn't complaining. *Scallop* is a tribute to Britten and the sea and a shell makes the song of the sea when we put it to our ear in childhood. Children climb over it, people leave flowers by it, others propose marriage there and Maggi knew for a fact that couples have made love in its shadow too.

In *The Time by the Sea*, Ronald Blythe seemed ambivalent about the sea as a creative force. Like many aspiring writers, he went to live in Aldeburgh to write. It didn't happen and, against the advice of his friends, he dragged himself away from this creative community to create the book that made his name, *Akenfield*. He needed solitude. Later, however, he recalled days with the poet James Turner in North Cornwall. 'We would sit on the dizzy headlands and let the Atlantic rollers drug us into mindlessness,' he wrote. Perhaps the sea is an anaesthetic and stops us thinking. (R. S. Thomas would disagree because, as he said, the sea drove him 'furiously to think', but that may have been because he was looking for God; interestingly, the closest he felt he came to God was in the abandonment of artistic creation.) For Maggi Hambling, this is precisely the point. 'I don't do enough thinking probably,' she admitted but then, she thought, it was important for a visual artist not to think too much. 'You'd never do a picture – you'd think yourself out of it.' The sea allowed her to empty herself and become a vessel through which the subject showed itself on canvas: 'Thought doesn't come into that.'

The sea enabled Maggi to find a state of mind in which she could create. From time to time, she tried to draw the wind. 'I suppose it's the same thing – this great energy, this great power, this great movement. If you're walking in a great wind, it takes you over, doesn't it? And you become part of this great surging force, and that takes you back to being in the moment, which is what you've got to be when you are painting something.'

For other artists, musicians and writers, however, the soporific state induced by the sea created a different kind of focus. 'At first I thought that to "look" at the sea was a landsman's compulsion,' wrote Ronald Blythe. 'Britten watched it all the time . . . It possessed its own talk. Tucked into a windbreak I would listen to a commotion of shouts and barks, birdsong, and little floating pennants of distant conversation. Up by the Martello the rigging of the Yacht Club could be orchestral. Fitted naked into the accompanying shingle on an August afternoon, I should have been writing, notebook and pencil being so near. But usually I did nothing. I listened. It was why I came there.'

## Explorations of Neptune

I can't offer anything less obvious in **Penwith** than one of the greatest walks in Britain: the South West Coast Path around Land's End. If you're not a wild-camping maverick, the sensible principle when walking this path is to book accommodation in advance and set modest mileage targets for each day of walking: it's strenuous, with lots of ascents and descents, and there is so much to enjoy that it is nice not to be route-marching as dusk falls. Despite the celebrated nature of this walk, I enjoyed long stretches barely seeing a soul when I was there in October although I've strolled parts in the summer when it is obviously busy. Most people head south from St Ives but I prefer south to north, and I made a late afternoon start from Lamorna, overnighted at Porthcurno (with its fascinating Telegraph Museum and the amazing cliff-edge, open-air Minack theatre) and then did a long day's walk around Land's End and up to Pendeen. The third day I continued with an easy walk to Zennor whereupon the path gets seriously strenuous to St Ives. Every tiny portion of this coast has amazing views and stories. My highlights: the tiny harbour of Penberth; the eerie columns of granite around Tol-Pedn-Pennwydh; the sun on the beach at Nanjizal, one of the finest, quietest southern coves; the oceanic sweep of Whitesand Bay; Cape Cornwall, 'the connoisseur's Land's End'; the ruined mines around Botallack (restored by the National Trust in such a sensitive way that you wouldn't know they had been); and the Gurnard's Head (both the real headland and the pub; the Tinners' Arms at Zennor is very nice too). The only lowlight is Land's End which is still a mess.

### OS Map

Explorer 102, Land's End

### *Nearest railway station*

St Ives to the north of Penwith and Penzance to the south are both yards from the coast path

### Websites

South West Coast Path

www.southwestcoastpath.com/

Porthcurno Telegraph Museum

www.porthcurno.org.uk/

Minack Theatre

www.minack.com/

Cape Cornwall

www.nationaltrust.org.uk/st-just-and-cape-cornwall/

Levant Mine

www.nationaltrust.org.uk/levant-mine/things-to-see-and-do/

botallack/

Botallack mining walk

www.nationaltrust.org.uk/article-1356403825884/

### The Llŷn Peninsula

**Plas yn Rhiw** is the atmospheric manor house formerly owned by the philanthropic Keating sisters, who became good friends with R. S. Thomas. They donated their house and the numerous landholdings around the village of Rhiw at the western end of the Llŷn Peninsula to the National Trust, and the house is a good starting or finishing point for a circular walk that cheekily skips past R. S. Thomas's old cottage and takes in both abandoned farms and gentrified cottages perching on the hillside overlooking Hell's Mouth. Turn right out of Plas yn Rhiw down the hill and then left onto the coast road. Bear right at the first fork and you'll turn onto a track which is the old coast road. On the left is the currently fairly derelict cottage belonging to R. S. Thomas. It remains the private property of his son, Gwydion, although ownership will eventually revert to the National Trust. If you continue along the old road, you rejoin the coast road. Cross it and take the left-hand footpath which you can follow across mostly abandoned farmland containing more typical vernacular cottages of

Llŷn. You can continue on paths up the hill to the top of Mynydd Rhiw, which is only 304 metres above sea-level but feels a lot higher, surrounded by water in all directions. Footpaths bring you back into the village of Rhiw. The Llŷn peninsula matches the Cornish peninsulas for scenery and reminds me of the west of Ireland with its pasture, tiny scattered cottages and spectacular beaches but is, of course, its own, unique place, a heartland of the Welsh language and a locus of pilgrimage. 'Unspoilt' is a belittling sort of word but Llŷn is exceedingly well preserved without yet being completely gentrified, although sadly much of its wildlife-rich marshland between its hills has been drained and 'improved' over the past century. R. S. Thomas's other former haunt, **Aberdaron** (complete with radical new National Trust visitor centre), is worth a visit. I'm going to have to return to see **Bardsey** – it was too rough to cross to the island when I stayed on the Llŷn.

### OS Map
Explorer 253, Lleyn Peninsula West

### Nearest railway station
Pwllheli, 11 miles (from Rhwi)

### Websites
Plas yn Rhiw
www.nationaltrust.org.uk/plas-yn-rhiw/
Aberdaron
www.aberdaronlink.co.uk/
Bardsey Island
www.bardsey.org

The **Suffolk coast** between the famous drowned port of Dunwich and Orford Ness is a place of extremes, although it is not conventionally beautiful. Inland are sandy heaths; by the sea are crumbling cliffs and shingle beaches. The most famous spot is now Minsmere, the RSPB reserve celebrated for its abundance of rare birds and mammals. Next door is the National Trust's **Dunwich Heath**, which is quieter and equally blessed with striking wildlife, from adders and nightjars to the fearsome ant lions which lay tiny insect-traps in the sand. Dunwich Heath is a fine place for a walk, with another excellent teashop in the old coastguard cottages which are not long of this world, such is the speed of the erosion here. South of the great bulk of Sizewell B is Thorpeness, a striking little Edwardian holiday resort created by a wealthy Scottish barrister. Maggi Hambling's *Scallop* is on the shingle just north of Aldeburgh (beach parking right there), which is a pretty town with a rich cultural life, particularly its annual festival. If you venture into this splendid region, you must visit **Orford Ness** (see Chapter 3).

## *OS Map*
Explorer 212, Woodbridge & Saxmundham
### *Nearest railway station*
Saxmundham, 7 miles from Aldeburgh
### *Websites*
Dunwich Heath
http://www.nationaltrust.org.uk/dunwich-heath-and-beach/
Maggie Hambling
http://www.maggihambling.com/
Ronald Blythe blog
http://wormingford.blogspot.co.uk/

## Further Reading

J. T. Blight, *A Week at the Land's End*, Alison Hodge, 1989 (1861)
Ronald Blythe, *The Time by the Sea*, Faber, 2013
Philip Marsden, *Rising Ground*, Granta, 2014
Byron Rogers, *The Man Who Went Into The West*, Aurum Press, 2006
R. S. Thomas, *Collected Later Poems*, Bloodaxe, 2004

# 6

# The Story of Neptune

*Wembury / The Carrick Roads / East Anglia*

Blakeney Point

Orford Ness

The
Carrick
Roads

Wembury
Point

It was a cloudy June day when I went to Wembury to meet David Pinder. I'd driven through the deep lanes of South Devon earlier in the spring and was struck by the movement of colour through the seasons – yellow primroses and celandines in early spring; the blue and white of stitchwort, cow parsley and bluebells in May; and now summer pink and yellow, foxgloves and buttercups.

The heights of North Devon end in vertiginous cliffs but the green pastures of the south gracefully roll towards the sea before ending in more modest rock faces. Even so, the views from the South West Coast Path are consistently grand, and the waves appear to be a long way down. The water is intriguing too, less luminous than the Cornish Atlantic but more oceanic than further up the Channel. It is a contradictory sea where currents and tides collide, and boats must beware. At Prawle Point, some way east of Wembury, a thin line of white water headed south, dividing the dark western sea from the paler blue east. High water was two hours earlier but the current continued to run up the Channel, from west to east, for three hours. This conflict, together with the prevailing south-westerly winds and the contours of the coast, created numerous ship traps, a polite term for a sailors' graveyard.

At the turn of the last century, Wembury was no more than a couple of houses and an extremely scenically positioned church overlooking a cove of grey sand six miles east of the Plym Estuary. By the turn of this century, its position close to Plymouth had encouraged 1930s ribbon development and 1970s bungalows. It left portions of what was once a spacious panorama of open pasture curving like a whaleback towards the Atlantic resembling the suburbs of the nearby city. I met David Pinder, a retired geography professor who helped the National Trust conduct an ambitious survey of the coastline when he was a student in the 1960s, at his home at the edge of Wembury. It was 1950s infill, and another small square of brick and concrete on a once empty coastline. 'Morally I shouldn't be living here but it seems a shame to waste the view,' he said, as we set off for Wembury Point.

Following a suburban road through the fields that now contained grids of streets and houses on a relaxed descent towards the cliffs, we reached a minor coast road. After a few twists west, this rather abruptly ended, and turned into a footpath snaking around an empty headland of rough pasture, gorse and wild flowers. There were no houses on this scenic promontory but it did not feel quite wild. The scrubby landscape gave an echo of recent occupation: it felt as if humans and their constructions had only just departed. Which, as David Pinder would explain, was exactly what had happened.

At first glance, this was a typically attractive stretch of the South Devon coastline. But, looked at historically, Wembury Point was a microcosm of our changing relationship with the coast around the country. Over the last half-century, the Point had been nearly developed, almost saved, built on, written off, threatened with development once again before it was finally, early this century, protected by the National Trust after a vigorous campaign by local residents. It showed how no piece of British countryside has been preserved without a strange melange of historical accidents: commercial disasters, wars, idealism, philanthropy and, occasionally, a dose of hypocrisy. It perfectly told the story of how we came to conserve the coast.

\*

The Romantics are the authors of modern conservation. They first expressed a desire to save wild nature and the 'natural' countryside as a response to the Industrial Revolution. A century later, it was the writings of William Wordsworth that inspired four Victorians – Octavia Hill, Robert Hunter, Hardwicke Rawnsley and the Duke of Westminster – to form an organisation that would change our relationship with the English, Welsh and Northern Irish landscape for good. At a public meeting on 12 January 1895 the National Trust for Places of Historic Interest or Natural Beauty came into being.

Today, when the Trust is often regarded as a rather conservative national institution, it is easy to forget that its origins lay in quite radical beliefs exemplified, above all, by Octavia Hill. Showing a pre-cocious commitment to helping the less fortunate, Octavia, so called because she was the eighth daughter of a banker called Mr Hill, began working for the Ladies Co-operative Guild, a charity helping distressed gentlewomen, aged just thirteen. In her later teens she befriended the art critic John Ruskin, an influential thinker in the late Victorian era as doubts grew about the Industrial Revolution and its social costs, and she became his human 'camera', sketching copies of pictures in galleries that he required for his work. Inspired by Ruskin's concern for the working masses, Octavia founded an organisation to acquire and repair slum property, developing strong ideas about the importance of green breathing spaces in polluted London. When she joined the Commons Preservation Society, she met its lawyer, Robert Hunter, who was working to stop London's commons being smothered by development. Without Hunter, the green spaces of Wimbledon, Tooting and Wandsworth commons, as well as Hampstead Heath and Epping Forest, would probably not exist today. During the campaign to save Hampstead from being obliterated by suburbs, they teamed up with the Duke of Westminster, a man of wealth, connections and ample estate.

The final member of the founding quartet came, crucially, from outside London. Hardwicke Rawnsley was an ebullient clergyman living in the Lake District who adored Wordsworth and became passionate about saving Wordsworth's Lakes. In 1863 he sought help from the Commons Preservation Society. The Commons Act of 1877 offered protection only to suburban commons within six miles of a town's edge but Octavia Hill also recognised that open country would benefit 'peasant and aristocrat' alike. 'Are we as a nation to have any flower gardens at all?' she wrote. 'Can we afford it? Do we care to set aside ground for it, or will we have beetroot and cabbages only?'

It was Hill who suggested the idea of a public trust to 'preserve' land for the public. 'Mark my words Miss Hill, this is going to be a very big thing,' predicted the Duke of Westminster, who became the hidden power behind the nascent National Trust. The Trust drew up its constitution, based on an American law of 1891 to establish public reservations in Massachusetts, and the campaign got underway, earning an approving leader in *The Times*. Rawnsley, a canny campaigner, knew the Trust had to make a quick impression. That same year, while staying in Barmouth with Fannie Talbot, an old friend of Ruskin's, he persuaded her to donate the land at Dinas Oleu overlooking Cardigan Bay. It became the National Trust's very first piece of property, dedicated to the public for ever.

From the very beginning, the Trust aimed to permanently preserve the 'natural aspect' of landscapes and their 'features and animal and plant life', as the 1907 Act of Parliament which formed its legal basis for holding land for the public, in perpetuity, made clear. This Act was an innovative idea and remains one of the most socialist arrangements ever embraced by Britain. By the turn of the twentieth century, popular revulsion at animal cruelty was well established (the RSPCA had been given royal patronage by Queen Victoria as early as 1837) and there were moves to protect rare birds and plants from egg collectors and flower pickers, but the concept of a nature 'reserve', a slice of land in which all wildlife would be protected, was an innovative one. Most local people saw the beach as a dumping ground. Wilderness was a wasteland. This is written into the coast via names such as Ash Can Gully in Penwith, Cornwall, where people once threw the detritus from their fires. As the coal tailings dumped on the Durham coast as recently as the 1980s demonstrated, this attitude took decades to eradicate.

The First World War and the Great Depression meant that the National Trust and its subversive ideas developed slowly and by 1928, it still had only 1,550 members. Although the Trust's first acquisition was coastal, its earliest campaigns were closely guided by its founders' spiritual connection with Wordsworth and thus on saving the Lake District, and also the Peak District, then besieged on all sides by the Industrial Revolution. The Trust's London connections, and links to the Commons movement, also meant that many other early acquisitions were downland sites – Hindhead Commons in 1906, Box Hill in 1914 – within a day-trip of the capital.

At the Trust's AGM in 1934, the Marquis of Lothian led a charge which has shaped how many people see the National Trust today. Britain's great estates were being demolished and destroyed: death duties had risen from 8 per cent in 1904 to 50 per cent in 1930, and *Country Life* estimated that sixty large houses (comprising a suite of state rooms and more than twenty bedrooms) and 600 'smaller' houses needed to be saved. The Trust's Historic Country Houses Committee was launched and dozens of threatened stately homes began to be passed to the Trust. For a while, this overshadowed moves to protect the coast, although there was a growing realisation that the seaside was under threat as never before.

The years between the wars saw the breakdown of the old order. It was a great liberation for many working people, who now enjoyed paid holidays and the mobility of motor travel for the first time, but it was not immediately apparent how a modern democracy would preserve any natural environment for its liberated citizens to enjoy. This was an era of 'homes for heroes' and the desire that survivors of the First World War must be provided for led to unregulated development and jerry-built bungalows wherever there was road – or beach – frontage. 'We are witnessing to-day what can be termed without exaggeration a national movement seawards,' wrote Wesley Dougill in a 1936 book produced for another emerging conservation group, the Council for the Preservation of Rural England. Dougill noted that along thirty miles of the south coast from Littlehampton to Goring, Worthing, Lancing, Shoreham, Brighton, Rottingdean, Peacehaven and Newhaven, it was impossible to lose sight of 'post-war houses, bungalows and shacks'. Similar sprawl afflicted the Dorset coast at Poole and in Wales from Prestatyn to Rhyl and Llandudno, 'a shoddy, unplanned and unsightly blight, entirely opposed to the natural character and beauty of the seaside'.

Developments like Peacehaven, on the cliffs near Brighton, were typical of the era: a roguish property developer sold land for families to build houses themselves, which began as shacks before evolving into more permanent sprawl. This, the Plotlands movement, empowered working people but it was also uncontrolled. 'The State is socialist enough to destroy by taxation the classes that used to preserve rural amenity; but it is still too Conservative to interfere in the purposes to which land is put by speculators,' wrote the historian George Macaulay Trevelyan in an essay called *Must England's Beauty Perish?*, published in 1929. Planning laws were passed belatedly, in 1932 and 1935, to restrict ribbon development, but many of their provisions continued to be circumvented by canny developers.

Wembury was subject to all these currents, as David Pinder explained while we walked around the empty headland. Above us, the cloud broke up and the dark-blue sea turned incandescent turquoise.

Cliffs jutted into the sea and retreated into hidden bays. To the west was the interwar suburbia of Heybrook Bay. Beyond was Plymouth Sound, perpetually populated with at least one low-slung grey naval frigate slipping into the dock; to the east, the wooded headland of Mouthstone Point. The object that turned a fine view into a spectacular one was the Great Mewstone, a wonky triangle of a rock jutting from the water barely 500 metres from the shore. It drew the eye, lent a pleasing sense of scale to the grandeur of the land, and was a constant temptation, calling we stick-in-the-mud mainlanders into Wembury Bay.

The Great Mewstone might have disappeared but for Wembury's first great escape from the tide of development around it in 1908. Proposals to build Britain's biggest commercial port, encompassing the whole of Wembury Bay, could have gone ahead had not a House of Lords committee dismissed the scheme's viability. The threat of development didn't go away between the wars, however, and the spread of car ownership placed Wembury within easy commuting distance of Plymouth. Like so many other great estates, Langdon, which included Wembury and Wembury Point, was broken up and sold in more than seventy lots in 1927. The Point was snapped up by a local property developer who built two small holiday camps with chalets and a roller skating rink. David pointed to a ragged outline of concrete marking an old sea swimming pool on the rocky shore; a large block of rubble was all that remained of its diving board.

Confronted by such rapid suburban sprawl, calls for the 'preservation' of Britain's coast took on a new urgency. In 1931 a priority purchase list drawn up in secret by Trust supporters featured the Dover cliffs, Seven Sisters in East Sussex, the Pembrokeshire coast and the Devon coast, including Wembury. This ambitious hitlist was abandoned in the wake of the Great Depression but in 1938, Ida Sebag-Montefiore, a prominent philanthropist who lived in eastern Wembury, gave the coastal parts of her property to the National Trust, establishing its first small foothold in the area. As the charity subsequently discovered, once it acquired a small plot of land, it could more easily win over a sometimes-sceptical local community and add more pieces to the preservation jigsaw.

Wembury Point was not saved by conservation, however. The Second World War halted the construction of homes across the Point but the Royal Navy then requisitioned the cliffs and turned Wembury Point into a gunnery school, despoiling the area by constructing ugly, functional buildings all across the headland. Big guns were fired far into the sea, over the little peak of the Great Mewstone, and this coastal firing range proved so useful that when the war was over, the Navy refused to hand it back. It seemed as though Wembury Point was lost for ever.

The war may have been the nation's great priority but it enlarged, rather than diminished, the conservation movement as the celebration of Britain's wild heritage and coastal scenery became imbued with especial patriotic feeling. Catching the public mood, the National Trust adroitly promoted itself via short films shown in cinemas that showcased our natural wonders in glorious Technicolor and by 1948 its membership had grown to 15,800. After the war, Clement Attlee's Labour government took the lead in 'conservation', a new term, imported from America, implying a more active management of land than passive 'preservation'. National Parks and Areas of Outstanding Natural Beauty were created which, in harness with the Town and Country Planning Act of 1947, helped local authorities stop coastal 'shack development' and conserve not only small reserves but entire landscapes. The Pembrokeshire Coast National Park came into being in 1952. Beyond government, the county wildlife trust movement blossomed after the war and Lincolnshire Wildlife Trust was the first to acquire significant tracts of coastline, halting developments spreading from Skegness to Mablethorpe. (This vanguard action explains why the National Trust does not own any of Lincolnshire's long coastline. Although the Trust is also sometimes accused of historically favouring ostentatious rocky scenery over subtler, low-lying sand dune and marsh, it hasn't had to step in to save much of our estuarine coastline because the Wildlife Trusts and Britain's second-largest conservation charity the RSPB have proved so effective in recent years at protecting these areas.)

Planning laws might have stopped the coast being swamped by bungalows, but new threats to our shores quickly emerged. The right to a paid holiday was enshrined in law in 1936 and the 1950s and '60s were the apotheosis of domestic tourism: disposable income was growing alongside car ownership although air travel was still beyond the reach of most workers, and so 20 million people spent two weeks on the British coast.

Despite the burgeoning holiday industry, the seaside was not a pretty place: industries were far more casual about pollution and raw sewage was commonplace. The Ministry of Defence owned 217 miles of the coast, much of it scarred by derelict fortifications from the war. Then there were the vast new atomic power stations which were constructed on the wildest spots because they were considered safer if far from seaside settlements. Calder Hall, now Sellafield, in Cumbria, was the first commercial nuclear power station in the world when it was connected to the grid in 1956; that decade saw a great programme of atomic construction, including power stations at Hinkley Point in Somerset, Sizewell in Suffolk and Bradwell on the Dengie peninsula in Essex. The nuclear plant at Dungeness, in Kent, was, with typical disdain, built on the largest shingle promontory in Europe, a wild place rich in unique plants and animals.

In 1962 the Trust decided that it needed a more forceful strategy for protecting the coast and, meeting in private, its Executive Committee proposed a new fundraising appeal. With a target of £2 million, an appeals director was appointed, a retired naval commander called Conrad Rawnsley, the grandson of Trust founder Hardwicke Rawnsley. Conrad shared his grandfather's panache for publicity and became the human dynamo behind the initial success of Enterprise Neptune, which he named after the Roman god of the ocean. But his radical vision and autocratic style threatened to tear the Trust apart.

Since the original gift of Dinas Oleu, the National Trust had acquired 187 miles of coast, but its acquisitions were more by accident than design. Now that it was launching a very public appeal to protect the coastline, it needed to know how much was worth saving. Here, David Pinder stepped into the Trust's history. In 1965 he was a student of an enthusiastic young geography professor at Reading University, John Whittow, who was asked by the Trust to survey more than 3,000 miles of the coast of England, Wales and Northern Ireland. During the summer holidays, Whittow, three staff and thirty-five students divided the coast between them and walked it on foot to record what they found.

When I had first arrived at David Pinder's house overlooking the Wembury coast, I'd had a cup of tea with him and his wife, Pam, as they remembered how they had taken the overnight coach from Stafford to St Austell and then another bus to the south Cornish coast to begin their epic survey of the coast of South Cornwall.

'We were engaged,' began David.

Pam interrupted. 'We were not engaged,' she said firmly. 'We were going out together and he asked me to go. We walked for three weeks from St Austell to Land's End, right along the coast. There was no coast path. We were jumping streams, fighting off dogs, forcing through hedges. The weather was very mixed. A rescue helicopter followed us at one point. At the end of it I decided I would marry him because we'd managed to keep our relationship going through all the difficulties. I thought it was a good test.'

They tramped between youth hostels with wet feet, soaked rucksacks and sodden clothes in the pre-Gore-Tex era. The South West Coast

Path, which now loops 630 miles from Minehead in Somerset to Poole in Dorset, existed only in fragments of rough track mostly used by fishermen. If clifftop paddocks were not overgrown with gorse and bramble, they were filled with rusted machinery and old tyres. Fences and barbed wire were laid across paths. No footbridges crossed Cornwall's violent streams.

For all its dereliction, David was impressed by the landscape. Where the coast was accessible by road, there were patches 'very badly damaged by early tourism' but large stretches were inaccessible and pristine. Undertaking this survey, he saw how the National Trust could invent a new kind of landscape: unspoilt but accessible, a beauty that people could enjoy.

The Neptune surveyors produced a trove of 1,314 annotated Ordnance Survey maps of the coast, recording three main categories of land use: coast developed beyond redemption; coast temporarily or semi-developed (such as caravan sites); and unspoilt land that the Trust might hope to buy. They are a fascinating snapshot of the coast in 1965, and of the aesthetic values of the day.

I'd visited David's old professor, John Whittow, a few weeks earlier. Like David, John had surveyed a long stretch of shoreline back in 1965 and was still working, even though he was in his eighties: he was currently overseeing an updated survey of the coast fifty years on.

'We couldn't just advise the Trust – "that's a pretty coastline,"' John had told me. 'We wanted to show what was available: pristine coast mainly under agriculture or forestry, or land that was partly developed such as beach huts or caravan parks, which we crudely and rather pejoratively called, "shack development". ~~~~tially be cleared.' He showed me some of the 1965 sur~ joined-up handwriting recorded: 'Large area of ~ Gross disfigurement of high quality coast.' Of ~ one of John's students had concluded: 'Winter epitomises coastal development of the wors~

of it is not visible from the coast road. A scene of shacks, chalets, caravans, holiday camps, bingo halls, candyfloss, bicycles-for-two, greyhound racing, stock-cars, etc. on a not very attractive stretch of coast, mostly of low cliffs. Unworthy of any attempt at protection or redemption – it is completely past it, except perhaps for a small buffer area to the north of Winterton. The only redeeming feature is that the disfigurement is concentrated.'

For all their attempts to be scientific, the Neptune surveyors were clearly guilty of making subjective judgements. 'Just finding that Norfolk assessment made me laugh because that's effectively writing off the county,' said John Whittow. 'Everyone has their own perceptions and the students weren't trained enough to be objective.' He would test them by showing slides of the coast between Dorset and Exmouth. An image of tower-block development by the beach was rated the worst by the students. Another picture of Beer, in East Devon, was ranked the best. Containing white cliffs, blue sea, a lightly peopled beach, it 'epitomises everything we think about the cultural heritage of Britain', he said. But he had cheated with his camera. When he took another photograph fifty yards further back, it included a huge caravan site in the foreground. The students ranked this photograph second-worst in the list. 'I suppose the vast majority of my undergraduates were middle-class children,' said John, 'but that's what they saw as their cultural heritage – unspoilt coastline.'

The Neptune surveyors' obsession with 'shack development' seems a quaint, rather ludicrous fear today when our coast is hardly dis–figured by any shacks at all. It also appears snobbish towards the beach huts and caravans that were a passport to an affordable holiday by the sea for so many. 'I don't like to see a coastal area covered in caravans,' admitted John Whittow, 'but that's being very selfish because people have the right to stay on the coast if they wish.' David Pinder also noted the tension between conservation and democracy: 'When we did the survey there was a basic assumption that chalet parks and caravan sites were bad, not least because many caravan parks were badly sited.' David's aunt and uncle had once lived in a Nottingham terrace with a view of a high wall and when they bought a static caravan on the Lincolnshire coast it 'transformed their lives'. They spent summers there; later, his widowed aunt still trundled into Skegness on her mobility scooter. 'The environmental loss does perhaps need to be weighed against the social gain,' he said. 'I'm not arguing for that sort of thing to be spread all over the coast, but I've come to realise it isn't just black and white.'

As David pointed out, the Neptune surveyors' fear of shack development was not simply class snobbery. At the time, it was a genuine problem. Caravan sites proliferated over stunning clifftops, white and beige boxes visible for miles around. And what started out as a wooden shack soon became a permanent brick dwelling, quickly surrounded by other houses. The main reason we are untroubled by shacks today is that most of them have been supplanted by brick suburbs.

Thanks to the intrepid efforts of John Whittow and his students (who worked all summer only for expenses – the Isle of Wight coast, for instance, cost 30 shillings), the Neptune campaign concluded that 900 miles of the British coast could be saved. Approximately another third was judged by the surveyors to be simply of little scenic, historic, geological or ecological interest, and a final third was beyond redemption, apparently desecrated by development. Interestingly, this dismissive judgement included military installations such as Wembury Point.

Enterprise Neptune was launched with a great flourish in the spring of 1965, appealing for £2 million to save the coast. The Duke of Edinburgh was signed up as Royal Patron and on 23 April, St George's Day, Armada beacons were lit across the nation, as a way of involving local communities and catching the eye of many more: even in landlocked Borsetshire, a beacon was lit in *The Archers* soap opera. A lavish 27-minute film, *The Vanishing Coast*, quoting Shakespeare's *Richard II* ('This other Eden, This fortress built by Nature for herself'), showed the glories of Britain's coast in expensive aerial photography. It also railed against its increasing ugliness, with shots of giant refineries and hand-painted signs saying: 'PLEASE DO NOT BATHE HERE – 190 YDS FROM SEWAGE OUTFALL'. The film was funded by oil company National Benzole, a sign that Neptune initially enjoyed the backing of some big corporations who would later be accused of despoiling the coast. That May, the Duke of Edinburgh spoke at a grand lunch at the Mansion House which raised £64,000 and the government announced it would donate £250,000. Although the Trust struggled to find affordable land along the White Cliffs, Neptune swiftly made its first purchase: Whiteford Burrows, a 670-acre peninsula on the Pembrokeshire coast.

Enterprise Neptune was an immediate success. Envisioned as a temporary campaign, it went on and on, raising £2 million by 1973 and enabling the National Trust to rapidly overtake the Ministry of Defence as the biggest private coastal landowner, safeguarding 100 more miles of coast in just four years. But Neptune's triumph also nearly tore the Trust apart.

Conrad Rawnsley was full of good ideas. Lighting the Armada beacons was one; another, vetoed by the Trust's Executive Committee on the grounds of cost, was to buy one of the 'little ships' that rescued British forces from Dunkirk in 1940 to deploy as a floating publicity machine. Rawnsley was also ambitious and effective campaigning cost money. He created a 'Field Force' under his control of six regional directors and thirty county commissioners, with 100 district supervisors and 500 wardens. To the other parts of the Trust, this was empire-building and Rawnsley certainly possessed an imperious touch. When the Trust's chairman, Lord Antrim, asked Rawnsley for a Neptune briefing note and then departed from it in his speech, Rawnsley wrote back: 'If you know it all, please don't ask for a brief. If you don't, then ask for one by all means, but have the courtesy to read it.' In another incident, Rawnsley gave a Christmas bonus of £500 – then an annual salary – to one of his Neptune recruits without getting authorisation. Despite the fact that all of Rawnsley's Field Force below director level were volunteers, the Trust's leadership became increasingly worried about Neptune's spiralling cost. Insisting that the campaign should not cost more than 5 per cent of the amount raised, or £75,000, in 1965, the Executive Committee ordered the expenses of Rawnsley's volunteers to be 'drastically curtailed'.

But in the end, it was ideals, not money, that caused a permanent rift between Rawnsley and the Trust. Rawnsley believed that the National Trust had become an Establishment organisation that had abandoned his grandfather's vision. Privately, he told the Trust that Neptune was for 'the man in the street' and it was 'a thousand pities' that this was not the Trust's public image. Preservation of the coast was meaningless without accessibility and enjoyment, he argued, and so the Trust must promise more amenities. 'Where are the dinghy parks, the launching facilities for pleasure craft, the camping sites, the car parks, the access roads and paths, the lavatories?' he asked. In an organisation enraged by 'shack' aesthetics, seeking to promote caravans was sacrilege. The Trust's Publicity Committee insisted its duty was to preserve, not entertain, and Rawnsley's populism increasingly grated with the Trust's leadership. In the autumn of 1966, when told his position would cease to exist in 1967 as Neptune was to be absorbed into the existing structures of the Trust, Rawnsley went renegade. At a press conference near Plymouth to celebrate Neptune's latest coastal acquisition, the ashen-faced commander gave an impassioned speech about a charity he called 'the child of my grandfather's imagination'. The Trust was not financially bankrupt, he said. 'But there are other ways of being bankrupt. You can be bankrupt in ideas, bankrupt in the common touch, bankrupt in your sense of what the people need and in your alacrity to provide it.' He accused the Trust of becoming 'an inert and amorphous organisation proceeding by the sheer momentum given to it by those who continued to bequeath their wealth to it, as often as not to escape death duties'. The press were delighted by such intemperance, the Trust hierarchy less so: Rawnsley was suspended from duty.

The Trust had made a formidable enemy. When Rawnsley was prevented from speaking at the AGM in late 1966, he took out advertisements in the papers and easily attracted the signatures required to call an Extraordinary General Meeting. In February 1967 some 4,000 people attended what the *Sunday Telegraph* called 'a rowdy special meeting' that went on all day, with speeches interrupted by cries of 'shut up' and 'sit down' – raucous behaviour by Trust standards. Rawnsley envisaged drastic reform – the Trust was too aristocratic, its house opening hours too restrictive and not enough of its land was accessible to the public – but his proposals suffered a crushing defeat.

Nevertheless, the mood of members was expressed by a motion from John Betjeman, one of several public figures in attendance, who supported the Trust's leadership but wanted 'due consideration' taken of some of Rawnsley's concerns. Neptune's first leader did succeed in shaking up the Trust. An official reform committee saw the need to modernise the charity's stuffy committees and improve its contact with its 160,000 members. Rawnsley's career with the Trust was over but many in the organisation acknowledged that some of his criticisms were valid. As Trust secretary Jack Rathbone put it in a generous defence of Rawnsley: 'The Wind of Change which he has produced is, I am sure, a good thing for the Trust; so are many of his ideas and the boisterous and enthusiastic sea breeze which he blows over us.'

The Neptune survey of 1964 is a powerful statement of the conservation values of the day but it also shows how land judged 'beyond redemption', supposedly ruined by development, can spring back into life. As we walked around Wembury Point that afternoon, taking in the grassland filled with yellow buttercups, the dark-green patches of gorse and the grey rocks by the sea, David Pinder said he felt that he and his fellow surveyors didn't quite understand the power of nature at the time. They never envisaged, for instance, that the coal-wrecked beaches of Durham could be cleaned up. When it came to places like Wembury Point, the survey noted how much of the British coastline had been 'lost' to the Ministry of Defence. 'In fact, in almost all instances the MoD coastline was actually an excellent place of environmental protection,' said David. 'The flora and fauna are rich, they were relatively undisturbed and there hasn't actually been a lot of damage to the landscape.'

We were strolling through just such a scene and I was astonished when David told me how recently the Navy had departed from this empty headland. When he and Pam had moved to Wembury in 1991, they'd still hear the boom of the Navy's big guns from the Point. Until a decade ago, Wembury Point was a forbidden eyesore, cluttered with naval buildings. On my OS map, the bay was still marked as a danger area with red triangles all around and yet this no-go zone had created a de facto marine conservation park, rich in wildlife.

In 2001 the naval gunnery was finally closed. Technically, it was a brownfield site, a spectacular clifftop location ripe for development. Worried residents of Wembury's suburbs began to campaign against a new building programme on their coastline. (A smidgin of hypocrisy is an almost universal feature of local conservation: 'In traditional style the people that moved in then began to campaign against further development,' said David, including himself in this wry observation.) The government's support for Neptune, however, meant that the MoD had to offer the land to the National Trust before it could be sold to a property developer. With the fortieth anniversary of Neptune looming, the Trust launched an appeal and raised £1.6 million to buy and rehabilitate Wembury Point, which it had identified as a conservation priority seventy years earlier.

Unlike at Orford Ness, the MoD removed all the buildings at Wembury and, in 2006, the National Trust took over. Seven years later, we were walking along what was actually an old road, featuring a couple of speed bumps and the remains of a mini-roundabout, a surreal touch of suburbia on an apparently natural headland. A sign explained it would take forty years to 'return to nature', but it was happening already. David wondered if one or two of the naval buildings should have been retained, to remember our recent military history, but I could see why they had been stripped away here. There were still beautiful sea views when these high headlands became a jumble of buildings, but standing on an empty Wembury Point was a gift of peace and space. Here, on a coastline that had been spoiled and then saved, I could experience the full force of this grand collision of land and sea.

Places like Wembury and Orford Ness were perhaps easier to protect because they had belonged to the government. An evening on the Carrick Roads revealed the complexity of acquiring land in private hands and the occasional cunning required to seal a deal. This was creek country, a unique part of our coastline that at times took on the character of a tropical rainforest. Unlike the Atlantic-spumed north coast, the sheltered south shores of Cornwall are defined by their estuaries. These were not the broad expanses of low mud I grew up with in East Anglia but fingers of water with steep, completely wooded sides, where a canopy of dense oak woodland followed the contours to the very edge of the water. The creeks were capricious in colour: deep blue in the open and a vivid green where they lay in the shadow of the trees. Crossing one of these creeks on the King Harry Ferry, I could not immediately tell that these often stunted sessile oaks were clambering over substantial banks and cliffs and so they took on the character of gigantic natives of the Amazon.

Daphne du Maurier chose well when she made the neighbouring Helford estuary the sensuous setting for her romantic thriller, *Frenchman's Creek*. The twisting deep creeks of both Helford and the Carrick Roads are secretive places, the oaks hiding boats, and people, from view.

Du Maurier's love for creek country was shared by other influential writers, including her best friend's father, Sir Arthur Quiller-Couch, the literary critic, and his friend Kenneth Grahame, who was inspired to write river scenes for *The Wind in the Willows* by holidays on the Fal. The talkative, water-loving Ratty is said to be modelled on Quiller-Couch, a voluble man who was obsessed with sailing. For all our holiday passion for the oceanic coast, if we seek to base our whole lives by the sea we value shelter. Estuarine landscapes that offer respite from the wind as well as water views contain the most desirable real estate. No wonder developers lay siege to creek country.

'The open coast is arguably less under pressure than the estuary coast because it's where we as humans tend to stick ourselves,' remarked Phil Dyke as we strolled through a field scented with flowers and warm grass at Messack Point. Phil was the National Trust's coast and marine adviser, a former ranger who was now its leading thinker on coastal protection, and he showed me around his homeland, the Carrick Roads, shortly after my trip to Wembury. Walking through this sheltered meadow at Messack, a relatively recent purchase using Neptune funds, I had no sense that the coast was nearby: a sudden tang in the air was as shocking as biting into a sweet and finding it salty. I could see only grass and trees but above the woo of wood pigeons came the shrill cries of oystercatchers and a muddy, bubbling curlew.

As we walked, I caught glimpses of the dinky grey church of St Just, which I didn't immediately comprehend was on the far side of a hidden creek. And then Messack Point sprang its surprise: a glittering expanse of water surrounded by wooded promontories that constantly changed shape, revealing and concealing, depending on where we positioned ourselves. Lines of yachts were poised to race in the middle of this befuddling estuary, which reminded me of the outer reaches of Sydney harbour. On the more developed west side of the Carrick Roads were leafy multimillion-pound homes of Restronguet Point, perhaps the most desirable address in Cornwall after Rock. In the far distance, beyond the clustered houses of Falmouth, were the white domes of Goonhilly satellite station on the Lizard peninsula, and seven wind turbines which had been the first in Cornwall but had just been 'replanted' – the disingenuous industry euphemism – with far bigger machines. Ironically, the most visually distracting object on the horizon was a big white block to the north of Falmouth which housed Exeter University's new Environmental and Sustainability Institute.

That evening over dinner at Phil Dyke's home nearby, I met Peter Mansfield. An impish man with a big laugh, Peter was retired from the Trust but still said 'we' when speaking of its actions. One third of Cornwall's shores were protected by the Trust and, as one of the charity's land agents, Peter had many 'notches on his belt': he had overseen Neptune's purchase of eighty-six pieces of Cornish coast between 1980 and 1996. 'There was a great evangelistic enthusiasm,' he said. 'Shopping is fun! We went into spending in a big way.'

In Neptune's first decade, the money kept rolling in, from the government and big business as well as bequests from wealthy individuals, and the Trust secured 175 miles of coastline. In its second decade, it added another 99 miles, including many much-loved beauty spots: Studland, the Needles, Golden Cap, the Seven Sisters, Robin Hood's Bay and the real Frenchman's Creek.

Rather like the piratical hero of Du Maurier's *Frenchman's Creek*, the Trust occasionally resorted to daring tactics in its mission to protect the coast, and Peter Mansfield explained these machinations wittily. He was a protégé of Michael Trinick, a swashbuckling surveyor and land agent who became the Trust's mini-dictator in Cornwall from the

1950s to 1984, and was compared to both a pirate and a Celtic saint, as well as being nicknamed King Neptune. The Trust's aesthetically-minded historic buildings staff were nicknamed the 'lilies' while its land agents were called 'the hobnailed boot' as they cut deals to buy land and handled the brutal economics of managing it. When Trinick was first posted to Cornwall in 1953, the Trust owned just 20 miles of the Cornish coast; when he retired, it held more than 100. He established the principle of purchasing not just a narrow strip of cliff but inland to the horizon, or 'a farm's depth', whichever was further, to ensure coastal scenes remained unspoilt for as far as the eye could see. The wily Trinick was adept at charming elderly ladies, who were often generous Neptune donors, but did not necessarily tiptoe around them to do it. 'People are terribly shy of being generous, because they are terrified of being smothered with thanks,' he once said. 'He could be a bully but he was a giant of the landscape,' said Peter Mansfield.

Peter's job was to meet potential donors, or people with land to sell, and work his magic. His philosophy was to treat every visitor with great care. One person left the Trust money to buy part of the Lizard Peninsula based on the quality of its cream teas. Occasionally, Peter would charter a plane from Land's End airport and fly prospective donors over the coast. 'Anything looks good from a thousand feet,' he chortled. 'You don't see all the grot.'

Most people assume charities are a pushover but the Trust has a reputation for carefully guarding its Neptune cash. I teased Peter about this: when buying coastline, would he ever try to fleece the vendor? 'If you were dealing with a property speculator from Bristol or London you might drive a hard bargain,' he said with a laugh. 'You are a charity, and you have an obligation not to spend over the market price. But you're generally dealing with a person from the local area with whom you will have an ongoing relationship and you wouldn't want to do them out of a pound.'

Peter's most memorable deal was when an old lady left the Trust the most southerly manor on the Lizard Peninsula. Architecturally, the house was not of national importance but Peter persuaded the farmer who owned the adjoining piece of clifftop to sell up so that the manor would constitute a coastal, Neptune acquisition. After the purchase was approved by the Trust's executive, Peter discovered that the house came with 'encumbrances' – a £30,000 mortgage. Terrified he would lose his job for misleading his bosses, he visited the derelict building and found it on the verge of collapse. In a dark room, he opened a dusty trunk. Inside was an old dress with a Dior label. Coming from a family of Leicester shoemakers, 'I recognise a good bit of skirt when I see it,' he chuckled. Peter opened more trunks and discovered more fabulous couture dresses from the 1930s. *Blue Peter* featured the dresses in a fashion parade on television and they sold for £100,000. He was off the hook.

This kind of ingenuity helped Neptune purchase 500 miles of coastline by 1988. As well as the gains, there were some losses that Peter still regrets. Despite his best efforts in Cornwall, the Trust never acquired Land's End: in 1981 it met the asking price of £1.75m but was outbid. Peter consoled himself that the money was better spent on unspoilt coast elsewhere such as beautiful Cape Cornwall, which was given to the Trust by ketchup mogul H. J. Heinz and which Peter liked to call the connoisseur's Land's End.

Spectacular purchases gain headlines but more important for conserving our coast have been Neptune's many far quieter acquisitions, such as Messack Point. As evening fell, I sat looking out on the Carrick Roads, lights twinkling on the opposite shore and the occasional small boat slipping across the darkening water. Messack, a 200-acre beef and arable farm, had been bought for £950,000 from two brothers, who were retiring, in the 1990s. The Trust spent £100,000 on placing power lines underground, removing unsightly farm sheds, creating two miles of public footpaths where there had been none and introducing sensitive farming practices so pesticides would not wash into the water. They sold off the farm house for a bargain £450,000 and so it cost £600,000 – £3,000 an acre – to protect and enhance this unobtrusive coastal land. 'Is that good value?' Phil Dyke had asked. 'Of course it's good value.'

The necessarily prosaic calculations of Neptune's deal-makers were banished from my mind as I climbed into one of the obligingly horizontal-limbed oaks overhanging the Carrick Roads. I crept along the branch until I was suspended above the water and dangled my legs. Tiny waves ulped and oolped against the underside of the rock below and the oak's limbs reached down as if it possessed a fatal passion for the water: any grey branch that touched this salty nirvana soon lost its leaves and died. As the branches bent to the surface, tendrils of seaweed hung in the clear water, reaching up, as if trying to touch their green brethren in the air. This meeting point of leaf and seaweed was as disorientating and bewitching as the contrary mix of wooing wood pigeon and shrieking redshank and the colliding scents of hay and mud.

The water amplified every sound – barking dogs and the conversation of two men lazing on a boat moored 100 metres away – and the surrounding trees tried to snuffle it out. When a distant motor boat disappeared around a tree-covered headland, its noisy throttling vanished as suddenly as if it had been swallowed by a sea monster. The trees and the water may have been mentally discordant but they worked together, concealing and revealing the magic of this most coveted landscape.

It may have been thrilling to take Neptune's money and go shopping, as Peter Mansfield gleefully described, but then the reality of looking after all these new properties hit home. This challenge has bedevilled the Trust since its inception, and it was presciently grasped by Emma Turner, the gun-toting first 'Watcher' on Scolt Head Island. 'It is one thing to acquire these beauty spots,' she wrote in her memoirs, 'it is another thing to maintain them for the nation. The public for whose benefit they are acquired, does not grasp this fact. Money, and yet more money, is needed.'

Maintaining a house or garden is bad enough; 742 miles of seaside is terrifying. Owning a chunk of coast is a daily battle against every kind of unpredictability: the ocean, the weather, the wildlife and the randomness of public behaviour. During my visits to the Neptune coast for the writing of this book I encountered the following: a mysterious toxic substance washed up on a beach that caused a dog to die; a landslip; a shipwreck; a pop star landing his helicopter on a bird reserve; a member of the public protesting over the removal of blackthorn scrub where blackcaps were nesting; sea-borne roots of hemlock water dropwort, one of the most poisonous plants in Britain; a freshly dug tunnel into a hidden Second World War bunker; a stray cat and kittens living down another bunker, and an illegally erected bench. And I could write a whole chapter about the items dumped in Trust car parks, from dead horses to the carcasses of cows. 'It's normally cats actually. Cats and dogs in bags,' said Robin Lang, ranger on the Isle of Wight.

No wonder land is called 'liabilities' in internal Trust jargon. This firefighting costs a fortune. I imagined the National Trust to be flush with the money from its four million members but it wasn't, and could easily be bankrupted by its coastline alone: it costs, on average, £3,000 per year to manage just one mile of its coast. To prevent financial ruin, its purchases are governed by the hard-headed 'Chorley formula' which calculates the income-generating opportunities of each piece of land (car parks were good) and the size of the endowment required to stop it running at a deficit. The Trust property manager in charge of each area is supposed to manage a self-sustaining portfolio of properties: empty coastline might not make any money but it can be subsidised by a nearby stately home. One historic problem with the Neptune campaign was that the money it raised could only be spent on actually purchasing the land, but recently the Trust had overcome various legal hurdles and could now release Neptune funds to look after some of the acreage it acquired.

In practice, as National Trust rangers discovered every day, managing land is often about managing the people who visited it and the average ranger not only has to act as conservationist, but also teacher, police officer, estate manager, farmer, naturalist, carpenter, traffic warden, local historian and problem solver for every issue from dog poo in the dunes to erosion caused by the ocean. One local ranger repeated an old saying about the National Trust: 'Loved by the nation, hated by the locals'. The Trust is an easy target. Unlike most landowners, it has signposts on the land and is in the phone book. Its stance as protector of the nation's beauty raises formidable expectations, and when it doesn't behave as people anticipate – erecting moderately unsightly fencing close to the White Cliffs, for instance, to enable conservation grazing to preserve flower-rich clifftop grasslands – it causes outrage.

Some of this antagonism harks back to the days when conservation was known as preservation, and naturalists put fences around wild places to keep people out, with some justification at the time because Edwardian nature lovers collected flowers, butterflies and birds' eggs on a rapacious scale. The first wardens of the earliest nature reserves were more like gamekeepers (indeed, they often were former gamekeepers) and this desire to protect the land from the people shaped the character of many wildlife charities' landholdings until quite recently. Because of its legal obligation to provide public access, the National Trust was always different. When the Trust's nature conservation subcommittee was formed in 1944, it presciently recognised that many parts of our 'natural' landscape, from chalk downland to woodland, required human intervention to maintain their richness of species. Sanctuaries 'to which all forgo access' were said to be seldom necessary, except for breeding birds.

This commitment to letting people enjoy places of great natural beauty was ahead of its time. But there is also a timeless tension between public access and conservation, which is still played out within all conservation charities, including the National Trust. Most contemporary conservationists publicly claim there is no conflict between people enjoying nature and wild things thriving. In many cases, there isn't: the Farne Islands' 40,000 visitors help several species of ground-nesting bird who nest deliberately close to the well-tramped walkways to stop their chicks falling prey to black-backed gulls. On Inner Farne, the highest densities of Arctic tern nests are found in the grassy courtyard outside the rangers' accommodation, the most disturbed spot on the island.

People need to be involved in a landscape to care about it and yet I saw how it wasn't as simple as opening the gates of every nature reserve when I walked along the deserted beach of Scolt Head Island in Norfolk. I was an intruder. Every hundred yards, I caused an oystercatcher or a ringed plover, or both, to sidle away from their nests scraped in the stones just above the high-tide mark. These timid birds scuttled along the beach, laboriously leading me away from their young before flying out to sea and around behind my back to return to their eggs.

They were no longer imperilled by egg thieves as they had been in my childhood, but there was one six-legged predator driving the ringed plover from Britain: man and his dog. There are so many more people on our remote beaches than just ten years ago. Even when we love nature, even when our dogs are well behaved, our presence is enough to scare the birds. With a steady trickle of Sunday walkers, a nest would be deserted, its eggs cooled and spoiled.

Sixty-two pairs of ringed plovers nested on Scolt's four miles of beach: this modest number was now the best site in England. To the east of Scolt were the mainland beaches of Holkham and Wells, another four miles of equally ideal habitat for the ringed plover. And yet, no pairs nested successfully here any more because both beaches were increasingly popular with holidaymakers, including myself. Further along the Norfolk coast at Blakeney Point, only accessible by boat or by an exhausting, three-mile trek along the shingle bank, there were ten pairs of nesting ringed plovers. In 2009 the National Trust belatedly forbade dogs from large swaths of the Point during the nesting season. The ban proved controversial with many locals, and rangers endured regular clashes with dog-walkers. 'You do get a lot of aggro. I've been told to eff off a few times and threatened with a punch and I can understand it,' said Paul Nichols, a Blakeney ranger. 'You've walked four miles in glorious isolation and suddenly you've got someone telling you what to do.' As Eddie Stubbings, Blakeney's head ranger, said: 'It's the time-old challenge of balancing protection of wildlife with access and education.'

Coastal visitors can be nudged by sleight of hand. Notices saying 'Beware – adders' is a classic conservation tactic – not untrue, but useful. On Orford Ness, the danger of unexploded bombs works well to keep people on the paths, where they cannot erode its fragile shingle ecosystem. But the trend now is to dispense with bossy notices in favour of encouraging people to make the most of being outdoors. We are less willing to curtail our freedom to enjoy wild places and this attitude can turn the coast and the creatures it contains into our plaything, only worthwhile insofar as it entertains us, and not somewhere for animals and plants to live untroubled by humans. Anyone who writes to inspire people to visit wild places risks accusations of hypocrisy, but I don't believe we should make every centimetre of the coast accessible. Ultimately, ringed plovers cannot nest on a busy beach.

When they are not managing people, the National Trust's coastal rangers manage wildlife. This can be thrilling, arduous or ethically challenging. On occasion, like the evening I jumped into the rear of the Double Cab Defender feeling like the junior member of a criminal gang, it could be all three. Dave, a studious, dark-haired resident ranger on Orford Ness, Suffolk, was behind the wheel. Ron, a voluble, white-haired National Trust volunteer, was in the passenger seat. Ron was head to toe in camouflage (a concept named during the First World War and developed on Orford Ness) and his large pink fingers clutched a .243 rifle. We were doing nothing wrong and had nothing to hide. Except our nocturnal activity, shooting foxes, was a pretty secretive affair. Conservationists euphemistically called it 'predator control' because many people hate the idea of shooting one animal to preserve another. Sometimes rangers received death threats from animal rights extremists who whispered abuse down the phone from their bedrooms in Surbiton. More often, wildlife lovers cancelled their membership of conservation charities that dared discuss this kind of conservation 'management'. But wherever there were endangered ground-nesting birds to protect – terns, avocets, ringed plovers – organisations from the RSPB to the Wildlife Trusts quietly authorised men with guns to take out a few of their principal predators. On the almost-island of Orford Ness, the National Trust was no different.

'You could put a strong case for the futility of it, but we practise predator control,' admitted Grant Lohoar, head ranger on the Ness. During his twenty years there, he estimated that 750 foxes had been executed. Once one is killed another smoothly takes over the territory, even on the peninsula, accessible to a fox only via a dangerous swim across the River Ore or a long trudge down the shingle spit from Aldeburgh. Nevertheless, the disappearance of terns on Scolt Head Island in North Norfolk was an illustration of what happened if nature reserves did nothing about the fox population. The previous spring, Ron had shot five cubs and their mother, so there were fewer foxes on the Ness this year. Two weeks ago, he shot a lactating vixen. No one had seen any cubs since. Ron hoped it meant they had died: the weather had been cold and the cubs should have perished from pneumonia, providing no foxy relatives looked after them.

As the clouds turned orange over the Suffolk coast, we bumped slowly across the King's Marshes, ancient grazing fields reclaimed from the sea and named after Henry II, who built Orford Castle. Between humps of gorse, the curved ends of an old Nissen hut stood like bookends, the building between them having long vanished. Last year's thistle heads still waved in the breeze.

A brown hare with dark-tipped ears lolloped away from the Land Rover. We were in the vehicle because it spooked the wildlife less than a person on foot. It also gave us an elevated position to peer over reedbeds and into ditches.

A local man and farmer's son, Ron gave up a night every fortnight to fire his gun on the Ness. A wildfowler, a villager who held traditional rights to shoot on the marshes, he had the restless eyes of a shooter and was a far more knowledgeable naturalist than I would ever be. He bombarded Dave with questions about the residents of the Ness. 'Are there any spoonbills still around? Have the shovellers gone now?' Ron loved the birds not simply for the sport and bore no grudge against the fox either. 'I like a pair of foxes but not ten pairs.' I had supposed a few would keep the rabbits down but Ron disagreed. He'd seen a fox stride through a field of rabbits, oblivious, to grab some chicks on a nest.

Ron also excelled at picking out tiny movements in the landscape. 'Cuckoo on that post there. It's got something in its mouth. Just ate it.' We bounced closer to take a look. Suddenly, Ron swung the gun from its resting position pointing into the footwell and aimed it at the bird. This was slightly alarming but he was using his rifle sight to inspect the bird. 'I haven't got any bullets in there,' he explained, handing me a small gold spike on the end of a slender, streamlined gold cylinder called a 'soft-nosed' bullet. Here was another of Orford Ness's distortions of scale for it resembled a miniature warhead.

Next up, by the fence, was a short-eared owl, richly feathered in chocolate brown, orange eyes staring at us. 'Beautiful, absolutely gorgeous,' purred Ron. By the old sea bank, he exhaled joyfully. 'It's tufty,' he exclaimed as he identified a tufted duck. Finally, I picked up a flash of orangey brown moving through long grass. 'Fox,' I whispered. Dave cut the engine and in one surprisingly fluent movement Ron was out of the door and round the back, resting his gun on the Defender's pickup tray.

I could still see the fox's ears in the meadow. So could Ron. It was actually a Chinese water deer. He climbed back in the vehicle. 'I can part his eyes if you like,' he offered, with boyish enthusiasm. Dave stayed silent. I felt silly for the mistake but Ron was excited.

'Here we go, first one of the night. That got the heart beating. The old trigger finger was itching but I'd calmed down my breathing by the time I got halfway along the truck.' He was visualising what would have happened. 'There would have been a pop, the animal would have flown up in the air and that would've been it.'

With the light fading on Orford Ness, we plugged Ron's lamp into the cigarette lighter of the Defender and fed the light through the rear window. Ron took up position on the back of the truck, gun over his shoulder. I stood beside him. A powerful yellow light swept along ditches and embankments like a wobbly lighthouse beam. No foxes had appeared at dusk. So now we were going lamping.

Ron played his beam along the horizontal lines of the Ness, looking for eyes. The first pair, on the track ahead of us, were pink: a hare, predicted Ron, and sure enough, a hare bounded away. A group of slightly yellowy eyes appeared in a field. These were sheep. A fox's eyes, explained Ron, showed up a bright bluey-white.

By concrete fence posts that contained no fence, Ron detected a pair of eyes, close to the ground. He tapped the roof of the Land Rover. Dave cut the engine. Ron conjured a small plastic whistle from his pocket which he blew to imitate the cry of an injured rabbit. No curious fox face appeared. A fox, he explained, will quarter an area, moving up and down and back and forth to identify the precise location of a sound like his piped rabbit scream. 'You'd think he'd stick his head up and have a look,' said Ron. But it didn't. He tried another shooter's trick: unscrewing a lid and waving a tiny vial in the air. It contained fox gland and its pungent perfume was supposed to lure a sniffing fox out of hiding. Still no creature popped up.

We bumped along more tracks and then onto the shingle. Driving through great troughs of stones sounded like we were forcing through a flood of water. The lights of Aldeburgh shone on the horizon, five miles away; the only light nearby was the firm beam of the lighthouse on Orford Ness. Coming into view every seven seconds, it was a melancholy prospect. A month after our shoot, the lighthouse would be decommissioned and it would spend its senility in the dark, waiting to fall with this quickly-eroding coastline.

The flat nothingness of the Ness was teeming with animals after dark. 'There's something in that blimmin' grass. It keeps giving us a flash of its eyes.' Ron swept the beam across once more. 'It's the littlest water deer you've ever seen in your whole life. It isn't much bigger than a baby rabbit, little sod.' I kept spotting bluey-white eyes but they always turned out to be Chinese water deer. Ron's lamp picked out the eyes of a stoat and then an otter.

It was nearly midnight. Ron passed the time by telling some good stories. There were fewer fish now, and so herons had to eat what they could. He recently passed one struggling with a conspicuous lump in its slender neck. When he returned a few hours later, he found the bird keeled over, dead. He took his knife, slit its throat and found it blocked by a rat.

Ron believed in UFOs but was sceptical about the sighting in nearby Rendlesham Forest. 'We've got to be pretty naive to think we're the only species living on these planets,' he said, but he knew a guy who had been lamping in the woods when the UFO landed and Ron was convinced the light people had seen was just his lamp. 'I bet they had shot a fox and were flashing about, looking for it,' he said.

And what about the theory that the UFO was stored in the upper level of the Cobra Mist building? Ron didn't answer. 'All I can say is its cloaking capability must still be working very well,' Dave said, laughing, 'because I've been inside and there's nothing there.'

Bang.

Ron discharged his first shot of the night. I looked in the beam and there was nothing. Ron swept his lamp along the sea bank again. Bang. This time, after the shot, a pair of eyes glanced our way and disappeared over the bank. A fox.

Ron thought he had hit it but had seen nothing after the second shot. Was it dead? Injured? Or unharmed and fleeing?

We hurtled over the paddock to where we had seen it and marched up and down through the hefty tufts of grass looking for a fox, or its trail. There was nothing. No carcass, no blood, no clues; just dark grass. Ron had missed.

It was thirty minutes past midnight. We returned to the jetty so Dave could give Ron a lift in the boat across the dark waters to the mainland.

It's a shame we couldn't find the body, I said.

'It's a shame I didn't kill the thing in the first place after all that messing about,' replied Ron, clearly cross at being outfoxed.

The scourge of the gulls and plovers was on the loose on the Ness and it would live to fight another fortnight at least.

## Explorations of Neptune

**Wembury Point** is perfectly pleasant for a potter but you get the best from this stretch of Devon coast by walking a decent chunk of it on the South West Coast Path. It is 15 miles on the path west to Plymouth but I'd recommend heading east from Wembury Point. The coast path takes in the Great Mewstone and Wembury's picturesque church before crossing the River Yealm (with the help of a seasonal ferry which you need to book in advance by telephone). On the far side, the route climbs out of ancient oak woodland to join the sweeping scenic drive around Mouthstone Point built by Barings banker Lord Revelstoke (the great-great-grandfather of Diana, Princess of Wales) in the 1880s to impress visitors.

*OS Map*
Explorer OL20, South Devon
*Nearest railway station*
Plymouth, 7 miles
*Website*
www.southwestcoastpath.com

The creek country of **the Carrick Roads** is probably best explored by boat because its lustrous tree-lined edges are not particularly well served by footpaths (the South West Coast Path does not attempt to follow every twist of these complex embayments). A good starting point is the National Trust gardens of **Trelissick**, one of the most scenically positioned stately homes in the country. As well as the obligatory cafe, there is a secondhand bookshop and a gallery housing Cornish art. Beyond lies classic parkland. I wandered south following the land as it curved towards the point, which was a lovely spot to contemplate the waters. It is possible to take the King Harry Ferry on foot and walk down the eastern side of the Fal to St Mawes, where the true sea begins again but for three miles from the ferry you have to walk on a busy road. If you are driving, you can dip into Turnaware

Point, also owned by the Trust, and look back at Trelissick. And if you prefer to escape the crowds of Trelissick, the Trust has opened up new footpaths (unmarked on most maps) on its old farm around Messack Point. These offer the quintessential creek experience: thick woods, warm meadows and the sudden appearance of water. There is limited parking on the roadside close to Messack Farm.

**Trelissick**

Feock

Near Truro

Cornwall TR3 6QL

**OS Map**

Explorer 105, Falmouth & Mevagissey

**Nearest railway station**

Perranwell, 4 miles

**Website**

www.nationaltrust.org.uk/trelissick-garden/

## Further Reading

Charlie Pye-Smith, *In Search of Neptune*, National Trust, 1990

Merlin Waterson, *A Noble Thing: The National Trust and its Benefactors*, National Trust, 2011

# 7

# A Better World

*Lundy / Brownsea*

Lundy
Island

Brownsea
Island

Alone on a rocky cliff high above the ocean, I found an indentation through the vertiginous, sweet-scented meadow and followed it on a zig-zag down. In the clear water far below, the pale tummies of two seals showed brightly. I felt the descent in my body: a hollow rush of vertigo, jelly legs, lungs seeking extra air. Below me were Montagu's Steps, a series of crumbling concrete posts and stumps of rusted metal, the ruins of a route built to retrieve wreckage from one of hundreds of vessels – a roll-call including *Ethel, Belinda, Mary, Edward Arthur, Thomas Crisp, Francis Anne, Ariel, Fiona, Charles* and *Millicent* – that struck a stretch of our coastline that seemed strategically placed to wreck ships. Twisting and turning, I found a short flight of reassuring stone steps, then a section of iron railings. I didn't dare clutch them in case they came away in my grasp. The swirling ocean was closer now, dispensing great slaps to the rocks. Finally, a sheer granite drop, pockmarked with the fragments of a metal ladder that once descended the final ten metres into the Atlantic. I stopped and squatted on the rock. If I slid into the water I would be like a mouse in a sink, unable to clamber out, sluiced in the icy swell until I was done for.

So I sat, stunned by my proximity to great heights, big depths and the might of the ocean, alone. Minutes passed. I realised I was stuck, rendered immobile not by fear but by some compelling force on this small island. I singled out one herring gull and watched it ride the eddies in every direction around the cliff; it seemed to go minutes without a wingbeat. I felt a sudden surge of exhilaration, a rush of ecstasy, gratitude, peace and heartfelt love for this spot, this moment in time. This is the best place I have ever visited, I thought. It is amazing. Perhaps three minutes later, I felt calmer than ever before. I stayed put for forty-five minutes or so, I wasn't really counting, and then climbed away. Ever since, I've wondered what happened there, on the rocks by the ocean.

Nineteen miles west of where the north coast of Devon halts at Morte Point is a piece of granite half-a-mile wide and three miles long, 143 metres above sea level: this is Lundy. There are virtually no trees on this lump of Dartmoor towed into the water; there are no hedges either but there are three stone walls: Threequarter Wall, Halfway Wall and Quarter Wall. Between these boundaries, various life forms cling to this ostensibly barren land: twenty-eight permanent residents, 13,000 cabbage plants, three hundred ewes, forty-five scheduled monuments, eighteen ponies and pigs, geese, feral goats, sika deer, manx shearwaters, puffins and pygmy shrews. Islands are exceptional places; islanders delight in difference, and Lundy has its own variety of cabbage, its own postage stamps and once had its own currency. It has the first written record of nesting peregrines (falcons were taken from Lundy by Henry III in 1243), the world's oldest private postage service, the first ever 'no take' fishing zone, the first ever marine conservation zone, and probably the last pub in Britain to get a licence.

It may be a meaningless cliché that we are an island race but it is true in many senses, including the fact that our big island is blessed with a surprising number of inhabited islets. It is no surprise that we have sought to conserve so many small islands as wild sanctuaries because throughout human history they have been escape pods from the developed world. Scolt Head Island (1923) and the Farne Islands

(1925) were among the National Trust's first purchases; the Trust snapped up swaths of the Isle of Wight; couldn't wait to get its hands on Brownsea Island; and looks after numerous tidal islands from St Michael's Mount to Northy Island.

Nothing better illustrates our changing attitude towards the coast than the fate of these islands. In the past, they were prisons; now they are infatuations. In *Mansfield Park* it was scornfully said of the naive ten-year-old heroine Fanny Price: 'She thinks of nothing but the Isle of Wight, and she calls it *The Island*, as if there was no other island in the world.' Here Jane Austen anticipated the Victorian era's adoption of the Isle of Wight as a holiday escape. It was the first of many idealised worlds, portals in which people fled everything from contemporary morality to tax. As objects of desire, these places were usually only owned by the very rich. A stay on Lundy soon revealed why: an innocuous island soon becomes a treacherous swallower of money.

The sky was thick with cloud when I set sail from Ilfracombe aboard the MS *Oldenburg*, a dainty, immaculately painted black-and-white passenger ferry. On first impressions, Lundy was more like a big boat than a lonely idyll. I and other members of the outdoorsy middle classes straggled up the steep track to the village two-by-two: elderly couples in matching walking sandals, hunky rock-climbing dudes, a school party. High on the rocks, we were surrounded by glorious blue water but, as on a ship, we couldn't get to it. Like the forbidding cliffs of North Devon, the edge of Lundy plunged directly into the water, leaving little room for beach. The island was as well equipped as a cruise-liner too: I had packed for three days of self-sufficiency (a prerequisite for a small-island dweller) with a rucksack-load of pasta and pesto, but the pub served three meals a day and the shop sold everything. Diesel generators chugged like a ship's engines by the camping field.

I erected my tent alongside six others in the field and walked northwards. People and clouds quickly melted away. Looking down from this land of 95 per cent cliff, with a hazy blue sea melting into the sky, I felt I was floating, completely unanchored. 'You wanted no trees,' wrote Charles Kingsley, when he visited Lundy in 1849, five years before he wrote his novel *Westward Ho!*, later appropriated by property developers seeking to lure visitors to North Devon; 'the beauty of their rich forms and simple green was quite replaced by the gorgeous balance of the hues, and beyond and around all, the illimitable Atlantic – not green – but an intense sapphire black-blue, such as it is never inshore.'

I wondered if three days would be too long to explore a featureless rock but the sea alone was enough to fill every day. The ebb between the slowly arriving swell caused submerged rocks to dip their black heads out of the water like seals. Further out, cloud shadows turned distant ocean into land, creating a delta-like pattern as if there was a river emptying over the western horizon. Looking east, I heard an engine on the water and the MS *Oldenburg* appeared beyond the headland, surprisingly small next to Lundy. My link to the mainland was already motoring away. Through binoculars, I could see the heads of day-trippers glinting in the sunshine, turned back towards the paradise from which they had been ejected.

Every rock was named on Lundy and on the eastern side, beyond steeply sloping banks of bracken, foxglove and Lundy cabbage, were stony beaches. From the heights of the island, these looked pebbly but, zigzagging down – Lundy was all about the reverse summit – the pebbles were actually big round stones, white and speckled with grey like the eggs of an enormous reptile. Even though the island's eastern flank faced into the Bristol Channel, I had never seen clearer water. It revealed dark forests of kelp, which were thriving in the marine conservation zone. Living within the four species of kelp were spectacular lifeforms we might assume were confined to tropical waters: spider crabs, wrasse of all sizes, anemones as fat as fists, delicate pink coraline algae, fish with turquoise spots, and tiny seven-legged starfish. Two seals bobbed upright like bottles in the swell.

We had been excommunicated from this watery society for many millennia and so I had to make do with terrestrial glories. A rose-chafer beetle dazzled emerald in the sunlight and a green-veined white butterfly flew past on the cliff-top meadows, scented with yellow kidney vetch and the dainty white and pink stonecrop. Thud. Whack. Two bad-tempered Soay sheep clashed horns with headache-inducing crunches. I mistook them for goats until I came across a cluster of nannies with a magnificently saturnine billy loitering nearby. Soon after, I had a close encounter with a family of sika. Three curious teenage deer gazed at me with moist eyes. Their parents were more fearful, as grown-ups are. One of the soulful youngsters took a trembly step towards me. When I said 'hello', he and his sisters looked at me some more. By the time I scribbled 'button noses' in my notebook, they turned and trotted away.

For all its four-legged fauna, Lundy was defined by its birds. 'Lundi' meant puffin in Old Norse. Larks sang in stereo. Sparrows emitted tuneless chirps from low stone sheds in numbers I hadn't heard since childhood. Stonechats moved anxiously between rocky outcrops, chat-chatting with their rocky calls. The cliff edge vibrated with the disconcerting grumble of nesting seabirds: fulmar, shag, kittiwake, guillemot, razorbill and the puffins. Some made gorilla noises, others sounded like a crying baby, and occasionally there was the laugh of a joker. Heavy-winged cormorants moved low over the water. A lesser black-backed gull flew around my head twice to inspect me. A peregrine got up fast, as did a racing pigeon, its probable target.

It was easy to see how Lundy could be the UK in miniature: a 1:300 scale model. Both were long, thin islands running north to south, with plenty of islets in the water beyond. Lundy's land jetty, like Southampton or Felixstowe, was in the sheltered south-east, and its only grand house was here too, close to the thriving metropolis of The Village (which didn't need a name because it was the only one). This boasted the Marisco Tavern, a shop and the church, and a range of old stone farm buildings, many now converted into holiday homes, and it bustled, relatively speaking, like London. To its north were the green midlands, grazed with lowland sheep. Further north, the sheep were a hardy Hebridean variety as enclosed fields became open moor. A lone stone house, Tibbetts, was Lundy's Edinburgh. Just like east and west Britain, the island's eastern shores were softer while its western cliffs grandly defied the waves unbroken by land until the eastern seaboard of the United States. Lundy had struck plenty of visitors as a mini-Britain: a ruined house at the northern tip was called John O'Groats.

This pleasing little analogy did not reflect reality. Lundy was far less populated and the way humans used its land was much simpler. But it was also a reductive comparison because this not-quite parallel world was its own place, complex and contrary, possessing a long and colourful history. It had been a hermitage, a pirates' nest, a king's retreat, a convict settlement, an assassin's refuge and had experienced four broad patterns of human habitation: the eras of criminal endeavour, exploitation, dictatorship and tourism.

The island's early human history was defined by its inconvenient position in the centre of the channel leading to the once-busy port of Bristol. If passing ships were not blown onto its rocks, they could be targeted by its pirates. Lundy's pub was named after William de Marisco, a renegade landowner who became the de facto king of Lundy in the thirteenth century and was executed by Henry III. The king became so exasperated by piracy emanating from Lundy that he established a garrison on the island. The islanders were victims of piracy too. Lundy provided shelter from storms and as many as a hundred boats would drop anchor by its eastern shores during a westerly gale. When members of a Dutch boat came ashore in the seventeenth century saying their captain was seriously ill, residents saw no reason for suspicion. A few days later, a message came from the still-stationary ship that the captain had died. The crew asked permission to bury him in Lundy's graveyard and the coffin was brought to the church. When the sailors asked to be left alone to perform their service of mourning, unsuspecting locals waited meekly outside. Suddenly, the doors were thrown open and the grief-stricken Dutch sailors had morphed into French pirates, armed with cutlasses taken from the 'coffin'. Islanders were robbed of their chattels, livestock were mistreated and Lundy's cannon was thrown off the cliff. The pirates left with their booty as mysteriously as they had arrived.

The era of exploiting Lundy's riches began with an improbable source: its bird population. In the eighteenth century, islanders fixed large nets on the rocks and removed the entangled bodies each morning. Puffins, then known as 'parrots', were their main target, alongside kittiwakes and they caught '1,800 dozen' – more than 20,000 – in a good season. Twenty-four puffins made one pound of feathers, which sold for one shilling on the mainland. Puffin eggs were flogged to sugar refineries; rarer eggs were sold to collectors. Mainlanders joined this slaughter, particularly when the Victorians took a fancy to plumes of feathers in hats. The groundbreaking Sea Birds Preservation Act of 1869 forbade the raiding of nests during the breeding season but this ended on 1 August. Then, at daybreak, according to an 1885 account, every boat from the small Devon port of Clovelly headed towards Lundy. 'In many cases the wings were torn off the wounded birds before they were dead, the mangled victims being tossed back into the water.' On a single day, feathers from 700 birds were sent back to Clovelly.

From 1834 to 1916, Lundy was owned by the Heaven family who had lost their Caribbean paradise when slavery was abolished in the West Indies. They lavished the compensation paid by the British government on a completely contrasting escape: Lundy. Reverend Hudson Grosett Heaven was the foremost of Lundy's many eccentrics. When a cable was laid from Hartland Point to the island, the Reverend dispatched his first telegraph: 'The Kingdom of Heaven rejoiceth.'

Finding Lundy to be a drain on resources, the Heavens leased the east coast to the Lundy Granite Company, which soon employed 299 workers on the island. Had this operation persevered, there would be little left of Lundy now. But the company only lasted five years. 'The first thing they built was the pub and the second thing they built was the church,' said Derek Green, the current general manager of Lundy. 'All the guys working here were drinking most of the time and the guy in charge was an alcoholic. Productivity was pretty rubbish. Same old story.'

The era of nation-building continued but the dictatorship became more benevolent when Lundy was purchased by the Harman family. Martin Coles Harman was a City banker and hoped to impress colleagues with hunting, shooting and fishing. An old-fashioned sportsman-naturalist, he was also a keen birdwatcher and loved wildlife so ardently that he introduced onto Lundy the mute swan, peacock, red grouse, grey partridge, moorhen, goldfish, guinea pigs, rock wallaby and red, roe, fallow and sika deer. The swans flew away and other species died; only the Soay sheep and sika deer thrived.

Simple islands have a habit of scuppering grandiose schemes. In the hope that tourism might offer a stable financial future, Coles Harman was persuaded to lay out a nine-hole golf course in 1927. A launch night was attended by two professional golfers and 150 VIPs with the island's fishermen instructed to catch at least seventy-five lobsters for the occasion. At its peak, Lundy Golf Club had twelve members. Its course cost far too much to maintain. By the end of the following summer, it was abandoned. I mistook its old bunkers for neolithic remains.

Reg Tuffin, Lundy's eighty-one-year-old Postmaster General, first visited in 1955 and became a regular holidaymaker before landing a 'retirement' job on the island. It was 'very run-down' in the 1950s but still 'wonderful' and it felt like staying in someone's home, he remembered. 'The hotel was quite tatty. The roof leaked when it rained. You'd move your bed and put your wash basin down to catch the drops. It was run on a shoestring and the staff were extremely happy if visitors helped keep the place going. I'd spend hours doing hay-making and collecting glasses around the bar.'

Martin Coles Harman died in 1954, and his son, Albion, then ruled for fourteen years as 'the Joint Overlord of Lundy'. He devised his own currency, Puffinage (exchange rate: one Puffin = 1p). The Crown took umbrage and prosecuted him. Albion would be gratified to know that one Puffin now fetches £20 on eBay. The royal family must have been pretty relaxed about this typical expression of Lundy sovereignty for the Queen Mother paid an informal visit in 1958. 'We like to believe that the freedom from police, civic dignitaries, and minute to minute programmes gave her the entrancing smile and manner she carried with her all afternoon,' recorded Stanley Smith, the shopkeeper who also penned the island's newspaper, *The Lundy Review*.

When Lundy came up for sale in 1969, there were rumours it would become a Butlin's holiday camp, a casino or a prison island. Or perhaps another private buyer would build a lair from which to conquer the world. Such scenarios appalled the public and Sir Jack Hayward, later the owner of another financial sinkhole, Wolverhampton Wanderers, donated £150,000 so the National Trust could buy it. Perhaps because there were some misgivings within the Trust over the cost of maintaining the island, it was leased to the Landmark Trust, a charity founded in the same year as Neptune to protect ruined properties. They still manage it for conservation and for the public.

*

The vast majority of the island's population at any time of year were visitors. On my first day, the population was 135, of whom only 28 were 'permanent' residents. None of these was born on the island and all worked for the Landmark Trust. In one sense, Lundy could be seen as the most extreme example of Britain's struggling coastal economy, where industry has died, farming is struggling and jobs are somewhat inadequately provided via holidaymakers. Here was a society entirely built for and by tourism.

The challenges its permanent residents faced were the same as in much larger societies: money, energy, conviviality and the search for a good life. At this tiny scale, however, these struggles could be touched by everyone. The man responsible for the survival of Lundy's human society was its general manager, Derek Green, a tough-looking Scot of middle years. Green was attractively blunt, a trait endemic to Lundy. 'There's no other authority on the island. I have to be the fireman, coastguard, ambulance man, policeman, harbour master and sometimes the vicar,' he said when we went for a stroll around the island. Prime minister? 'I've been called lots of things,' he muttered. After the Heavens and the Harmans, I wondered if Lundy attracted eccentrics. 'It's compulsory,' said Derek, who looked the least eccentric person imaginable. In our society, he theorised, a lot of people cling to a nine-to-five job. 'Opportunities to work in a place like this are becoming more and more attractive to get away from that mainland culture. If that makes us a little bit eccentric, I guess we are.'

Throughout Lundy's human history, the biggest challenge has been to keep the island afloat financially. 'The finances have always been shaky,' said Derek. Today, the island's income came from its modest number of annual visitors (15,000 to 20,000 each year; the Giant's Causeway in Northern Ireland receives 600,000), its working farm, European environmental farming grants, and unique exports such as stamps and meat. The Landmark Trust built its own slaughterhouse which was permitted to butcher wild animals and so sales of venison and lamb (Soay sheep were classified as wild) provided valuable extra revenue.

The island breaks even – 'just', said Derek – and if the depreciation of assets was taken into account, it would make a loss. Infrastructure is expensive. An unobtrusive new track to the jetty cost £1.75 million. 'It's like a boat,' said Derek. 'You know that saying? The two best days in a man's life are when he buys a boat and when he sells the boat.'

Lundy, of course, was not run to make anyone a fortune but protected as a place of conservation. Some of this was subtle. It took me a while to spot the purist approach to notices on the island. There were none: no nature trails, no signs 'to the puffins'. This made the staff's jobs harder – 'Where's the puffins?' was an incessant question – but the absence was crucial to the character of the place: it stopped Lundy feeling like a scale model or a tourist attraction. It still felt like a real community.

I rather primly disliked the thundering diesel generator, concealed within a low stone shed, but residents pointed out it was the fulcrum of the island. 'It keeps the hot tea flowing, it keeps everyone's lights on,' said one. Everywhere I went, I saw a slight but fit-looking man with a worried look, dressed in a bright blue boilersuit. The island's engineer didn't move at island pace, he moved much faster. Eventually I tracked him down in a low-roofed shed which housed one Massey Ferguson tractor, one JCB, two John Deeres, three Land Rovers, four quads and three of the island's five generators. A giant fuse box, more than two metres high, controlled the electricity for all Lundy's properties and Roger Fursdon, a lovely man who tended a miraculous garden in his minimal spare time, had to make running repairs on all of this and almost everything else imaginable, including the community's 200,000-gallon water tanks.

His dusty shed was known as the Covered Yard. 'It gives an appearance of being old but in here beats the heart of the power requirements of the island,' said Roger, leading me to the rear door. We stepped inside and I was transported into a miniature power station. The control room was dominated by tall green metal units dotted with red, blue and yellow buttons and black knobs. Through a glass window were three generators rather similar to hefty car engines: an 8.3L, six cylinder turbo-charged, that produced 117kW; a 5.9L six cylinder turbo that did 70kW; and a veteran 5.9L turbo that produced 65kW. Because we were approaching power-hungry lunchtime, an extra engine started up with a chugging heave. On average, the generators used 10–15 litres of diesel per hour but at peak times – New Year, say – it could rise to 25 litres. Twice a week, the *MS Oldenburg* brought 4,000 litres of diesel to the island, which was transferred by tractor into the island's storage tanks.

'Lundy is a sponge for money and it has been throughout time. Electricity costs money, especially when you're burning diesel to run it,' said Roger. The turning point for human comfort on Lundy came when Lottery funds paid for the new generators. Storage heaters could be installed in the houses, which previously had gas fires and dehumidifiers because they were so damp; finally people could stay on the island all year round, in what Roger called 'relative comfort'.

These days, Lundy's residents were far more sensitive to their impact on the environment than mainland folk. Incredibly, until 2003, rubbish was burnt and pushed off the cliff. 'If you suggested we do that today people would look at you as if you were mad,' said Derek Green. Its water supply was mostly rainfall run-off taken from Lundy's streams and its piglets were fed vegetable waste from the restaurant. It was unrealistic of me to expect a small island to be an ideal society, especially since I didn't have to live there, but I still balked at the diesel generators. In such a sensitive landscape, defined by its protected status and conservation goals, surely its visitors could survive on renewable power?

Derek was not keen. There was just one farmhouse and some dorms on the small island of Flat Holm, off the coast of South Wales, and these used solar energy. 'There's infrastructure everywhere. There's panels upon panels,' he said. 'It detracts from the natural beauty of the place. We're trying to keep any infrastructure to a minimum. The aesthetics are one of the most important things for us – to keep Lundy as unspoilt as possible. Aesthetically, renewables fail to deliver that. I'm not anti-renewable, but they have to be in the right place and sympathetic to their environment.' Even a small turbine would be visible from everywhere on Lundy, which campaigned against the Atlantic Array, a proposed wind farm which was abandoned in 2013, much to the delight of Derek Green. Lundy actually had a 55kW turbine in the 1980s. 'It did the job, it produced power throughout the night,' said Roger, who thought that solar could be hidden on shed roofs where it would not be visible except from the air. It would, however, require significant capital investment, and you'd still need diesel generators for backup.

Money and power were a perpetual challenge on Lundy but visitors were more intrigued by the social lives of its tiny population. Most residents were couples in their forties whose children had left home and who were looking for a change. 'You tend to find unusual people on the island, in good ways and bad ways,' said Issie Winney, who was studying the island's sparrows for her PhD. 'Mostly in good ways.' Roger believed Lundy attracted people who wanted to escape society. Until he travelled to other remote places, he didn't realise that this was the norm on small islands. 'You often meet people on islands who haven't quite made it on the mainland.'

How did the inhabitants of a tiny island get on? The answer was: carefully. 'You're always renewing your friendships every morning – you're saying "hi" and finding out how people are, which is lost on the mainland,' said Issie. 'It's a small place and if there's a problem amongst the staff, tension rises and someone ends up leaving.' Although I did not expect Lundy to spill any turpitude to a writer like me, Issie recalled an old scandal involving a former inhabitant who slept with half the women on the island while his wife was working there too. 'I was quite impressed,' she said. 'You're seeing everyone, every day. How can you get away with that sort of thing?'

Apparently privacy was possible in such a tiny community. Reg, the postmaster, said an interesting thing though: there was no privacy from your job. 'You've got to enjoy what you're doing otherwise it would be the most awful place imaginable.' He escaped his fellow inhabitants by 'never' going out for an evening. For some staff, their private space was their room, where they had a slow internet connection and could just about go shopping online. Most, however, found their own quiet spots outdoors. 'Residents have to enjoy the island in some way,' thought Issie. 'If computer games were their solace, they've generally not lasted.'

For all the privacy and care with personal relationships, there was still room for romance. Roger had met his Italian wife, Patrizia, on Lundy. 'I'd been off the island to buy a Land Rover and a tractor. I saw her on the boat,' remembered Roger. 'I didn't take any notice – you see a lot of people on board. She came over as a volunteer and asked me where the seabirds were. I said, "Out on the cliffs," and I showed her where to pick up the path. Then she wanted to find other things so she came back and asked me. Gradually, we became friends.' Roger paid her a return visit to Italy, just as a friend. They stayed in touch and, after a year, she told him she had applied for a job on Lundy. They married in Bologna, nine years ago. They had, said Roger in his understated way, similar interests. 'She loves plants and gardens. She's a bit of a loner as well. We're quite well suited.'

If Lundy's residents tended to be escaping the mundane mainland, so too were its visitors. Apart from the climbers, most came for the birds. A decade ago, rats were preying on burrow-nesting manx shearwaters and the island's seabird numbers slumped, but a £100,000 scheme to eradicate the rat population had seen manx numbers increase by

300 per cent to more than 3,000 individuals. In 2004 the birds bred successfully for the first time in living memory.

The manx shearwater is the nearest thing to a British albatross, completely at one with the ocean but clumsy and easily picked off by peregrines on land. I went to search for these strange, nocturnal birds during the day, when most were safely asleep in their burrows. Beccy MacDonald, the island's ranger, played a recording of their call (like the groaning of a very poorly dog) to elicit a reply from deep inside the burrow. After five attempts, a long, grumbling response came from the female, sitting on chicks while her partner was finding fish at sea. The island's puffin population was recovering, at eighty, but its gannets had been gone since 1897, disturbed by the dynamiting of the cliffs to build the island's North Light.

The monotonously cheeping sparrows were far less spectacular but even these were unique. Issie Winney was the ninth-generation PhD student working on the University of Sheffield's House Sparrow project. Lundy was a perfect natural laboratory because almost no sparrows emigrated or arrived on the island. By 2000, the native population had been decimated by rat poison (unconnected to the manx recovery programme) and forty sparrows were introduced from South Yorkshire. Across the UK, house sparrows declined by 71 per cent between 1977 and 2008 due to pesticides, development and 'improvements' such as fewer leaky roofs and less spilt grain. On Lundy, there was more traditional farming, with animals kept outside, plenty of insects and 110 nest boxes, and those forty sparrows had become more than 120 today.

People might find privacy on Lundy but there was none for the sparrows. Each bird sported four tiny coloured rings. The colour combination enabled researchers to identify individual birds. Individuals were also fitted with radio frequency identification tags, and receivers were placed on nest boxes, so comings and goings could be monitored. One researcher found that fledglings peeped into almost every nestbox, like first-time buyers looking for a home. Cameras were also fitted to nestboxes, recording shocking *Springwatch*-style dramas such as a blackbird trying to scoff baby spadgers.

Issie was interested in sparrow personalities. She sought to measure variations in behaviours and see how these affected their existence. 'What makes a successful sparrow? What doesn't? Or are there more ways of living your life?'

These were profound questions for any creature. Lundy's lab enabled Issie to consider selection and evolution but also genetics and see how behaviours could be inherited over generations. She measured boldness and curiosity: babies were checked at ten and twelve days and placed in a container for thirty seconds to see how active they are. Some didn't move in this foreign environment; others were constantly looking around. Swapping chicks between nests, she and other researchers found that behaviours were inherited but also socially acquired. In just ten days, baby sparrows picked up characteristics from their foster parents.

'I see the sparrow and think, you're beautiful and you're under-appreciated,' said Issie, who was happy to eschew Lundy's more spectacular birds. Visitors, however, were on a mission to see its rarities. Years were remembered by them: '52, the American robin; '56, the Sardinian warbler; '87, the Eastern phoebe; '90, the ancient murrelet, which saw the *Oldenburg* sailing to the island twice a day, while Clovelly boats doubled their prices. The little shearwater of 2010 led to twitchers chartering boats and climbing cliffs when they arrived, at night, which rather alarmed the coastguard. The golden oriole seen shortly before I visited had less chance to attain legendary status because it was swiftly eaten by one of the island's peregrines.

On the far side of the camping field were two middle-aged men living under three tents with an array of camping gadgets that were sensible precautions for a nuclear holocaust. We got chatting. Shaun Barnes was a garrulous monumental mason turned wedding photographer who wore a New Agey shell around his neck. Ken Ebsworthy was a quiet toolmaker with short grey hair who was recovering from a serious illness. They were school friends and were on a birding tour of the island . . . for *four weeks*. They were full of surprises.

'Everyone always asks, what the hell do you do on a little tiny island for four weeks?' said Shaun, who was evangelical about the place. 'You couldn't get bored. You could spend the whole day in Hell's Gates where the seabirds come and go. There are the rock pools and shells and Lundy jewels – ground-down glass remains from the castle – to collect, and watching the manx shearwaters at 2 a.m. under the stars when everyone is asleep or drunk. It's class.'

Perhaps Shaun and Ken were so fascinated by Lundy because they grew up in Bideford on the north coast of Devon. As boys, they would scour the Torridge for otters or take an old army telescope to search for peregrines and dream about Lundy. It was there, out at sea, appearing and disappearing depending on the weather. It represented mystery, said Ken. 'It's just that urge – I wonder what's over there?' A childhood fantasy, it now returned them to their boyhoods because of its small fields, bird populations and peace. Apart from the generators, there were no man-made sounds. 'Stop and listen and there's nothing. It's impressive. Even on Dartmoor there's that background hum of man, of machinery,' said Ken quietly. 'There's so many little reminders of childhood. You tend to connect better. I'm forty-eight years old and I've never been abroad but I've been here God knows how many times. To me this is leaving the British Isles. It's only twenty miles from where you live but it's a completely different world.'

The thrill of rare birds formed the rhythm of their stay. Unexpected arrivals were a gift of the south-west wind. The weather broke, the birds arrived. 'Tomorrow we could get the rarest bird in the country and it will be here for two days and then it's gone,' said Shaun. But the island to them was more than ticking off a glamorous rarity, it was the rose-chafers, sheltered gullies, the sea, the freedom, the names of convicts engraved in a cave. 'Cancel your ticket home and we'll show you springs, copper mines, mesolithic flints in rabbit burrows, Queen Mab's grotto cave . . .' enthused Shaun.

'Basking sharks, sun fish . . .' murmured Ken in agreement.

The flints did not occur naturally on Lundy so Stone Age people had brought them over. Shaun was very taken with these tribes who, he theorised, walked to Lundy on the sheets of ice that tied it to the mainland. 'That Ice Man, chiselling his flints, was no different from us. He would've set off for the better world – we're just the same.'

Darkness was yet to fall when I climbed 147 steps to the top of the Old Light, the disused lighthouse on the highest point of Lundy. From the wrought-iron balcony halfway up its great glass enclosure I could see the whole island stretched out below my feet. As the lighthouse glass moaned in a gathering easterly, I felt I could be flying. The moon cast an orange light on the darkening water and a second star appeared in the pale blue firmament, moving at the pace of an aeroplane. Ken had told me to to expect the International Space Station at 10.36 p.m. and there it was, haring across the north-western sky.

Those with more experience of Lundy than me came closest to its truth. Felix Gade arrived in 1926 as the equivalent of general manager Derek Green and, apart from a short period after the war, spent the rest of his days at No. 1 Paradise Row. 'I have lived close on half a century of my life on Lundy,' he wrote in his memoirs. 'Others, perhaps, look upon me as a poor specimen without ambition; a man who could, in the 20th century, live upon a square mile of rough land, an island, with little or no prospect of ever improving my position. Those people who think in terms of sumptuous houses, expensive motor cars, yachts, and the other things of wealth and position, are welcome to treat me with contempt. They do me no harm.'

I loved this. The rest of the world did seem silly and materialistic when confronted by the eternal values of the rock and the ocean.

'Lundy gives far more to you than you give to it,' said Roger Fursdon. 'It's a hostile environment but in other ways it's very welcoming and very calming.' Issie Winney put it this way: 'If you stay here for any time, you have this immense feeling that this small lump of granite in the middle of the ocean is the world. Your mind changes.' Reg Tuffin told me that, 'To sit by the sea and watch the sea, before you know what's happened half the day is gone.'

I felt this exactly. I got stuck by the sea on Lundy. For months afterwards, I wondered what bewitchment occurred when I felt so ecstatic and becalmed on the ruin of Montagu's steps by the western ocean. It may have been a bit of a bodily trick, adrenalin pumping after a frightening descent. It may have been a holiday romance, the island infatuation of an old-fashioned Romantic who finds a form of religious ecstasy in the natural world. I don't really think Lundy is the best place on the planet. Looking back on my feelings there, is like looking back on my emotions as a teenager, which seem absurd to my older self. But they are true in the moment that they occur and we should not disown them afterwards. And I wasn't alone with such sensations. Plenty of people felt what I had on Lundy. In 1972 a holidaymaker called Betty Hindson told the *Illustrated Lundy News* of her days there. Back home, friends asked her what she did, and she told them she walked, watched seabirds and looked at the sea. It sounded so dull, she wrote, and yet she found herself staring at Lundy's grey shores, 'enslaved for ever by what I can only describe as peaceful exhilaration'.

On my third day, the island was foggy, smothered by low cloud and mizzle. I had thought three days would be an extravagantly long time to explore Lundy; I had interrogated this land for every hour I was awake and yet I had barely scratched its surface. I hadn't seen The Earthquake, a natural rock formation, or The Fog Battery, a derelict nineteenth-century building with two old cannons, or The Devil's Slide, the climbing magnet that was the largest single slab of granite in Europe. I was moving so slowly now I only just caught the boat, which mysteriously sailed well ahead of schedule at 4.06 p.m. Within eight minutes, Lundy had disappeared, as if it had been a mirage all along.

Lundy harboured a disproportionate number of eccentrics but its outlandish history was trumped by a dome of dark trees in Poole Harbour. The perilously narrow dune called Sandbanks was home to some of the priciest real estate beyond Mayfair and it did not feel English, or at least not the England I knew. Suburban streets were studded with corpulent villas, done up like ships in tinted glass and chrome, demolished and rebuilt by each new owner. That the most tasteful was home to a famous football manager, a profession not known for its aestheticism, was saying something.

Before catching the boat for a five-minute trip, I knew nothing about Brownsea apart from reading that it was the largest of eight islands in the harbour and featured a rare population of red squirrels. I wondered how 500 acres surrounded by the affluent suburbs of Bournemouth that received 130,000 visitors each year could hold any wildlife, or mysteries, at all. Like many otherworldly coastal places, however, this water-bound sanctuary was crammed with animals, enigmas and eccentrics.

As I approached on the little boat, Brownsea showed up as a mass of dark pines, some slumping sandy cliffs, a castellated country house in a jumble of red brick and stone, several grey-stone coastguard cottages and a faintly ludicrous landing jetty ornamented with twin turrets. On the jetty lurked a man in tatty brown trousers clutching a pair of binoculars: John Lamming had been a National Trust ranger here for the last thirty years and, as one of twenty-seven permanent residents, was the ideal entrée into island society.

Brownsea had been home to hermits and royal fortifications before its present incarnation as Britain's favourite nature reserve. Between these familiar island incarnations, it acquired a less enviable reputation as an ideal world for some of the nation's strangest visionaries. Mr Auditor Benson, its first private owner, paid £300 for Brownsea in 1722. Benson was a poet and architect and his nickname was 'Mad'. He hired a botanist who stuffed the place with rare plants, including 10,000 saplings, and after a year on the island Mad Benson developed such a sudden dislike of books that he took his castle's library and burnt it on the beach. Another owner, the Hon. G. Augustus Cavendish-Bentinck, filled Brownsea with priceless Italian sculptures, on which a pretty Mediterranean snail hitched a lift and was only discovered two centuries later, still thriving in the castle grounds. A third, Sir Augustus Foster, was our man in Washington in 1812 where he presided over a diplomatic row that culminated in the most recent occasion when the United States declared war on Britain. He saw Brownsea as an ideal retirement home from the diplomatic service but became so depressed after seven years on the island that he cut his own throat in the castle.

At this point, Brownsea's history became particularly odd. While Sir Augustus's widow, Lady Albinia Foster, was trying to sell the island, she was visited by Colonel William Petrie Waugh and his wife, Mary. When Mary noticed a piece of white mud stuck to the ferrule of her umbrella, she deduced that there must be china clay just below the surface of Brownsea. The colonel engaged a geologist who estimated it contained £1 million pounds' worth of clay; an engineer's report also valued the island's clay at £100,000 an acre. Barely able to contain their excitement, the Waughs snapped up the island for a bargain £13,000 in 1852 and were loaned large sums to launch their venture. The colonel was inspired by the Great Exhibition of 1851 and, true to the Victorian spirit, did not scrimp in turning his new world into the Branksea Clay & Pottery Company. He added a gothic tower of Portland stone to the front of the castle and its extravagant redecoration included a study lined in embossed leather that the colonel had admired at the Great Exhibition. He also reclaimed 100 acres by building a sea wall around St Andrews Bay and built a village he called Maryland for his workers.

Digging into the island, the colonel's labourers were soon producing sanitary ware – mainly sewage pipes – in good quantities. The hive of activity concealed one small problem: the clay failed to create the fine porcelain predicted by Mary and the expert reports. Convinced their society had been graced by a go-getting entrepreneur, the tradesmen of Poole rowed to Brownsea one day to ask the colonel to become their Conservative parliamentary candidate. The colonel was away on business and Mary was rather deaf. Not hearing their request and increasingly paranoid about their failing business, she believed they wanted their debts paid and promised the bemused tradesmen that her husband would soon do so. On the boat home, the local businessmen discussed the Waughs' accounts with each other for the first time and discovered they were collectively owed a substantial amount of money and so began legal action to recover it. In debt by more than £250,000 and faced with the collapse of his enterprise, the colonel fled with his wife to Spain, with whom there was no treaty of extradition for bankrupts. The colonel may have committed fraud but, curiously, local opinion never turned against him. A popular rumour held that Lady Albinia Foster, far from being a luckless widow tricked into selling Brownsea far too cheaply to the greedy colonel, had herself planted the high-grade porcelain clay to facilitate the sale.

The golden age of Brownsea as a rich man's playground arrived in the Edwardian era when it was purchased by Charles and Florence Van Raalte, a Dutch family grown rich on cigar manufacturing. Jack Battrick, who was born on the island in 1909 and wrote a memoir of his life there, admired Charles, who was charming and handsome with his dashing trimmed goatee and monocle. The island became a sporting estate, a country retreat and a working farm, growing daffodils for flower markets. The Queen of Romania was a visitor;

Guglielmo Marconi, the inventor of radio, met his wife on Brownsea; and on 1 August 1907 the most celebrated guests arrived: a group of young men from different social backgrounds brought to camp in the woods with Lieutenant General Robert Baden-Powell. It heralded the birth of the Scouting movement.

During this happy era, the resident population of Brownsea grew to 270, as husbands, wives and their families were employed on the estate. There was a school for youngsters like Battrick, and islanders played in the Brownsea Island Band, beat pheasants for shooting parties and caddied for aristocrats traipsing over its nine-hole golf course. But Battrick's idyllic childhood abruptly ended in 1927 when the island was sold to Mary Florence Bonham Cox-Christie for more than £100,000. Perhaps the greatest of all Brownsea's eccentrics, Mrs Christie had a completely different vision to transform the island into a better world: she wanted to rid it of human beings.

Mrs Christie loved animals but did not appear to much care for people. When she bought a vacant clifftop plot next to her grand house in nearby Southbourne and refused to sell it to the Bournemouth Corporation for parkland, she declared: 'Nobody wants to live near a space open to the public with their present day bad manners and untidy way of throwing bottles and paper about.' The unspoilt shores of Brownsea had been imperilled by plans for a luxury hotel and marina but Mrs Christie gave it over to the animals more completely than the most idealistic conservationist. She appointed a new steward who was instructed to stop workers' wages and remove everyone from the island – including one family who had lived and worked there for four generations over ninety years – within twelve months. An armed guard was dispatched to patrol Brownsea's shores to enforce 'Keep Out' notices erected around it. Mrs Christie's security detail was a twenty-six-year-old Danish PT expert called Bertha Hartung Olsen. One day, a local man called Mr Batt and his eighteen-year-old daughter defied written warnings from Mrs Christie and rowed to

Brownsea to dig for fishing bait on its mudflats, as Mr Batt had been doing for years. Ms Olsen spotted the pair and, after checking that Mr Batt's daughter could swim, flung her into the water. The case went to court, Ms Olsen was fined 40 shillings and left Britain. This story delighted the press, who became fascinated by Mrs Christie, 'the Lady of the Lonely Isle'.

Brownsea ran wild. Commercial projects, including farming and bulb-growing, were halted and all domestic animals were given a right to life until nature intervened. Horses were not to be harnessed; cows were set free, unmilked and unmanaged. One lived to thirty-six. Mrs Christie banned hunting, shooting and fishing and any form of trapping: eyewitnesses – probably not very reliable as they included a reporter who sneaked onto the island and wrote a sensationalist account of its dereliction – claimed it was overrun with rats.

Having been evicted, eighteen-year-old Jack Battrick got a job at the hotel on Sandbanks overlooking the island. 'The bizarre life of the mainland, so different from our accustomed island way of life, made us feel like orphans, sometimes total outcasts,' he wrote. For a while, his younger sister was the only pupil left at Brownsea Island school. Battrick paints a scene more reminiscent of the Highland Clearances than the south coast of England.

The day after the last of the human population left the island, in July 1934, a great fire began in the parched pine woods. In his memoirs, Battrick makes no suggestion that this was vengeful arson but it seems a mighty strange coincidence. Islanders hated Mrs Christie so much they called her the 'Demon of Brownsea'. For seven days and nights, the fire raged uncontrollably. Mrs Christie's brave efforts alongside firefighters from the mainland helped save the castle but much of the woodland was destroyed. It was probably at this moment that its large population of sika deer fled across the harbour onto the mainland and began a successful colonisation of Britain that continues today. More fires raged on Brownsea during the Second

World War when Mrs Christie was compelled to allow military men onto her property, where they established a series of decoy lights to lure German bombers away from Poole docks. On one night in 1942, two hundred bombs were dropped on Brownsea, destroying the village of Maryland.

Mrs Christie 'was an absolute fanatic but she succeeded in her aim', concluded Jack Battrick: despite the controversies and the fires, Brownsea became an impenetrable thicket of rhododendron and Scots pine, a haven for some wildlife. In her nineties, the Lady of the Lonely Isle lived alone in one room of the castle, washed in cold water, and survived on bread, butter and boiled eggs cooked on a camping stove. She died in 1961 and the island was inherited by her grandson, John. Fifteen buyers soon hovered over this delectable piece of real estate, one proposing to construct the largest marina in Europe. Local people campaigned to save Brownsea and the Treasury agreed to accept the island in lieu of death duties if the National Trust would take it on. The Trust required £100,000 to be raised to look after the island; the key donor was the John Lewis Partnership, which took a long lease on the decrepit castle in eighteen acres of grounds and runs it to this day as a private retreat for its staff. The National Trust also leased two-fifths of the island to the Dorset Wildlife Trust and created a smaller area for a Scout camping ground. With these partners, it opened Brownsea to the public as a nature reserve in 1963. There was a happy ending for Jack Battrick too: after years of exile, he was given a job as the Trust's assistant warden and returned to see out his days on the island.

Dark storms were swiping the mainland but it was bright on Brownsea. After making a cup of tea in his old coastguard cottage, the Trust ranger John Lamming led me through a back gate to his little electric utility vehicle. We hummed across Church Field, where a dozen peacocks strutted by the handsome church constructed by Colonel

Waugh from Portland stone. It still held services every Sunday during the tourist season. A mile long and three-quarters of a mile wide, Brownsea consisted of two ridges of sandy, wooded high ground separated by a valley. Like other small islands, it felt far bigger than its actual size, and was stubbornly mysterious. The low thud of large yachts crisscrossing Poole Harbour penetrated the pine woods, but Brownsea itself was silent. There were no cars, no bikes and no dogs or cats, although some of the rangers used Land Rovers and a few of the island's permanent staff were permitted to keep a well-trained dog. Most visitors enjoyed a simple boat trip across the harbour, followed by a picnic on Church Field and a spot of red squirrel watching. 'A lot of people come across and say, "How lucky are you!" because they think it's utopia,' said John, who was a modest man with a deep knowledge of his adopted home. 'They assume all we do is wander around the island with binoculars. It's then you tell them about emptying the rubbish bins or cleaning out the sewage works.' (The latter proved a painful expense for the Trust which spent a fortune upgrading the island's sewage works to comply with modern regulations and ensure there was no risk that the modern conveniences for its 130,000 visitors would pollute the island's precious lagoon.)

Despite the privations of terrible transport links, a slow Internet connection and the claustrophobic character of living where you work, John had lived here since 1980, when his passion for birds led him to seek a job on Brownsea. His wife worked in the National Trust cafe. John soon realised the island was more than a splendid spot to admire overwintering avocet, black tailed godwits and Brent geese. 'The reason why Brownsea is a Site of Special Scientific Interest isn't because we've got wading birds or red squirrels, it's because of our range of habitats within a really small space,' he said. 'We haven't got any tundra but we've almost got a bit of everything else. It means the diversity of species here is fantastic.' Squeezed onto Brownsea's 500 acres are deciduous and coniferous woodland, heathland, open grassland, freshwater lakes, reed beds, alder carr, a brackish lagoon, salt marsh, seashore and seawater. The wading birds that most of us normally see in pairs or tens arrive here in hundreds or thousands: 1,500 avocet, 1,000 oystercatchers. More than 850 species of moth and 23 dragonfly species, including three nationally scarce species (the small red damsel, downy emerald and ruddy darter), have been recorded here. Thirty-two species of mosquito have also been found on the island, including four species that bite humans, and these nearly stopped its transfer to the National Trust: builders renovating the castle as part of the conditions-of-sale were so badly bitten they threatened to leave.

For all Mrs Christie's veneration of wild animals, Brownsea's natural diversity was threatened by her tenure and, when the Trust took over, the island had been strangled by invasive species. Two hundred peacocks patrolled a rhododendron jungle which extinguished all sunlight, and most life, from heath and woodland. Sand lizards and adders became extinct, as did other native animals and plants. We upset natural balances particularly easily on small islands, which vividly illustrate how species can be destroyed by the monstrous ecologies we inadvertently create. Even so, the hybrid wilderness of twentieth-century Brownsea must have held great mystery and charm, and the island was the setting for a 1974 gothic horror story, *The Bornless Keeper* by P. B. Yuill, and several Enid Blyton adventures.

Walking through the island in spring, it was difficult to imagine the former rhododendron thicket. Most of Brownsea was wooded but I could glimpse Poole Harbour through the dappled shade from almost every spot. Woods of Scots pine, sycamore and oak were lined with mossy furrows, a remnant of the old daffodil-farming days, and interspersed with small patches of restored heathland and grassy clearings, on which a green woodpecker yaffled noisily. It took forty-eight years to clear the rhododendron, a muscular, deep-rooted plant which keeps sprouting back no matter how brutally it is hacked back. On the Dorset Wildlife Trust patch alone, an area equivalent to fifty-six football pitches was removed by 10,000 volunteers. Even today, the plant was vigorously shooting up again, growing a metre each season, and required regular doses of weedkiller.

As we passed an oak festooned with magnificent grey lichen, the silence was interrupted by a vivid croak nearby: one of the two pairs of nesting ravens. Everything appeared as if under a microscope here, especially on a still day. I soon saw a red squirrel up close, its ears short and perky like a stereotypical devil and a black streaked tail, far daintier than the heftier grey squirrels that had eradicated them from southern Britain.

Brownsea may have been attacked by exotic plants but here was an example of a small island as an ark, its population of 187 red squirrels surviving because the greys, which were introduced into Britain from North America in the nineteenth century, had been unable to cross the water and outcompete or spread disease among the indigenous reds. This was a puzzle because greys were competent swimmers and had been found on nearby Round Island as well as halfway down the similarly tidal waters of the Solent. Instead, it was the weaker reds who had mastered Poole Harbour. Some years ago, a population of red squirrels was introduced from Cannock Chase in the Midlands onto Furzey Island, which was separated from Brownsea by just 200 metres of water at the lowest tides. Scientists who studied the squirrels of Furzey found that 10 per cent of its reds did not have Cannock Chase squirrel DNA but the DNA of Western England reds, which were now only found on Brownsea and the Isle of Wight. This suggests that some of Brownsea's squirrels had migrated from Brownsea to Furzey. In the summer of 2013, two reds made the considerably longer crossing from Brownsea to the villas of Sandbanks where, sadly, they didn't survive for long.

I was put up for the night in the Old Vicarage, a cavernous building by a ruined tractor buried in the woods. It housed the Dorset

Wildlife Trust warden, Chris Thain, his two assistants and various volunteers. After warning that a volunteer who was also a spiritualist had reported the building was crawling with ghosts, Chris, a balding, bearded man who rather resembled a vicar and had a sardonic sense of humour, kindly took me to the castle bar for the night. As happens on small islands, here I encountered everyone I had glimpsed so far on Brownsea, from the young people on the boat to the older man who was holidaying with his mother.

It was a country house restored in the taste typical of John Lewis and its out-of-season atmosphere was rather like a ship, where the crew got along with banter and in-jokes. The rangers soon regaled me with the island's multitude of stories, such as the rumour that a murderous husband had visited for the day and shoved his wife down one of the old clay mines. My favourite mysteries, however, concerned the creatures that made it across the channel, and those that didn't.

Brownsea was perfect for ground-nesting birds like terns because it was bereft of mammalian predators. The rats that plagued Mrs Christie were almost eradicated, mink had been removed too and, unusually, there had never been any foxes, stoats or weasels. This was surprising when sika and roe deer regularly swam between Poole Harbour's islands alongside grass snakes, which had colonised Brownsea in recent years. It was even more surprising given that a wealthy resident of Sandbanks fed foxes in her garden, and cubs played on the mud at low tide. Perhaps they were so well fed on Sandbanks that they had no need to emigrate. 'They are probably eating caviar,' chortled Chris.

The biggest conundrum, however, concerned Britain's biggest surviving carnivorous mammal. Until recently, more than a hundred hedgehogs snuffled around Brownsea at night. In less than a decade, they had been almost wiped out. The prime suspect in this mass-murder mystery was only spotted in 2008 when a BBC cameraman returned from a night filming sika deer saying he had seen a badger.

The rangers were astonished. Brownsea was intensively monitored for wildlife and they had never found any trace of badger. The cameraman hadn't got any footage but the rangers scoured the island and eventually found a badger-shaped hole in an old sandpit. After a stake-out that went on for many evenings, they eventually spotted this elusive animal. Badgers and hedgehogs mostly feed on similar invertebrates such as beetles and worms but if food is scarce, badgers will devour its smaller rival and can wipe it out. Reuben Hawkwood, Brownsea's head ranger, found a hedgehog skin turned inside out, which was characteristic of a badger kill. And yet the badger had only been spotted about four times over the past six years. Brownsea's sandy soils seemed unpromising but when I snooped around the sett, it was definitely still occupied. The rangers suspected a solitary badger had been swept across the channel from Furzey. But badgers can swim as well as dogs so was there only one long-lived badger or several? Had a small population existed, unseen, on Brownsea for decades?

Predators make a big impact on a small island and it was difficult to see how humans could always protect the diversity of a place like Brownsea. Conservation dilemmas were stark when surrounded by a small stretch of water. Even with regular culls, the sika population had soared since John Lamming first arrived on the island. The deer prevented the natural regeneration of the pine trees, which were crucial for the survival of the red squirrels. More difficult, perhaps, was deciding how best to manage bird populations. In the 1960s, Brownsea's wardens walked through its herring gull colony smashing their eggs to protect its terns, which the herring gulls attacked. Now the declining herring gull is protected and so their nests are not destroyed. Ravens and buzzards have only recently recolonised Brownsea but these fine birds helped destroy a burgeoning colony of little egrets and continue to pick off nesting waders. (Badgers enjoy the eggs of ground-nesting birds as well.)

'Everyone says, "Why don't you do something about it?"' said

Chris Thain. 'We have to take the long-term view and avoid doing something knee-jerk which everybody wants you to do. We're not the gamekeeping fraternity.' After thirteen years on the island, Chris had concluded that nothing stayed the same, particularly as the growing number of storms apparently caused by climate change were now creating dramatic erosion which ultimately threatened its freshwater lagoons. 'Twenty-five years ago, we were always looking over our shoulder trying to recreate past glories,' he said. 'Now we're hurtling into bigger issues we can barely get our heads around. We're peering into a murky future that is very, very difficult to read.'

The Revd Theophilus Bennett, a nineteenth-century vicar of Brownsea, applauded the island for the fact there was no catching of trains, no burglaries, no election fights, no insubordination, no poverty. 'Nothing, in fact, that makes the hair prematurely grey, that furrows the forehead with lines, and ages men before their time.'

Even on a busy day, it was easy to find yourself alone, just as on Lundy. Before and after my trip to the bar, I wandered to Brownsea's edges. An island you can traverse in a few minutes is nirvana for water watchers. The character of the sea changes in all four directions. On Brownsea, so does the view of the mainland. When I sat in a creaky wooden bird hide looking east over the lagoon, black-headed gulls shrieked noisily, masts of yachts poked above the sea bank and the villas of Lilliput and Parkstone glittered on the far hillside. To the west, however, there were no human settlements visible among the dark lines of trees and, as the sun set, I climbed to a grove of bare sycamores above the crumbling cliffs and looked west and south towards the fingers of Sandbanks and Studland, separated by the narrow exit from Poole Harbour into the English Channel.

Watching the water when concealed in the woods is a secretive small joy that makes you want to hug yourself. I sat, sheltered and unseen, as a heron stalked the foreshore and a small boat chugged in the channel, its wash making diminutive waves rush in. The seashore sounds of curlew blended with woodland noises, the chinking of blackbirds at dusk and the big song of tiny wrens in low bushes. Eventually, the peace was broken by an alien *crack-cracking*. I thought someone was throwing stones but it was a gnarled hawthorn which erosion had placed on the edge of the slumping cliff, where it creaked, preparing to fall onto the beach below.

The water mirrored the silver and yellow of the sky and darkened with it. The wind dropped to nothing and a precisely cut crescent moon appeared high above. As the breeze departed and a storm stalled in the western sky, the water ushered in every sound from the bass notes of a passing barge to the airy swoosh of a flock of dunlin scooting overhead.

It was not wilderness but there was a peculiar comfort in watching the world go by from a quiet place. Buoys shone with red lights and tall posts marking Poole's channels flashed green. Workaday boats became fairytales at night, lit up on the water. The chain ferry clanking between Sandbanks and Studland twinkled with white lights. A cross-Channel ferry resembled a block of flats cut loose on the water. Just as when we are granted membership of a private club, so we are quickly seduced if we're admitted to an exclusive island. Sitting in the woods by the water, I felt as mysterious as the dark silhouette of Brownsea was to everyone unfortunate enough to be stranded on the world beyond it.

## Explorations of Neptune

There is no secret to walking on **Lundy**: get there, and roam. There are no signposts and even the 1:25,000 OS map is fairly useless on such intimate terrain. If you are on the island only for a day-trip, I would take the main track north, which runs from the village up the eastern side of the island, past the house at Tibbett's Hill and on to Lundy's wild northern end, three miles from its south. You can then follow a smaller path down the north-western side, where you'll find the puffins and reach the lighthouse, which is definitely worth the climb. If you head west from the lighthouse, you'll pick up a smaller cliff-edge track which heads down to the south-west corner of the island. I'm not recommending this because it is dangerous but just north of the south-west corner, if you are so foolish, it is possible to pick up a little indentation in the grass which leads down to Montagu's Steps, the crumbling relics of the path built to salvage the wreck of HMS *Montagu*. This offers a rough, dangerous route down almost to the shore. If you slipped off these rocks you'd never climb out again. Lundy's beaches are virtually inaccessible, although I had more joy getting down to one of the rocky coves on its eastern flank. Even more so than Lundy, **Brownsea Island**'s size militates against any kind of set walk. Much of the northern half of the island is closed to visitors to protect wildlife but a gentle hour's stroll along the western cliffs from behind the castle, past the Scout camp and along to the ruins of Maryland gives you a good sense of the island, and nice vistas of Poole Harbour's undeveloped western side. The best bird-watching spots are in the hides overlooking the lagoon on the eastern side of the island.

### OS Maps

Lundy: Explorer 139, Bideford, Ilfracombe & Barnstaple

Brownsea: Explorer OL15: Purbeck & South Dorset

### Nearest railway station

Lundy: Barnstaple, 12 miles to Ilfracombe; boats from Ilfracombe or Bideford

Brownsea: Poole station 0.5 miles to Poole Quay; summer season daily boats from Poole Quay and from Sandbanks Jetty

*Websites*

Lundy

www.landmarktrust.org.uk/lundyisland/

Brownsea

www.nationaltrust.org.uk/brownsea-island/

## Further Reading

A. F. Langham, *The Island of Lundy*, History Press, 1994

Gail Lawson, *Brownsea Islander – Jack Battrick*, Poole Historical Trust, 1978

# 8

# After Life

*Seven Sisters / Land's End / Arnside Knott*

Arnside
Knott

The Seven Sisters

The Land's End

It was virtually the first hot afternoon of the year when I arrived at the Seven Sisters and everyone seemed disorientated by the violent onset of summer. Visitors descended the metal stairs at the crumbling cliffs at Birling Gap still wearing their coats. On the beach, a woman wore a knitted cardigan over her swimming costume. I stumbled across grey stones in trousers and a hooded top. Only the very young were appropriately dressed, in trunks and bikinis, faces turned to the sky as they floated in inflatable dinghies on the flat green water.

The Seven Sisters are how the White Cliffs appear in the minds of many around the world. They are a classic gateway to England, the country's highest chalk cliffs, calm ramparts of brilliant white sailing into the turquoise waters below. To some, the White Cliffs are blemished by the port of Dover and its industrial chatter, and we can see them in their full glory only from a ferry crossing the channel. In contrast, the Seven Sisters have the grace to show themselves from every angle. When I was down on the shingle, the cliffs dazzled above. When I strode the irresistible coast path, its yellowing sward walked to the dimensions of a bowling green, sinuous white headlands reared like waves for each Sister. On the landward side, the Downs were broad and unspoiled by development, thanks to local people who saved it from becoming another Peacehaven and donated three-and-a-half of the unsullied Sisters to the National Trust between the wars. These sweeping views were grandiose but they offered less showy gifts as well. Right at the cliff edge waved the luminous blooms of the yellow horned poppy.

When I returned to my car to collect my trunks for a swim, a 4x4 with yellow-and-red emergency stripes and lights on top performed a slow circuit of the car park at Birling Gap. Later, as I walked up one of the Sisters, the car drove past again, with watchful slowness, on the nearby road. At the end of the afternoon, I saw it for a third time, stopped in the car park on the heights closest to Eastbourne, window wound down, its driver talking to someone. 'Beachy Head Chaplaincy' was painted on its rear. Despite the glorious day, the chaplains were on constant patrol.

Walking high cliffs on a clear day is the nearest a stroll can get to flying: it is exhilarating, joyful and life-affirming. Like most people, I felt a tremor of thrilling fear when I got too close to the edge and briefly contemplated my own mortality. I hadn't associated the romantic Seven Sisters with its neighbour, Beachy Head, its name a corruption of the medieval French for 'beautiful headland' but now possessed of the same dark power as places associated with specific tragedies: Lockerbie, Hungerford, Dunblane. Regardless of the half-a-million people who enjoyed hiking, picnicking or proposing marriage here each year, these cliffs were better known as one of the world's 'most notorious' suicide spots, as if one of the most beautiful places in England was an international criminal.

In the seventh century St Wilfrid was shipwrecked close to Beachy Head and claimed that Saxons were throwing themselves from the edge during a famine to leave more food for the others. Records of suicides date from the 1600s and the Victorians' creation of a scenic road over the top of the Downs was reputed to increase the number of deaths here. As suicide rates in the western world have risen, so too at Beachy Head: in 2004 thirty-four people died here, the highest annual number recorded. The cliffs do not always present an obvious edge and in places the high Downs gradually curve beyond view, grass thinning to chalk before turning sheer. In one such spot, out of sight, is a small metal cross set in a concrete base, an unofficial memorial made by Keith Lane for his wife Maggie, a petite, vivacious woman who was one of those who took their life in 2004.

Keith had met Maggie five years earlier when she turned up at his local for a quiz night. Both in their late forties, and recovering from failed relationships, they quickly fell in love and married at Eastbourne Town Hall. After several years of uncomplicated happiness, Keith, who worked as a window cleaner, found a bottle of vodka under their kitchen sink. Maggie denied it was hers but it marked Keith's awakening to his wife's growing misery. Her bubbly nature masked a difficult childhood during which she suffered physical abuse, and the present was tough too: Maggie had lost her job and was struggling with the menopause, and her social drinking gradually became secret drinking.

Life was increasingly tense at home and, one day, Keith returned from work to find Maggie had tried to kill herself with antidepressants. She received psychiatric treatment and joined Alcoholics Anonymous but despite Keith's support, recoveries were followed by relapses, binges and two further overdoses of antidepressants. Maggie also told Keith about a nightmare in which they fell off Beachy Head, hand-in-hand.

On 2 March 2004 their outlook momentarily brightened: Maggie found a new job. At lunchtime, she phoned Keith. He felt uneasy because her speech was slurred but he was reassured when she asked him to put some jacket potatoes in the oven that night; she would make chilli when she got in. When he finished work, he bought a new CD as a treat and began cooking the potatoes. Maggie never came home. Keith rang her mobile several times and, at 10 p.m., his doorbell rang. It was the police: their car had been found at Beachy Head; a police helicopter had been deployed.

The next day, he went up to Beachy Head himself and searched, desperately hoping she would be passed out under a bush. That night, however, police found a body on the rocks below the cliff and Keith was called to identify his wife. Devastated, he tried to lose himself in his work. A week later, having risen early to clean windows, Keith felt a compulsion to go to Beachy Head. It was 5.30 a.m. and a woman sat alone, head bowed, on a bench. She was writing what turned out to be her suicide note. Keith sat down beside her. 'I hope you aren't going to do what I think you're going to do,' he said. The suicidal woman was hostile; she had a right to do it, she muttered. Keith burst into tears, overwhelmed by this sadness, and still reeling from his own recent loss. The woman got up and ran towards the cliff. Keith sprinted after her and rugby-tackled her at the edge. Luckily, the police were searching for her and arrived to help.

Keith had saved a life but he was still consumed by guilt for the life he had not managed to save. An idea formed in his head: there should be twenty-four-hour patrols of Beachy Head and, between work, he set out to do two or three each day. It was a kind of grieving, and it helped him feel close to Maggie.

Because she left no note, and no one saw her jump, the coroner did not record her death as suicide but as an open verdict. Officially, around twenty people kill themselves at Beachy Head each year, travelling not merely from Doncaster, Manchester or Leicester but from Germany, Finland and Switzerland. Keith believed the true figure was closer to fifty, which is supported by scientific studies. Of 250 fatal falls at Beachy Head between 1965 and 1989, 134 were recorded as suicide with another 100 open verdicts. Of these, 97 had three or more factors indicating suicide, such as taking a taxi from a psychiatric hospital straight to the cliffs.

An informal media blackout minimises the coverage of most

incidents, but the more dramatic deaths at Beachy Head invariably make the headlines: the occasional celebrity, a terminally ill Falklands veteran, 'suicide pacts' between people meeting online, elderly couples, a medical student, a father-to-be, an aspiring UKIP politician, a man who faced criminal charges with his eighty-one-year-old mother. The tragedy that attracted the most attention in recent years was when the bodies of Neil and Kazumi Puttick were found in 2009 wearing rucksacks carrying children's toys; with them was the body of their disabled son Sam, who had died of pneumococcal meningitis two days earlier. A flurry of suicidal visitors followed this publicity, as predicted by sociological research which shows that the reporting of suicides can lead to a spike in the suicide rate. It would be wise to recognise, however, that the words Beachy Head do not drive people over the edge any more than its supposedly bad energy cited by some spiritualists: if someone who is determined to end their life is not alerted to the possibility of Beachy Head, they are likely to find another way.

In the months that followed Maggie's funeral, Keith interrupted a few people simply enjoying a quiet walk on the cliffs but he also learned to spot those wrestling with more profound problems. His second rescue came when he saw a man sitting on the cliff with his legs dangling over the edge. Keith went over and did the same. If he said the wrong thing, Keith realised, the man would simply disappear. So they sat in silence for a bit and then Keith struck up a gentle conversation. The man showed him a photograph of his young children, and they talked some more. Eventually, Keith got him away for a pint at the pub that improbably sits at the top of Beachy Head. They discussed the man's estrangement from his wife before Keith put him on a bus home.

Keith's strategy was to identify desperate people, sit with them, and quietly seek a connection. 'If I made eye contact, and if I sat with them for any length of time, I knew I'd got them,' he told me.

Usually, he would talk about Maggie, finding it helped people focus on something outside themselves for a few seconds. Through his own raw grief, he could also show them what they would be leaving behind. 'You're talking from the heart rather than from the book. You can't teach someone that,' he said. As he wrote in his autobiography, *Life on the Edge*, 'My experience always seemed to give me some kind of authority. Whether or not my story inspired respect, empathy or merely made people inquisitive, they seemed to want to listen to it and that was good enough for me.'

For three-and-a-half years after the death of Maggie, Keith carried out his patrols. It gave him moments of elation but also despair. He saved twenty-nine people, but there were losses too. One or two of those he saved returned to the cliffs days later or took their lives another way. One morning he passed a man on the cliffs and wished him good morning. When the man calmly returned his 'good morning' he felt reassured but an instinct told him to watch him. When the man glanced around, Keith knew he was a potential suicide risk and quietly asked if he could have a few minutes of his time. 'He just looked at me, took his glasses off and jumped,' he remembered.

Others, however, got in touch to thank him. The first woman he saved later approached him in the shopping centre in Eastbourne and told him her life was back on track. At the time, Keith was still consumed by guilt and grief over Maggie and drinking too much. One night, 'completely smashed' on a bottle of vodka, he took a taxi to Beachy Head to throw himself from 'Maggie's spot'. He stopped himself, and gradually began to recover.

When he received an award for his first life-saving effort, it was reported by local and then national media, for whom the story of a window cleaner driven to save lives by the death of his wife was an irresistible blend of tragedy and heroism. There are a few other people like Keith around the world and even if they do not court publicity, it soon courts them. At the equally spectacular clifftop spot in the eastern suburbs of Sydney, a local man called Don Ritchie became known as 'the Angel of the Gap' for saving more than 160 lives between 1964 and his death in 2012. Ritchie would approach them at the edge, smile and ask if he could help them. 'I was a salesman for most of my life and I sold them life,' he told friends of those he saved.

Around the time Keith began roaming the cliffs, volunteers for the Beachy Head Chaplaincy Team, an evangelical Christian charity, started patrolling the area as well. Keith welcomed their work and donated money to them in the beginning but, over time, tension developed. On occasion, Keith's cliff-top interventions without any safety equipment alarmed the authorities whose rescuers always wore safety harnesses if approaching someone on the edge. Keith's irresistibility to the media generated publicity which the chaplaincy group believed could encourage more unhappy people to visit Beachy Head. On several occasions, chaplains confronted Keith. 'So-called professionals' told him he shouldn't be patrolling the cliffs. So he took a course in person-centred counselling and found this professional approach exactly mirrored the techniques he had intuitively developed himself. Keith also believed that some people in the mental health system who had endured lengthy battles with the authorities would not find succour in a police officer or a chaplain in uniform on the cliffs. 'People tended to trust me because I wasn't a figure of authority, I was just a guy who'd lost his wife,' he wrote in his autobiography.

Disillusioned by friction with the chaplains but also finding that his life was moving on, Keith stopped his patrols in 2007. 'I wasn't really aware going through that period of three-and-a-half years that it was part of my bereavement,' he said. 'It was my way of coping. I was channelling all my energies into preventing other people going through what I was going through. It wasn't until I moved on that I got everything into perspective.' He had grieved for Maggie but eventually rebuilt his social life and met and fell in love with Valerie, who became his wife.

The number of deaths at Beachy Head declined during the years of Keith's patrols but he is careful not to claim any credit for this. In an operation costing £200,000 a year, the well-organised chaplains, who now number twenty-five, have saved plenty of lives too, but the Beachy Head Chaplaincy Trust's statistics still show a curve of desperation leading upwards. In 2006 they undertook 138 'rescues'; in 2012 they made 305. In the first week of 2014 alone, they intercepted fifteen people who were 'despondent' or suicidal. 'Unfortunately there were two deaths at the cliffs this week, which is a particularly sad start to the year,' they recorded.

Why choose Beachy Head? Its reputation, obviously, has something to do with it and Keith Lane believed that the rise of online forums discussing suicide options led to an increasing number of depressed visitors, who perceive its cliffs, erroneously, to guarantee instant death rather than an awful injury. I wondered if the beauty of the place could be a draw for some people but Keith said this was rarely mentioned. 'I've had one or two who have said to me, "What a beautiful place to die." That's a difficult one to get around because yes, it is,' he said. But, generally, seriously unhappy people are not having rhapsodic moments on the cliffs like the rest of us. The beauty of a place is meaningless, or mocking, for the seriously depressed. As Keith put it: 'Anyone who normally admires the beauty has gone there to have a nice day out.'

The Beachy Head Chaplaincy Team currently has a 'vision statement' aimed at ending suicide at Beachy Head. The Golden Gate Bridge in San Francisco is now netted to prevent suicide. The cliffs at Beachy Head are owned by the local council, not the National Trust, and are part of a country park and the South Downs National Park. The authorities could spend millions on fencing along the cliffs, 'but where do you stop?' asked Keith. 'Do you stop at Birling Gap because that's not Beachy Head? A fence would ruin the beauty of it. Essentially, it's a wonderful place to stand and enjoy the view –

one of the best views in England.' He believed more deaths could be prevented by campaigning for better mental health provision and closing suicide websites, but 'you will never, ever stop suicide. It's something I had to learn. Every time someone jumped, I took it personally. I thought I'd failed. I thought I could go up there and save everyone. In the main, the people that you save are the people who really want to be saved. I've had to watch people go over and there's nothing you can do to stop them because that's what they want to do.'

It is only human nature for its notoriety to be a source of morbid fascination, but like every local person, Keith would rather the cliffs around Beachy Head were known as a beauty spot rather than a suicide spot. The former is a far more accurate designation, given the thousands who enjoy it every year.

These days, Keith was more focused on his nine grandchildren, and looking after Valerie, who has Parkinson's, but he still went onto the cliffs on the anniversary of Maggie's death and to tend to her cross. 'It's a place of peace for me now,' he said, 'just tinged with a little bit of tragedy. I don't have any bad thoughts up there.'

For all the sad endings by our shores, many people choose to spend their last years, months or days in much calmer contemplation of our coast. The sea is a mirror, as that great mariner Joseph Conrad wrote in his classic study of the ocean. Perhaps being beside it reflects the state of approaching death: the world is behind us and ahead is nothing, at least, nothing we can discern. W. G. Sebald thought this when he considered why hobby fishermen sat on the Suffolk shingle with a thermos – with a little radio giving 'forth a scarcely audible, scratchy sound, as if the pebbles being dragged back by the waves were talking to each other' – when there was little chance of catching a decent fish. 'They just want to be in a place where they have the world behind them, and before them nothing but emptiness,' he said.

For those approaching the end of life, a more symbolic place of departure from this world might be Land's End. One theory is that the prehistoric stones of Penwith are chamber tombs, which suggest that many centuries ago our most westerly point was considered an exit lounge to another life. The ancients believed that souls must journey out to sea to a mystical place of rest beyond the western horizon; the west's symbolic association with death may be one reason why Christian churches are built facing east, the dawn a comforting symbol of new life.

Perhaps the slightly baffling contemporary popularity of Land's End is linked to a folk memory of this spiritual connection although it is more likely a consequence of the eighteenth-century Romantic quest for majesty, wilderness and mightily large rocks. Nevertheless, at the start of the twentieth century, W. H. Hudson noticed that many tourists who flocked to Land's End seemed to regard the view westwards with a contemplative reverence. He wrote of the elderly men he watched, gathered there, alone, 'sat mostly in dejected attitudes, bending forward, their hands resting on the handles of their sticks, some with their chins on their hands, but all gazed in one direction over the cold grey sea'. Although the men were all strangers, they bore 'the same look of infinite weariness on their grey faces and in their dim sad eyes, as if one thought and feeling and motive had drawn them to this spot'.

Hudson wondered what they saw out to sea. He imagined they were not picturing joyful scenes of their imminent welcome in a sparkling heaven but actually desired 'a silent land of rest'. Here, he thought, these grey pilgrims would cast aside wearisome 'passion and striving' and would experience 'neither joy nor sorrow, nor love nor hate, nor wish to know them any more; and when he remembers his fellow-men it will comfort him to think that his peace will never be broken by the sight of human face or the sound of human speech, since never by any chance will any wanderer from the world discover him in that illimitable wilderness'.

It's a nice piece of imagining but I am a little unconvinced by W. H. Hudson's powers of empathy: I think his writing is far more perceptive about birds than people.

But perhaps his flight of fancy reflected his own hopes for the end for many of us derive great comfort from the coast at the end of our lives. Extreme old age is often considered a time when our horizons shrink and we return to a remembered childhood. When we forget the present, we can still recall ancient holidays on the beach. Past associations may encourage people to retire by the sea, but there are more prosaic reasons too. Young people look on retirement as a confined existence but retirees are freer than they've been since they were children, no longer tied to a particular place for jobs, schools, children or elderly relatives. The coast is a place of freedom, as well as contentment and solace towards the end of our lives.

On a dark November day, I drove to Arnside Knott, on the edge of Morecambe Bay in Cumbria, to explore why a sea view was one thing so many of us sought in our final years. I'd been to the Knott before, chasing its rare butterflies, and marvelled how Arnside, a slice of Victorian suburbia clinging to the hill, resembled a tiny independent kingdom with a population solely consisting of white-haired people. It was happy to be overlooked as the rest of the world raced past on the M6, drawn to the more dramatic uplands of the Lake District. Well equipped with sheltered accommodation, its streets were peppered with those slightly insulting signs showing a stooped and stick-wielding old couple, as if everyone over seventy was going to topple into the road like skittles. Most of all, it had benches galore, each with a stunning view over the silver water of Morecambe Bay to the west.

I visited a large Victorian house of stone and slate on the edge of the Knott. It was clean, well heated and noisy. The din was not the old-persons'-home cliché of the blaring television but all the well-meaning safety equipment: entry buzzers, bleepers and secure doors. Despite this, many elderly residents sat asleep in rows of high-backed chairs.

Jack Armitage, who was eighty-nine and came from Halifax, had retired to Arnside with his wife, who had now passed away. They'd discovered the area during their 'extensive honeymoon' touring the Lake District. The beauty of Arnside was its views of the mountains to the north but he considered 'the main ingredient' to be the great sweep of Morecambe Bay. 'The first thing that appealed to us is its innate attraction as a natural place of beauty. My wife and I were fortunate in as much as we travelled all over the world, as far as New Zealand. We kept coming back to Arnside. Wherever we went, although there were some fine spots, the peace and natural surroundings around here – nowhere did we find them excelled. It's incomparable.'

It brought to mind one of the most brilliant passages of writing about the sea by Ronald Blythe who, in *The Time By the Sea*, described the pleasures of watching 'the sea hit the rocks like a restless sculptor with all the time in the world to shape them' on the cliffs of North Cornwall. 'My head becomes a tabula rasa on which the ocean is welcome to write poetry or gibberish without any guidance from me. Is this why old people retire to the south coast or Florida? Why their most treasured possession is a deckchair? Not a bed in the opium den but a seat where the most wonderful monotony can drug the watcher into forgetting past, present and future. Should it be warm enough there is no reason why, at Eastbourne, sea-nirvana should not be reached by elevenses.'

If the sea brought us peace, was this what we desired as we got older? 'I'm sure it's so,' said Jack Armitage. 'That and the memories of past experiences and happiness and the good times we've all had together.' An elderly lady sitting next to Jack, who was having her nails done by a visiting beautician, leaned over. 'Definitely,' she said.

Elsie Simpson was ninety-one and hailed from Bury. She remembered the simplicity of holidays at Fleetwood as a girl. 'I'm going back to the days when families didn't have holidays. Everybody was scraping the barrel. You were really somebody if you had a little holiday in Fleetwood,' she said. A boat used to sail to the Isle of Man. 'We thought that if we caught the boat we were going abroad.' She had returned to Fleetwood when she had a family of her own. 'Our little boy spent hours and hours with a bucket and spade on the beach and that's all he wanted.'

These days, the sea was something different for Elsie. There were no sandcastles being built on the treacherous sands of Morecambe but she enjoyed the constantly changing mood of the bay, and the way it told her what the weather was going to do. 'When you come up to retiring age, that is when it's peaceful,' she said. 'We've done away with the crowds and bothering with things and it's nice to be able to sit down and relax. The sea is a wonderful peace-maker.'

Just after three o'clock, with the day at an end, I climbed onto the Knott. Looking over infinite sand towards the yellow-bottomed clouds on the western horizon, it seemed impossible that the tide would ever pull the sea back to land. Great streaks of light and colour, purple-grey sand and silver slivers of water, were traced across the bay. To the south-west, the two great blocks of Heysham nuclear power station looked like mere houses in the vastness.

The Knott was better than a concert hall at collecting tiny sounds. A raven gargled, a pheasant fussed in the woods and some extra-ordinarily gossipy corvid conversations played in the bonsai yews growing on the rubbly limestone slope. The last oak leaves clinging to the branches gave a soft rattle. A dog squeaked, an iron gate banged and there was the approaching puff of a walker climbing the hill before the last light left.

The human activity – a chainsaw, a plane trail scoring the sky and the *bur-booh* of a train's horn across the bay at Grange-over-Sands – seemed utterly inconsequential against the constantly shifting, never changing expanse of Morecambe Bay. As the mist rose and thickened like lustrous white hair against Helvellyn and the darkening Lakeland fells to the north, the land looked wintery, implacable and very, very old.

The shore looked older still. The bay resembled a pre-modern plain, a great delta, devoid of humans, where an array of giant beasts trod instead. Tidal flats were the last wilderness, unconquerable by us. But it was more than that. The sea was simply the oldest thing of all. No man, wrote Joseph Conrad, 'ever saw the sea looking young as the earth looks young in spring'. The wind, he thought, was what made the sea look old and it was, too, older than everything, our ultimate source of life. Something in us revered it for that.

Imperceptibly, browns and greys leeched from the land and everything became purple: the clouds, the mountains, the woods, the mud. It was impossible to see where the earth ended and where the sea began. Finally, the whole scene was washed with the darkest shade of blue.

## Explorations of Neptune

The 100-mile South Downs Way reaches its climax on **the Seven Sisters** above Eastbourne where it careers along the cliffs and around the Downs in a fantastic, strenuous 21-mile circuit. This walk can be taken in either direction although it is probably easiest to start at Eastbourne and head north up the Downs away from the coast, over Windover Hill and down into the Cuckmere Valley. If you walk it this way you then climb the Downs and spend the final third of the walk striding (or staggering) along the Seven Sisters, with the chance of a swim at Birling Gap. If you would prefer a shorter walk, you could head straight for Birling Gap, and the National Trust's rather chic new visitor centre. From this low point between the Sisters there are spectacular walks east to the old lighthouse of Belle Tout and up the rolling Downs west towards Cuckmere Haven. Or you could park at the Eastbourne end of the Sisters, at the Beachy Head car park, and walk west from this high point.

*Birling Gap*

East Dean

Eastbourne

East Sussex BN20 0AB

*OS Map*

Explorer 123, Eastbourne & Beachy Head

*Nearest railway station*

Eastbourne, 2 miles

*Websites*

www.nationaltrust.org.uk/birling-gap-and-the-seven-sisters/visitor-information/

www.nationaltrail.co.uk/south-downs-way/

www.sevensisters.org.uk

If you are ever driving north to Scotland or the Lakes on the M6, take a fifteen-minute detour to **Arnside Knott**. It is one of the most beautiful, and overlooked, places in Britain. I love it for its butterflies: the most southerly populations of the Scotch Argus fly there in July, alongside big, golden and incredibly rare High Brown Fritillaries. But it is gorgeous at any time of year. It's an abrupt limestone outcrop, which offers steep little walks and spectacular views in all directions. It's the sort of place to potter, and have a picnic, rather than take a lengthy stroll, although it's worth a thorough circuit, taking in its lower meadows as well as its vertiginous cliff to the south. A longer walk is to head south on footpaths to Silverdale: this too, is part of the Morecambe Bay limestone, an intimate and biodiverse landscape and you can always catch the train back to your car. If you are driving to the Knott, the biggest challenge is finding it: drive into the village of Arnside on the B5282, under the railway line and turn left after the road runs along by the water. Follow this road through the village and around to the right. Look for a small lane on the left, signposted 'to the Knott'. This heads uphill, narrows and crosses cattle grids to a National Trust car park under the trees.

## OS Map
Explorer OL7, The English Lakes: South-eastern area
### Nearest railway station
Arnside, 1 mile
### Website
www.nationaltrust.org.uk/arnside-and-silverdale/visitor-information/

## Further Reading

W. H. Hudson, *The Land's End*, Wildwood House, 1981 (1908)
Keith Lane, *Life on the Edge*, John Blake, 2010

# 9

# Faith

*The Farnes / Morwenstow / Lindisfarne*

Lindisfarne
The Farne Islands

Morwenstow

It had been miserable down south but in the north it was a cool, clear evening. The curry restaurants of Seahouses were full but its harbour was empty and smelt of cold stone and seaweed. By the water were four wooden huts like bookies' stands at a race. Each one was hand-painted with carefully judged adverts about its offerings. Billy Shiel's USP was his MBE. Hanvey's was 'landing on NT bird sanctuary'. Golden Gate was 'dogs may land'. Serenity was 'view those inquisitive grey seals'. All offered exactly the same thing: tours of the Farne Islands, in small boats run by local families who once made a living from fish.

The Farne Islands are an archipelago, a word which possesses misleadingly exotic associations for what is a collection of treeless rocks in the North Sea. Their number differs depending on who you ask and the state of the tides: Inner Farne, Knocklin Ends, Little and Big Scarcar, Little and Big Harcar, The Wideopens, The Kettle, Megstone, Gun Rock, Brownsman, Callers, Crumstone, North and South Warnses, Clove Car, Northern Hares, Longstone, Brada and Knivestone, the outermost island, which sounds like a menace for ships.

All were invisible on this May evening but for four low lines of rock on the calm water, dark shapes under the slowly diminishing brightness on the northern horizon. The graceful serenity of this simple view of earth, fire, wind and water dwarfed all the human activity in Seahouses. The scale of the landscape and the calm of the evening might make us ponder the modesty of our endeavours next to the potency of a benevolent God.

The next morning, all goodwill had been withdrawn and replaced by a domineering power. The wind that scudded the clouds whipped the sea into implausible violence over a short stretch of water between coast and island. The boat bucked up and lurched down and we knew a wave was about to strike because the pilot cut his engine to take each hit. Clinging on and seeing nothing but spray during this twenty-minute rollercoaster, I eventually noticed an unusual number of seabirds on the water: razorbills, black-and-white and handsome; guillemots, the northern-hemisphere penguin; shags, their tufted crest showing only because it was May; kittiwakes, the smallest and noisiest species of gull; and, most compact of all, the puffins, whirring through the air, wings moving like propellers. Shortly afterwards, dark rocks and low cliffs dashed with guano loomed out of the storm. Rounding a corner and slipping into a modicum of shelter from the heaving sea, we landed on the small jetty of Inner Farne.

Given their vulnerability to elemental forces, both tranquil and violent, it seemed appropriate that the Farnes were the birthplace of hermitic life in Britain. Lundy or Brownsea were islands on which survival seemed possible, but Inner Farne was little more than an exposed piece of rock in the North Sea. It offered no quantum of comfort to St Cuthbert, which was precisely why he established a cell here in the seventh century, seeking an uncompromising place for self-abnegation and prayer.

The coast is a great consolation to many people, but I was coming to realise that I had written about my perception of it as befits a child of a secular age. In another era, my feelings of elevation, or humility, or ecstasy might be explained in terms of a religious faith. The coast has long been a place of pilgrimage and a destination for those on a quest to find meaning in their lives. What did this boundary between sea and water express, for us to vest it with such significance?

Christians did not invent the idea of religious activity by the sea in Britain or anywhere else but we have little record of how pre-Christian people worshipped on the coast. There are tantalising hints, such as the upturned oak root and circle of wooden posts we called 'Seahenge' when it was exposed on the sands of Holme-next-the-Sea in Norfolk in 1998. This early Bronze Age ceremonial site was controversially removed from the beach for safekeeping but its meaning remains elusive: Seahenge was probably a mortuary ring where the bodies of the dead were placed, but did it actually reveal anything about our ancestors' relationship with the sea? The disappearance of the east coast is so striking that at the time of its construction, 2049 BC, Seahenge would not have actually been situated on the beach.

So many parts of the Neptune coast have been touched by faith through the centuries. Christianity arrived in Britain with the Romans but the pagan Angles, Saxons and Vikings drove the faith to the western fringes. The religion returned to the shores of southern England in the year 597 when Augustine was dispatched from Rome on a proselytising mission by Pope Gregory the Great. The Roman Empire never quite reached Ireland, but Christianity had trickled into the country nonetheless and took on its own distinct identity. Monks and their monasteries were important in the early Christian tradition in Ireland and their concept of *peregrinus*, Latin for pilgrim, was particularly influential. The first Irish pilgrims were missionaries and, in 563, Columba was among those monks who travelled to where God told him. The Scottish island of Iona was the chosen destination and where Columba established his celebrated monastery. From here, monks took Christianity to what has become the holiest place on England's coast: Lindisfarne, or Holy Island.

On my way to the Farnes, I had started reading a fascinating history of Holy Island by the historian Kate Tristram, who was particularly good at explaining the motivations of the early Christian settlers on our shores. The fortunes of the region's great saints were inextricably bound up with the lives of their political masters. The Kingdom of Northumbria, a grand land encompassing Durham and Yorkshire as well as Northumberland, was largely established by Aethelfrith, a fifth-century English warrior known as the 'Destroyer' who once slaughtered 1,200 unarmed Welsh Christian monks who were praying against his victory. When he was killed in battle in 616, his children, Oswald and Oswiu, fled to Iona, where they were taken in by the monks and adopted Christianity. When Oswald recaptured the throne of Northumbria, he warmly welcomed the arrival of Aidan, a monk from Iona who decided to make a pilgrimage to Godless north-east England in 635. Supported by twelve monks, Aidan chose for a monastery the island of Lindisfarne. The tranquillity of island life would have appealed to the monks brought up on Iona; however, it was not a place of monastic seclusion but a pragmatic choice. It was within sight of Aidan's protector, Oswald, and the monk could walk at low tide to his castle at Bamburgh. The sea was also an important highway. The Irish were second only to the Vikings as the most skilled seafarers and Aidan's Irish monks were always zipping about in their little coracles from Lindisfarne. Unlike the rest of the population, they did not fear storms because 'God was in direct control of the sea', as Tristram put it in *The Story of Holy Island*. Aidan needed to be well connected because he was on a proselytising mission: opening a school to teach Christianity to local boys in English, and seeking to convert the rest of the population to his faith. At times, however, the Irish monk retreated from his busy mission to the remoter Farne Islands for contemplation, prayer and miraculous feats. During one retreat, Penda, the warlike King of Mercia, besieged Oswald and his people, attacking them with fire at Bamburgh. Looking back to shore, Aidan realised that the wind would drive the flames to consume the wooden castle, so he prayed, the wind changed direction and the smoke was blown back on the attackers, who abandoned the siege.

Aidan's monastery at Lindisfarne was a great success, but it was not until after his death that the Farne Islands were established as a beacon for solitude. On the night Aidan died, an aristocratic teenager called Cuthbert was guarding a flock of sheep when it is said he saw angels escorting a human soul to heaven.

After these visions, Cuthbert entered a monastery at Melrose and undertook preaching tours of lowland Scotland, where other monks feared to go. Energetic and humble (Bede, the brilliant monastic scholar of the eighth century and a key source for historians of this period, stressed that Cuthbert wore 'ordinary' clothes), Cuthbert was a persuasive teacher and also demonstrated gifts of healing, prophecy, driving out demons and a profound connection with nature. During a visit to his friend the Abbess Aebbe of Coldingham, he spent a night on the beach where he was warmed the next morning by the breath of two otters.

Cuthbert was transferred to Lindisfarne where, initially, monks were suspicious of this outsider. He overcame their opposition by smiling a lot. 'Cuthbert's cheerfulness seems to have been one of his outstanding qualities,' writes Tristram. After a decade at Lindisfarne, Cuthbert believed God was calling him to be a hermit. Tristram explained that the word 'monk' comes from the Greek word for 'alone', and many of the Desert Fathers, the heroic first monks who lived in the deserts of Syria and Egypt, embraced a solitary life. As this Christian tradition developed, it was considered wise for hermits to first live in the community of a monastery, where they could be supported before striking out on their own. Here, living alone, through fasting and prayer, the hermit would become 'one of God's frontline soldiers in the most difficult war of all, the heavenly warfare against the forces of spiritual evil', as Tristram puts it. 'If he won, that is, if he remained faithful, the spiritual benefit for the whole Church would be enormous. So it was no selfish vocation. The hermit was not cultivating his own soul.'

At first, Cuthbert moved to a tiny island cut off from Lindisfarne by the tides but it proved too close to his old life, and to visitors. He needed somewhere more remote and so chose Inner Farne. This was the only island in the Farne archipelago that held enough soil for Cuthbert to grow crops to eat. But it was also a spiritual choice: the Farnes were lashed by the wind and the sea, which would be conducive to prayer and were also reputed to be more densely populated with demons than any other locality. Before he was left alone, Lindisfarne monks helped Cuthbert build a stone chapel and a dwelling, surrounded by a high wall so he wouldn't spend his time admiring the view.

When I read this, I realised that I had completely misunderstood what might compel a religious person to seek solitude by the sea. I found the contemplation of the coast to be a source of great solace and yet this was extremely individualistic, almost solipsistic thinking. My love of sitting by myself on the coast was just another form of pleasure-seeking, no different from surfing a big wave or riding a jet ski, except for the exertion required. The twenty-first century was all about what the coast could do for us. John Fowles was fiercely secular but he condemned the narcissistic way in which we turn nature into therapy. For a person like Cuthbert, it was very different: a pilgrimage to the sea was a journey to seek discomfort in an inhospitable land, giving up every pleasure for a confrontation believed to benefit wider human kind. Hermit-monks were not pursuing a special individual relationship with God, they were supporting society through prayer.

So I had rather elevated expectations of St Cuthbert's Chapel when I finally stepped onto the Farne Islands. I assumed this small stone building which had been rebuilt many times would house great tranquillity. Set on the north-east side of the glorified rock that is Inner Farne, its door was reached off a sheltered stone-walled courtyard surrounded by a low barn and the domineering bulk of the four-storey pele tower. This castle-like stone fortification was built in the sixteenth century for monks who clearly demanded more comfort than St Cuthbert and required protection from the Scots raiding the coast. It was now home to ten National Trust rangers who lived on the island for nine months of the year and its castle-keep of a living room featured a wood-burner, a guitar, an impressive row of whiskies on a stone shelf, and a bucket catching a persistent drip in the corner.

My assumption that I would find peace in the chapel was perhaps a peculiarly contemporary expectation of religious places because they are now mostly empty rather than the bustling community centres of old. St Cuthbert's may have been deserted, but there was nothing tranquil about it. I closed the heavy wooden door behind me and breathed in cool, still air and damp stone, but the wind still howled and above it were the screams of Arctic terns hovering on wings of aluminium over the yard outside. Even now, not long from midsummer, Inner Farne was bleak, wet, grey and without any sensory comfort. The constant wind set me on edge and there was no peace either, only a raucous city of birds. It seemed the height of folly to live here, within sight of the tormentingly fertile green fields of Northumberland. Enduring such torment was, of course, precisely Cuthbert's point.

Ancient history may remind us how much of our thinking is shaped by the characteristics of the era in which we live but it can show the timelessness of interactions between individuals and society too. Despite his great saintliness, Cuthbert was compelled by political pressures to return to the mainland after ten years selflessly battling demons: the much-admired monk had been made a bishop without his knowledge, let alone his consent. Reluctantly, therefore, he became Bishop of Lindisfarne and travelled the region, like Aidan before him, converting, healing and prophesying. He had a strong presentiment of his coming death and, after his final Christmas at Lindisfarne, took his little coracle back to his hermitage. In his final two months on Inner Farne, he was visited regularly by monks, who lit a torch when he died to signal the news back to the monastery. His body was brought to Lindisfarne, where the monks planned to raise his bones after eleven years to symbolise his entrance into sainthood. After the required period, his coffin was opened and Cuthbert appeared to be a man asleep, untouched by decay. His capacity to heal others also continued in death: a violently possessed boy was given a small piece of earth taken from the place where the water used to wash Cuthbert's body had been poured away and was completely cured; a paralysed man was healed by wearing the shoes in which the saint had been buried. The political stability in Northumbria, unusually governed by one family throughout the seventh century, also proved conducive to promoting the cult of St Cuthbert, who was energetically celebrated by Eadfrith, made bishop of Lindisfarne in 698, the year Cuthbert's body was discovered undecayed. Eadfrith went on to produce the Lindisfarne Gospels, a masterpiece of Anglo-Saxon art and literature which survives to this day and was made 'for God and St Cuthbert'.

Of the hermits who followed Cuthbert to Inner Farne, only a few survive in historical documents. Aethelwald, Cuthbert's immediate successor, made his monastic cell more draught-proof by fixing a calf-skin in the corner where he prayed. A piece of the calf-skin washed in water cured the facial disfigurement of the next hermit, Felgild. The successor who most wonderfully conforms to our expectations of hermits was St Bartholomew of Farne, a man who embraced three names and extreme austerity. Born Tostig, to Scandinavian parents in the early twelfth century, he changed his name to William and enjoyed a riotous youth before being ordained in Norway, fleeing an arranged marriage and becoming a monk at Durham, where he took the name Bartholomew. A vision of St Cuthbert encouraged him to become a hermit on Inner Farne where he endured great privation for forty-two years. He slept on rocks, subsisted on fish and bread from his own corn and wore a ram's skin, which became black with dirt in accordance with the idea that his soul grew cleaner as his body became dirtier. For years his only companion was a pet bird but he was eventually joined by Thomas, the former prior of Durham. Fragrant Thomas was initially offended by Bartholomew's disastrous personal hygiene and the two quarrelled, but eventually they got on well. For all Bartholomew's hostility to neighbours and his habit of rebuking the rich and powerful, he was known, like St Cuthbert, for his great cheerfulness. He roamed his island singing psalms and when he died on Inner Farne in 1193, the monks attending him heard a noise 'as of mice dancing or of sparrows creeping about on the roof with beaks and claws'. Miracles were soon reported at his tomb.

The human instinct for comfort is insatiable and the Benedictine monks who lived on the Farnes from 1255 until the dissolution of the monasteries under Henry VIII developed an easier lifestyle. They cultivated three acres of barley and pasture to support two bulls, three cows and three heifers, sheep, pigs, six capons, six hens and a cock, some of whom were put out on Brownsman, which was also cropped for hay. Supplies so they could survive when it was too rough to cross to the mainland included half an ox, three sheep in salt, 200 red herrings, twenty dried codlings and five codfish, a bushel of oatmeal, six quarters of wheat, twelve quarters of coal, and twelve-and-a-half quarters of barley malt. These monks were practical men, skilled butchers, carpenters, thatchers and fishermen who exported seal oil and luxuries such as porpoise and seal calves for religious festivals in Durham. Something of the character of the early hermits endured on the Farnes, however. A fourteenth-century hermit, believed to be John Whiterig, an Oxford graduate, wrote of a vision in which he asked Jesus how he could be saved. In Whiterig's vision, Jesus replied 'with gaiety and kindness' and 'Love, and thou shalt be saved'. Whiterig was also a great believer in cheerfulness. 'The Farne Islands give us at least three examples of happy hermits,' wrote Kate Tristram. The hagiographers who recorded the lives of the saints would have us believe that they were innately cheerful, but perhaps living by the sea added to their joy and helped them spread it to others.

If St Cuthbert and St Bartholomew embody the monastic experience of the coast, a more recent Christian seaside tradition is illuminated by the singular figure of Robert Stephen Hawker. An amusing cast of dodgy vicars crops up in coastal fables, exposed for their complicity in smuggling or wrecking. One version of a tale that recurs in similar form around the country stars an unnamed vicar of East Portlemouth Church, which stands by a glorious, treacherous section of the Neptune coast in South Devon. He was halfway through his Sunday sermon when a parishioner entered the church and whispered in his ear. The minister continued his sermon but, eventually, could contain himself no longer. 'There's a ship ashore between Prawle and Pear Tree Point, but let's all start fair!' he exclaimed, tearing off his gown and running from the church, pursued by parishioners eager to join him in stripping the wreck of all its valuables. On the Isles of Scilly, a Parson Troutbeck is said to have offered up this supplication: 'Dear God, we pray not that wrecks should happen, but that if it be Thy will that they do, we pray Thee let them be to the benefit of Thy poor people of Scilly.' Later, Daphne du Maurier took inspiration from such tales in her gothic horror, *Jamaica Inn*, in which the creepy Vicar of Altarnun turns out to be the ringleader of a brutal wrecking gang who terrorise the north coast of Cornwall.

It was on these bleak cliffs that Hawker, the nineteenth-century vicar of Morwenstow, engaged directly with the mythology of the reverend-as-wrecker, setting himself up as a heroic figure, living among 'a mixed multitude of smugglers, wreckers and dissenters of various hue', seeking to save ships, give dead sailors a decent burial and expel evil from our shores. In many ways, Hawker perfectly fits the stereotype of a Victorian cleric, a romantic, intellectual vicar and poet inspired by the sea but also compelled to endure a kind of hermitage – the physical and psychological isolation of a remote coastal parish. The truth of his life by the sea has been obscured by his monstrously unreliable biographer and fellow clergyman, Sabine Baring-Gould. Perhaps Baring-Gould can be excused his unreliability on the grounds of his overburdened existence: he fathered fifteen children, wrote the hymn 'Onward, Christian Soldiers', and published 159 books including the melodrama *Mehalah*, set on the Essex island of Ray – another magical island of Neptune. But Hawker's own imaginings, exaggerations and downright lies add to the complexity of his character and his relationship with the coast.

Remoteness is a quality largely erased from the map of southern England but it is still tangible in Morwenstow. No good roads lead to this northerly edge of the north coast of Cornwall, and there are no safe ports or beaches either. 'The very land itself had an oceanic quality about it in its huge swells and unfeatured plateau,' wrote H. J. Massingham in 1952. 'No place in England could be more remote from the levelling powers of modern civilisation.' Approaching from the east, cross-country, on a grey day, the high, treeless countryside looked desolate even in July, and was filled, like all empty country places, with industrial installations: vast sheep farms, coniferous plant-ations, wind turbines, fields of solar panels and huge white satellite dishes identified only by a discreet road sign: 'GCHQ'. It must be the least gentrified piece of coastal Cornwall.

When I arrived at Morwenstow, a dark granite church facing the ocean half-a-mile beyond, there were fourteen cars already parked on the green by the thriving tearooms in Old Rectory Farm and I felt disappointed: it became immediately harder to visualise the austerity of this rural parish in Victorian times. The roads here in Hawker's day were still too rough for horse-drawn coaches in many places. No railway penetrated the claustrophobic wooded valleys and bleak tops of its north until a line reached Bude in 1898, twenty-three years after the vicar's death. Copies of *The Times* were similarly waylaid, arriving in Morwenstow three days after it was published. Hawker told a friend how every 100 miles from London was said to turn you back by a century from the present day: by his calculation, it was 1610 in Morwenstow.

The hamlet's handsome church, pinnacled tower poking above gnarled, lichen-splattered oak, beech and sycamore, was unspoilt and virtually unchanged since Hawker's day. Half-a-mile beyond the churchyard, visible in the 'v' of the small steep valley which provided a modicum of shelter for Morwenstow, was the ocean: turquoise grey sea, flecked with choppy white. Beyond tall cliffs that threw lines of jagged black rock into the water, the horizon was a smudge of grey. Beyond, nothing until Labrador, Canada.

'The coast from Tintagel to Hartland is almost unrivalled for grandeur. The restless Atlantic is ever thundering on this iron-walled coast,' wrote Sabine Baring-Gould, perfectly capturing a Victorian clergyman's sense of the sea. 'To me, when staying three miles inland, it has seemed the roar of a hungry caged beast, ravening at its bars for food.' Baring-Gould saw that the waters off North Cornwall had none of the tameness of the German Ocean and none of the 'green crystal' of the sea that arrives before Torquay on the south coast. 'It is emphatically "the cruel sea", fierce, insatiate, hungering for human lives and stately vessels.' Hawker's life here was defined by these prospects, but his relationship with the sea had started far earlier.

The eldest of nine, Hawker was born in Plymouth in 1803 and moved to the coast of North Cornwall after his father became a vicar. By the age of ten he had read Shakespeare, Scott and Byron. At thirteen he wrote:

*I love the ocean! From a very child*
*It has been to me as a nursing breast,*
*Cherishing wild fancies.*

These 'wild fancies' included attention-seeking and sometimes cruel teenage practical jokes such as delivering a coffin to the door of three spinsters who were so traumatised they fled the village for Plymouth. His most celebrated jape played on coastal fable: Hawker rowed to a rock off Bude, wrapped his legs in an oilskin and donned a wig of lank seaweed in an excellent impersonation of a mermaid. Crowds gathered to listen to its mournful songs. Accounts of his stunt vary but it ended either when he got cold, sang 'God Save The King' and dived into the water or when he overheard a farmer threatening to pepper this apparition with buckshot and hurriedly slipped into the sea.

Aged nineteen, Hawker married Charlotte I'ans, a wealthy and well-educated woman who also happened to be forty-one. It was an untruth spread by Baring-Gould that I'ans was his godmother but she did help fund Hawker's degree at Oxford University, where he threw champagne breakfasts and entertained his wife's two older sisters with such solicitude that he was nicknamed 'the man with three wives'. He was bright, extrovert, attractive – and unreliable. Like other eminent Victorians such as John Ruskin and Oscar Wilde, Hawker won the Newdigate Prize for Poetry while at Oxford. But he was the only one accused of plagiarism: his prize-winning poem is startlingly similar to one of Macaulay's poems which won the Cambridge prize a few years earlier. Hawker did find lasting acclaim, however, as the author of *The Song of the Western Men*, a popular ballad about the imprisonment of a Cornish royalist which became almost an unofficial anthem for Cornwall.

After Oxford, Hawker returned to his roots and, in 1834, became the vicar of Morwenstow. For forty years he lived on the cliffs, cultivating his eccentric image and writing prolifically – poems, journals and racy 'real life' accounts of his life on the cliffs for London magazines. Although he never acquired the national recognition he craved, Hawker became an intellectual figure of some repute in the south-west and Tennyson said of one epic poem: 'Hawker has beaten me on my own ground.'

The Church of England's rural vicars in the nineteenth century famously fell into three categories: those who had gone out of their minds, those who were about to go out of their minds and those who had no minds to go out of. One West Country vicar did not enter his church for fifty-three years and kennelled the local foxhounds in his vicarage; another replaced his congregations with wooden silhouettes and swaddled his vicarage in barbed wire. Next to these, Hawker's idiosyncrasies appeared harmless albeit rather calculated showmanship. He was famously particular and used a swan's quill for writing, Latakia tobacco for his pipe and insisted on prohibitively expensive oak shingles for his church roof when local slate would have been far more suitable. His attire was especially arresting: he wore fishermen's jerseys with Christ's spear wound stitched into the pattern underneath a yellow poncho, a claret-coloured coat and a brimless purple hat in the style of the Eastern Orthodox church. He hated beards, loved cream (although the story that he lived off clotted cream is another fiction) and adored cats. He kept two deer, Robin Hood and Maid Marian, and was accompanied on his parish rounds by Gyp, a black Berkshire pig. When his sister objected to Gyp coming into her house, Hawker replied: 'He's as well-behaved as any of your family.'

Partly because of this flamboyance, and much to the frustration of Hawker, who was desperate for his verse to earn the acclaim enjoyed by, say, Tennyson, the Vicar of Morwenstow became best known as 'a kind of marine undertaker', as Jeremy Seal puts it in his exploration of the vicar's coastal adventures. The coast of North Cornwall was a magnet for shipwrecks: eighty-one around Bude between 1824 and

1874. If not deliberately wrecking ships, coastal residents were happy to strip the wrecks, and their victims, of all valuables. Charles Kingsley, a great promoter of the north coast of Devon and Cornwall, described its people as 'wild folk . . . and merciless to wrecked vessels which they consider as their own by immemorial usage, or rather right divine'. Hawker vigorously campaigned against heartless local attitudes to wrecked ships and made it his duty to bury the often anonymous sailors who were washed ashore. He was not shy about publicising his work and his magazine stories dramatised himself as 'the resourceful spiritual suzerain who performed his grisly duties with compassion and calmness', according to his biographer Piers Brendon.

The fame acquired by Hawker's sensational accounts of shipwrecks and his determination to give their tragic victims a Christian burial probably explained why the beautifully proportioned Church of St Morwenna and John the Baptist felt like a shrine to the cult of Robert Stephen Hawker. By the door was a sepia photograph of the ageing vicar signed, 'Yours affectionately, R S Hawker'. Fixed high on the wall of the northern aisle was the salvaged figurehead of the *Caledonia*, the wreck that made Hawker's name. The dull grey light spilling onto the south aisle came through a stained-glass window featuring illustrations including the *Caledonia*'s figurehead and the historic wooden lychgate to the churchyard and the dedication: 'To the greater glory of God and in memory of Robert Stephen Hawker, priest, forty years vicar of this parish'. There was a rood erected in his memory in 1934. Hawker's thirst for immortality would have been slaked by such memorials and by the preservation of his own touches inside the church: an engraved wooden box on the ornately carved pews read 'Hawker's Alms Box' while a large tombstone marked the resting place of Charlotte, with the inscription facing the pulpit so the vicar could glance down at the words remembering Hawker's first wife as he gave a sermon. That just one of Morwenstow's many vicars loomed so large in the mostly medieval church was, in many respects, rather fitting for despite his typically Victorian megalomania, he was a far more devoted and energetic parish priest than other literary vicars such as R. S. Thomas. Hawker extensively renovated his rectory and church, established a school in the parish and funded the building of a road bridge to better link Morwenstow with the outside world. He is also credited with establishing the Christian tradition of the harvest festival by creating a special thanksgiving service each September. He said Matins and Evensong in his church every weekday. Often, the only person in the church was his wife; more often, he was alone.

The church was a fine memorial to Hawker but, for me, it deepened the conundrum surrounding the vicar of Morwenstow. The most common adjective in the visitors' book was 'peaceful' and yet Hawker was a noisy man with a turbulent life. Why did someone who apparently spent his whole life pursuing attention and craving fame choose to live in the remotest spot in southern England? Was his apparently illogical attachment to this spot because the coast here bolstered his faith in God?

To find an answer, I jumped the stone stile in the churchyard, crossed three paddocks where swallows swooped low in the mizzle, turned south along the coast path and followed the sign to the National Trust's smallest coastal property: Hawker's Hut. Between priestly duties, the vicar built a series of huts along the cliffs from driftwood he salvaged from the beaches. (Having attempted to reach the shore via a vertiginous path that ended in a vertical drop with a thin rope for guidance, I saw that this alone was quite a feat.)

The one surviving hut was about 5ft long and 4ft wide, and was invisible from above, set into the side of the cliff facing the ocean with a flowery, turf roof. It had no windows but a wooden stable door gave views west over the ocean. Rain was beginning in earnest, no one was around and the door was open: I stepped inside and found myself in Hawker's real church.

The hut's floor was stone flags and its walls were made of irregular, faded planks of rough wood. The roof was supported by sturdy beams featuring holes and worn wooden pegs suggestive of an older, maritime purpose. A narrow bench lined the walls, which acted as an extremely comfortable backrest because they sloped outwards. The rear wall of the hut was curved too, a pleasing touch which was redolent of the ships from where its raw materials came.

I latched the bottom half of the door and took Hawker's position, gazing at the TV-sized picture created by the frame of the upper half of the door. Half this frame was salt-and-pepper sky, one quarter was sea and one quarter was the waving of flowering grasses from the cliff outside. There was nothing on the water – Lundy, previously visible to the north like a spectacular Iron Age fort in the middle of the ocean, was out of sight around the corner. Suddenly, a gannet. Its solo flight, low over the green-grey water, only added to the loneliness of the scene. Despite its emptiness, this small portion of empty sea consumed my attention: it possessed the charisma of a giant being, a pulsing, brooding, shifting, calming, unsettling, reliable and utterly unreliable presence.

Most simply, the time Hawker spent in his hut stimulated his imagination and inspired his writing. Perhaps the changeability of the sea influenced his rather fluid approach to truth as well. When the *Caledonia* was wrecked in 1842, Hawker wrote how 'a mangled seaman's heart' was discovered on the beach. Unrecognisable lumps of human flesh, known locally as 'gobbets', were collected in baskets. After a wreck of 1859, five of seven corpses buried by Hawker 'had no Heads – cut off by jagged rocks!!' as he recorded in rather sensational essays he submitted to London magazines. When a body was found under a heavy boulder, Hawker claimed an engineer from the Bude Canal hoisted the rock in iron chains to allow the corpse to be pulled free, 'the altered, ghastly, flattened semblance of a man!'

These picaresque details were mostly invented. The writer Jeremy Seal shows that a substantial part of the vicar's account of the 1842 wreck of the *Caledonia* was a spectacular fiction. According to Hawker, the 200-ton brig was wrecked en route to Gloucester because it encountered a hurricane for which the captain had no warning after the cabin boy broke the barometer. After searching the rocks below Morwenstow, Hawker and his helpers found the captain's body still grasping bags containing his pistols and his brass logs (which supposedly demonstrated the captain's dying dedication to his job). Another seven corpses were washed up and promptly buried by Hawker who also discovered the sole survivor, a Jerseyman called Edward Le Dain. 'As he saw me leaning over him in my cassock-shaped dressing-gown, he sobbed, with a piteous cry, "Oh mon pere, mon pere!"' wrote Hawker, who said he looked after Le Dain for six weeks. Afterwards, the sailor was so grateful he gave the vicar the best Jersey cow he could find. Most implausibly of all, Hawker claimed that Le Dain named his first son after the vicar and lived to survive being wrecked on two further occasions.

In fact, there are only five bodies from the *Caledonia* buried in Morwenstow's valley-side churchyard, not eight as Hawker claimed. Le Dain was not found by the vicar but by a young man called John Adams, who later became a clergyman-poet like Hawker. Adams took Le Dain to his father's house in a nearby village, where he was nursed for several weeks before being befriended by Hawker. Le Dain never mentioned any broken barometer and the captain clutching his pistols was surely another of the vicar's imaginative flourishes. The most remarkable details were true, however: Le Dain christened his first son Edward Robert Hawker Le Dain and the lucky Jersey sailor really did survive two further shipwrecks.

I sat in Hawker's Hut and watched the ocean. From this height, the sea looked flat and solid but it was constantly changing. Little humps of dark green appeared and disappeared like imaginary dolphins. I couldn't hear the sound of individual waves breaking on the jutting slabs of granite that formed Upper Sharpnose Point, just an indefatigable low roar. It was not a day for those perfectly formed Atlantic rollers but the sea still bore a sense of arriving from afar, tempting us to follow it on an adventure. Despite this enticement, Hawker almost never left Cornwall. Perhaps he was scared. Perhaps he enjoyed being a relatively big fish in a small pond. It seems perverse that he cleaved so completely to Morwenstow when he hunched in his hut and complained he was 'as lonely as Lundy' in the winter months, portraying himself as an isolated martyr on a Godless promontory. 'Human nature is bad, English nature is worse but Morwenstow nature is vilest of all,' he wrote. Local barbarities included two children dying of starvation after they were driven from their home by their mother to collect firewood, and a man leading his wife to market by halter to sell her to the highest bidder. Hawker also feared that extramarital sex, 'the leprosy of England', was particularly prevalent in his parish.

R. S. Hawker's profound cultural isolation was identical to that felt by another R. S., Thomas, in West Wales a century later. And for all the hellfire he cast upon his backward parish, like Thomas, Hawker had sought it out, desperate to escape Victorian England which he viewed as 'a sea-girt charnel-house of crime'. His rejection of the mores of his age was acutely representative of it, for Hawker's nostalgia for a medieval past was very much part of the Victorian Gothic revival. The ocean inspired Hawker and reinforced his faith. He saw God in the sea. Its majesty belittled industrialism, utilitarianism and positivism, 'the ephemeral creeds of nineteenth-century man', in the words of his biographer Piers Brendon. The waves never ceased their work and the ocean, particularly from this bleak cliff, appeared everlasting and omnipotent. The violence of the sea also thrilled Robert Hawker but perhaps its relentlessness, which he experienced daily, was an indispensable sedative for this restless, highly strung man.

As he grew older, however, his own contradictions drove him to the edge of madness. He had sought to escape society but craved to be a celebrity within it and decried the fact that he would be remembered as a 'ballad monger' (for *The Song of the Western Men*) when he 'rescued with his own hands some at his cost all 33 corpses from the sea and laid them to rest'. He became increasingly vitriolic about the world of publishing, fantasised he was betrayed and picked quarrels with friends or denounced them in the most intemperate terms. His lack of money became an obsessive refrain despite his own tendency to be 'unscrupulous, if not downright dishonest, in money matters', according to Piers Brendon.

Robert Hawker believed in ghosts and saw a demon on one stormy ride by the sea. So it was probably a bad idea to begin taking opium. The drug became his dark secret. 'It violently excited him for a while,' wrote his brother, Claud, 'and then cast him into fits of the most profound depression. When under this influence he wrote and spoke in the wildest and most unreasonable manner.' According to Claud, he became addicted after the death of his dear wife in 1863 but he had posted morphine tablets to his friend Mrs Watson in 1857, so he probably began using the drug far earlier. During the six weeks of Charlotte's final illness, Hawker claimed he did not go to bed at all. Later in 1863, in grief, and almost certainly high, he wrote *The Quest of the Sangraal*, which critics consider his greatest poetic achievement.

For all his torment and paranoia, Hawker could still raise good cheer and, eighteen months after Charlotte's death, he was compelled to take his second ever train journey to London in an act of persuasion, to win round the mother of Pauline Kuczynski, a twenty-year-old governess. Pauline's mother forbade her marriage to a man forty-two years her senior but the charismatic vicar prevailed, and Kuczynski made her home in Morwenstow too. As implausible as his first marriage to Charlotte, it appeared a genuine love-match, although Pauline noted her husband was subject to 'the most absurd delusions'.

They had three daughters but Hawker's troubles returned: part of his church roof collapsed while he was preaching, the countryside was afflicted by potato blight and the taxman came calling. Around 1870, Hawker's opium addiction reasserted itself with a vengeance. 'What a life mine would be if it were all written and published in a book,' Hawker once said. He would be gratified to know his strange life by the sea has been the subject of three biographies, numerous studies, an appreciation society, a website and plenty of quiet pilgrimages.

His poetry has not weathered particularly well, but the one thing that Hawker created without any self-conscious eye on posterity has survived: his hut. In the years since Hawker, thousands of people have followed him here to contemplate the ocean. As some sat and watched, they chiselled memorials of their own into the wood: initials, dates, hearts. 1927, 1961, 1983, 1998. DJAK HAWKER. Kernow. Cat + Mouse 2012. There was something childlike about Hawker and the hut took me back to childhood dens, a comforting nest, a feeling of simplicity and safety, in the presence of an infinite power that the Atlantic Ocean so powerfully represented. Hawker's Hut was the perfect memorial to this strange, contrary Victorian, the great loyalty he showed Morwenstow and the faith, inspiration and comfort that sustained him for so long in such a lonely place.

The place on the Welsh coast to which more people have undertaken a religious pilgrimage than any other is the sacred island of Bardsey, resting place of 20,000 saints, off the western tip of the Llŷn Peninsula. It was not on Bardsey itself but at the very end of the Llŷn where R. S. Thomas, who chronicled his own search for God in his poetry, experienced the only mystical encounter of his life. Birdwatching 'became his form of prayer', R.S.'s friend Ronald Blythe told me, and Thomas wrote of the day he was walking, looking at birds, when he came to a clump of bare trees that he had never explored before. Stepping inside, he found it alive with goldcrests. 'The air purred with their small wings. To look up was to see the twigs re-leafed with their small bodies. Everywhere their needle-sharp cries stitched at the silence,' he wrote. Had he stretched out an arm, they might have perched on it. 'I became a tree, part of that bare spinney where silently the light was splintered, and for a timeless moment the birds thronged me, filigreeing me with shadow.' When suddenly they were gone, his sense of self reappeared. 'Where had I been? Who was I? What did it all mean?'

I think I know what he felt: many of us may occasionally experience something similar, although perhaps we couldn't describe it so eloquently, when we are alone in nature, and fleetingly feel at one with it. R. S. Thomas was fascinated by the idea that creation occurred during this momentary abandonment of self. He agreed with Coleridge: 'The nearest we can approach to God, he appears to say, is as creative beings,' wrote Thomas.

Many of Thomas's later poems pondered God's absence but the coast around him – the sea was his 'ever-present background', he wrote – gave him ways to contemplate his faith, even though it did not always offer meditative tranquillity. 'Beneath that smiling surface, what horrors!' he wrote. 'And as if conscious of the grotesques within it, the sea would sometimes become wildly agitated.' But occasionally, it seemed that its waves provided comfort. In *The Echoes Return Slow*, published in 1988 when he lived in his cottage by the ocean, he described lying awake on a still night, listening

*to the swell born somewhere in the Atlantic*
*rising and falling, rising and falling*
*wave on wave on the long shore*
*by the village, that is without light*
*and companionless. And the thought comes*
*of that other being who is awake, too,*
*letting our prayers break on him*

*not like this for a few hours*
*but for days, years, for eternity*

Some months after my visit to the Farnes, I drove north again to explore England's most holy island. For southerners, Lindisfarne has an arrival to die for: its castle clinging to a pinnacle of rock is visible from 15 miles away on the Great North Road. A tidal island, its causeway across the sands is only accessible for a few hours around low tide. An ugly dot-matrix sign gave crossing times and then the road bumped down onto the beach. TURN HERE IF TIDE COVERS CAUSEWAY, said one forbidding sign. DO NOT PROCEED IF TIDE COVERS CAUSEWAY, said another. The causeway was covered by a thin layer of water and sand blown across it by a scudding north-westerly. An elderly lady in a VW Polo barrelled through the spray ahead and, reassured, I drove on. Cars are ridiculous things away from a tarmac road and my vehicle soon surfed into a small wave which turned the steering to jelly. In the middle of an expanse of beach, the vehicle was buffeted by the wind; skiddy patches of green seaweed were unnerving as well. But the old lady ahead made it across and so did I, relieved to bump onto a normal road snaking around the sheltered south side of the island's dunes.

The castle high on its rock is the physical symbol of Lindisfarne but has little relevance to its religious history. Smaller than it looks from afar, the building, which was brilliantly refurbished by Edwin Lutyens as a holiday home for Edward Hudson, the founder of *Country Life*, was today plaguing the National Trust with its draughts and damp. 'We should be flying a union flag here,' said Roger Carr-Whitworth, the Trust's curator in the region, when I stumbled upon his assessment of the way the castle could be damp-proofed with due sensitivity to its design. I guessed Roger was one of the Trust's 'lillies' for he had a finely honed aesthetic sensibility: he was appalled when he visited five years previously and found that the castle flew a National Trust flag.

'It's not because I'm a fanatical Unionist. A castle like this needs a flag, and it doesn't need a National Trust flag.' I admired his passion and attention to detail.

Later, lingering by Lindisfarne's ruined priory, I discovered that the historian Kate Tristram, who had written so vividly about the interior lives of St Aidan and St Cuthbert, still lived on the island. The directions a friendly local gave me to her house – past the Post Office, right by the school, down the lane – sounded like quite a trek but, in the manner of small islands, it turned out to be no distance at all. I knocked, an unannounced stranger, and Kate welcomed me in, sitting in a plain rocking chair in a living room well heated by an electric fire that pretended to burn coal. She was a small, neat, smartly dressed woman, with white hair and earrings. She came to Lindisfarne in 1978 to run Marygate House, a Christian retreat, and was warden for twenty years. 'I didn't come here to be ordained,' she began. I had imagined she was simply a historian but she was a practising priest as well. When the vicar of Lindisfarne asked if she would consider becoming a deaconness, she agreed, and later became a deacon (able to conduct marriage ceremonies) and then a priest when the Church of England allowed it. At seventy, everyone must retire from office but Kate has continued as an 'associate priest'. Lindisfarne is a busy parish and St Mary's is a busy church, holding three services every day for congregations of visitors who come to the island laden with spiritual hopes and expectations. As well as the vicar and Kate, there are also two Anglican clergymen who have settled on the island and help out; two Readers, who take services; and three eucharistic ministers who can administer Holy Communion in people's homes: an embarrassment of ecclesiastical riches on an island with a population of 160.

Kate was born almost as far from the sea as it is possible to get, near Stourbridge in the Midlands. She was eight when war broke out, which stopped seaside holidays, and so she didn't see the ocean from seven to fifteen. When she was at school, the British navy was the biggest in the world. They sang patriotic songs, unthinkable now, while her home 'got every bomb that missed Birmingham'. And then she said an unusual thing. 'I never cared for the sea. It wasn't part of my natural childhood. I never thought I would settle by the sea. I never wanted to retire to a seaside place. To find myself living in the sea was a bit of a surprise.' So what happened?

She read history at Oxford after the war, took a Masters in medieval language and studied the two languages of Lindisfarne: medieval Latin and old Irish, 'the most difficult language I've ever had to learn'. Before she took the job on the island, she had visited several times and admired the vicar of the day, Denis Bill. 'I'm sure he was the man who brought the island alive spiritually, because it had gone,' she said. Denis walked around the village, getting to know the locals, and his wife became the island's popular nurse, which helped. He would pray in the church after rising at 2 a.m. in the summer, he started three daily services and founded the retreat centre, Marygate House. 'I wouldn't call him a saint because he would hate it but he was a man with strong spiritual sensibilities,' said Kate. 'Sometimes he felt the whole church vibrate with what he called presence. He didn't call it God or the saints, he called it presence. Things that were there. I was interested in that.'

Kate radiated a deep sense of calm that came, I guessed, both from her faith, and also from being able to place our lives within a sense of the centuries that have passed before. She wore this wisdom gently and was as witty and sensible as her writing. In her history of Holy Island, she described how other guidebooks claimed that ghosts of Lindisfarne monks were 'often' seen fleeing from the Vikings and the ghost of St Cuthbert was 'often' encountered in the priory ruins. In more than thirty-five years on the island, she had never heard of any such sighting.

There was, however, another reason she came to live on the island

and she told me about an experience she had when visiting one Saturday afternoon. 'I was just walking through the village and suddenly I felt spoken to. I didn't hear a voice – I'm not into hearing voices – but I felt addressed. The feeling was so strong that I stopped dead in my tracks and said, "Oh". Words formed in my head that said, "We are alive, you know, you can talk to us if you want to." That's the most dramatic experience I've had. I've never heard anything again. I wasn't hearing with my ears but I was picking up a message which was in the airwaves. That was one reason I wanted to come here permanently. People said, "Don't tell anyone, they will say you're going mad."'

Kate, like Aidan long before her, appreciated the way the tides were like a door opening and closing on Lindisfarne. When she was the warden of Marygate, prospective visitors would phone and inquire about the road onto the island. The visitors became quite indignant when she pointed out when they would be able to arrive and when they wouldn't. If she told them they could leave on the Sunday between 1 p.m. and 5 p.m., for instance, they would say, 'Oh, that won't suit us at all,' as if Kate could change the arrangements. 'We are powerless, you see,' she said. 'I've no doubt that something in Aidan responded to the pattern of the tides as an expression of the comparative weakness of human beings. It imposes a natural check on human pride. Why do so many people get stuck on the causeway? It's because human beings don't believe that anything can get in between where they are and where they want to be.' I didn't tell her about my own close encounter with the causeway.

I got a sense of where visitors hoped to be on Lindisfarne when I stepped into St Mary's Church, its beautiful stained-glass windows and unplastered rough stone walls giving it a Celtic demeanour. Its visitors' book was unusually ecstatic. 'Wonderful peaceful place.' 'We are privileged to be here at Lindisfarne.' 'At one, at peace with the LORD, such a special place for us.'

I wondered about the pressure of great expectations. 'We do get a lot of people who are seeking,' said Kate. 'Some people say it's got a special atmosphere and that's all they will say but a lot who come are used to Christian language and they will say they are looking for inspiration from the saints or for God to become more real to them.' Kate called it spiritual presence. 'In one way or another they come here to pray for clear answers. They may feel that God is more available here. He isn't, but if this is what people pick up, let them use it. If they find God here, let them come and take away whatever they take away from the place. People like Aidan and Cuthbert and many more loved and cared about the island. Aidan wasn't handed it. He chose it. If it turns out when I'm out of this world that God used people so that human beings could continue coming to Lindisfarne and feeling closer to him, I shouldn't find that surprising.'

Kate accepted that there were contrasting reactions to Lindisfarne too. 'Some people hate it. They will not come through our church door because they don't like the feeling that something is grabbing at them. Our parish church is a beautiful little building in itself but there are people who prefer to sit on the tombstones and hold the family dog even though we welcome the family dog inside the church.'

When I left St Mary's, there was a family dog sitting in the graveyard but no dissenters lurked by it; its owners were savouring the calm stillness and old stone inside.

Kate had resolved her 'quarrel' with the sea. 'I'm friends with it now. There is something in us that still responds to the rhythm of the waves. People can get very peaceful by sitting on the shore and watching wave after wave break. If we find a place where we can see a good stretch of the horizon, the sheer vastness of it, whatever our own troubles are, they become smaller if we see the wide open sea and the eternal tide breaking on the eternal rocks. People do find a spiritual message in that.'

## Explorations of Neptune

The **Farne Islands** are simple to explore: turn up at Seahouses harbour, hope the sea isn't too rough and book a tour on one of the many local boats offering official half-day tours. Most of the islands are bird reserves and closed to the public but Inner Farne is open and there are also trips to Staple Island. Check online for seasonal opening times. Tours do sell out in the summer. A short drive north lies **Lindisfarne, or Holy Island**. If you are more adventurous and have more time than me you could walk on the St Cuthbert's Way, a long-distance footpath, onto the island via its causeway. Most people drive and, like all popular tourist destinations, most visitors (including me on my last trip) only spend time in a tiny portion – in this case, the southern tip of the island, wandering between the National Trust castle, the village and its priory and church. This means you can easily have the rest of the island to yourself. If you want to walk an easy circuit, park in the big visitor car park and walk the half-mile through the village to the castle. East of the castle you can pick up a path running up the east side of the island towards Emmanuel Head. This curves away towards the west along the back of the big, deserted northern dunes. You can turn south onto an arrow-straight, mile-long track leading back to the car park or continue west and follow a slightly longer path along the edge of the pasture, which rejoins the main road onto the island.

### OS Map

Ordnance Survey 340, Holy Island & Bamburgh

### Nearest railway station

Berwick-upon-Tweed, 10 miles (from the causeway)

### Websites

www.nationaltrust.org.uk/farne-islands/
www.nationaltrust.org.uk/lindisfarne-castle/

Like many remote parts of the Cornish coast, the busiest bit of

**Morwenstow** is the South West Coast Path. The 15-mile stretch south from Hartland Quay (just south of Hartland Point, arguably the remotest corner of southern England) to Bude is reputed to be the toughest of the entire 630-mile route, with tall, treacherous cliffs and vigorous ups-and-downs created by the path crossing ten steep valleys. One of those is home to St Morwenna's Well and, three fields inland, the elegant church of St Morwenna and St John the Baptist at Morwenstow. For those slogging along the coast path, a detour into the cool church (and the neighbouring teashop or pub a few hundred yards on at Crosstown) is an ideal lunch break. If you don't fancy the coast path, there are several pleasant circuits you can walk around Morwenstow.

This circular walk is less than two miles but feels longer because there is so much to see. Park on the green by Rectory Farm teashop, enter the churchyard by the lychgate. The church is a fascinating shrine to Victorian vicar Robert Hawker. If you walk to the east end of the churchyard, a public footpath runs down and along the side of the old rectory, rebuilt to Hawker's eccentric tastes (check out the chimney pots). Follow this path into the wooded valley bottom and then turn left across pasture on a footpath towards the sea. This climbs and joins the South West Coast Path, on which you turn left (or south) as it descends to the well of St Morwenna. Follow the coast path up out of the valley and almost at the end of the second field you cross you'll see a sign to Hawker's Hut, which is tucked out of sight on the edge of the cliff. Beyond Hawker's Hut to the south are the treacherous reefs of Higher Sharpnose Point. As the coast path descends again, it was possible when I visited in 2014 to take a tiny footpath down to the black beach but this involves a dangerously steep scramble and a roped section and so is only for the very intrepid. Otherwise, just beyond Hawker's Hut, a footpath runs inland along the southern side of the field boundary and into the pretty village green of Crosstown, where the pub awaits.

**OS Map**
Explorer 126, Clovelly & Hartland
*Nearest railway station*
Barnstaple, 29 miles
*Websites*
www.southwestcoastpath.com
www.nationaltrust.org.uk

## Further Reading

Piers Brendon, *Hawker of Morwenstow: Portrait of a Victorian Eccentric*,
    Jonathan Cape, 1975
Kate Tristram, *The Story of Holy Island*, Canterbury Press, 2009

# 10

# The Shores of the Future

*Northey / Cemlyn / Northern Ireland*

The oldest official battle site in Britain, where the Essex men of Earl Byrhtnoth met the marauding Vikings in 991, is a gently sloping field beyond the cowsheds of South House Farm. When I walked there in sunny late February, the only sign of conflict was two hares eyeballing each other, not yet mad enough to begin their duel. I had no sense of the impending sea as I traced its edge towards Northey, a triangular-shaped island of 300 hectares in the Blackwater Estuary. Maldon, famed for its sea salt, was sensibly high on its hill to the north-west and the surrounding farmland did not appear particularly low-lying, even as ditches of reeds rattled in the wind. Then the lane rose to a grassy bank and I got a shock: the salt marsh on the other side was higher than the pasture I'd just walked through. The land was more vulnerable than it first appeared.

Northey is famed as a place of retreat – from the waves and from invading armies. The 3,000 Vikings who landed here were initially barred from crossing the causeway to the mainland by a local militia led by Byrhtnoth, a Saxon in his sixties. Shouting across the tidal channel, the Danes promised to sail away if paid in gold and armour. According to the fragmentary Anglo-Saxon poem that commemorates the battle, Byrhtnoth ('bright courage' in Old English) replied: 'We will pay you with spear tips and sword blades.' Just three of Byrhtnoth's men could defend the causeway across the channel because it was so narrow but the earl rather chivalrously drew back to allow the Vikings onto the mainland so the two armies could meet and fight. Interpretations of the poem vary: Byrhtnoth showed either overbearing pride not to pay off the Vikings, or the implacable courage of an earl with a peasant army who fought against the odds to his death. Either way, he was hacked to bits on the battlefield and the king, Aelthelred the Unready, paid 3,300kg of silver to buy off the Viking forces, the first – but not last – instance of Danegeld in Britain.

More than a thousand years on, we are engaged in an expensive new battle with the sea. We are also still fighting among ourselves, debating whether we should draw back from Northey and other places besieged by salt water. This fight can be cast in both interpretations of Byrhtnoth's battle: as a courageous crusade against the odds, or haughty human folly. Northey today is notable not just for Byrhtnoth's retreat but for our drawing back from the sea. In 1991 it became the first piece of British coast to undergo 'managed realignment' – where we removed sea defences and let the waves in. The coast is changing before our eyes, and so is our relationship with it. A desire to defend it at all costs is shifting with the shores.

A causeway lay ahead, a deceptively simple track snaking across tidal flats for 250 metres to the island, a low lump of green pasture and a wiggly line of telegraph poles. Stern notices warned of access by permit only which entailed a phone call to the local Trust office, which I had made, and I now strolled onto one of Britain's forty-three unbridged tidal islands which can be walked to from the mainland. The causeway was covered in slippery green seaweed; the mud on either side, the Essex coast's signature, was almost as incandescent as water, the colour of henna with patches of twinkly bronze. Blue sky and clouds turned sepia in its reflection. It was firm, the consistency of cheesecake, but when I pressed on it with my boot it felt I would never again reach solid ground. I'd heard that a ranger inspecting Northey's old sea bank recently sank up to his waist.

Northey was as enchanting as any island, the ordinary made strangely thrilling when bundled into a circular package and separated from the mainland by a sometime strip of water. I took a little lane twisting through a thicket of blackthorn, its bridal white flowers already in bloom, past a small chestnut whose sticky brown buds glistened in the sunshine. A group of twenty-five Brent geese glided overhead and landed on one of Northey's four grass fields with a late flurry of wingbeats. They joined a group of several hundred and I stopped and watched these plump birds with white rumps and necks of coal black in the brightness. Murmuring, they walked in a deliberate fashion, a line strung across the pasture like police conducting a fingertip search, plucking at the grass with their beaks. Northey was an internationally important overwintering site for 5,000 brent geese, and the Trust's tenant farmer moved his cattle off the fields to allow them to devour grass all winter.

The geese's four grass fields made up less than a quarter of the island. The rest was salt marsh. At the end of the lane, where the fields dipped down to the marsh, was a small farmhouse and an eccentric four-storey structure of dark wood surrounded by faux-medieval walls that was built in the 1930s by Norman Angell, a Nobel Peace Prize-winner and League of Nations activist (islands attract idealists). These two properties and the island itself had been donated to the Trust by Angell's descendants in 1978 and then, as was customary, the houses and farmland had been leased back to the family. The farmhouse was still a family residence, the wooden tower a holiday home with splendid views over the Blackwater Estuary.

In 1991 Northey became the testing ground for 'managed realignment'. Rather than shore up expensive and eroding hard sea defences, the Environment Agency, the government body responsible for all kinds of water management including flood defence, agreed an innovative approach with the National Trust to redraw a portion of Northey's coastline. The sea would be allowed into pasture and a new sea wall would be built further inland. First called 'set-back', then 'managed retreat' and now 'managed realignment', this concept has been cherished by academics for several decades but the phrase incurs the suspicions of many coastal residents: giving up land to the sea sounds like giving up. If people's homes are at risk, realignment becomes particularly controversial. As so often on islands, Northey's experience was a microcosm of a bigger problem that will be played out along our eroding coastline for decades to come.

Holland, which depends on its sea defences for its survival as a nation, has just 280 miles to protect. The British coastline stretches for an indefensible 10,800 miles, although most of this is rocky Scottish coast untroubled by erosion. According to one academic measurement, 28 per cent of the 2,300-mile coast of England and Wales is disintegrating by more than 10 centimetres each year. For all the contemporary concerns about climate change, increased storminess and rising sea levels, much of our coastal loss is caused by natural geological processes and for centuries we have successfully turned back the tide by fortifying our shores ferociously: 45.6 per cent of England's coast is buttressed by sea walls, groins or artificial beaches, compared with just 7.6 per cent of Ireland.

England's east coast is young, mostly taking shape 8,000 years ago after the last Ice Age. Geologists say it is still adjusting to the present sea level. The Holderness coast in the East Riding of Yorkshire has retreated by nearly three miles over the last 2,000 years. The release of the great weight of the ice sheets at the end of the last Ice Age caused a 'springboard' effect which is still pushing up Scotland and Northern Ireland relative to sea level while southern Britain sinks at a rate generally estimated to be 1 millimetre each year. Since the beginning of the twentieth century, scientists have also recorded a 19-centimetre rise in mean sea level, raising the prospect of coastal flooding.

Scientists fear that climate change will exacerbate these trends. In 2013 the Intergovernmental Panel on Climate Change increased its projections for sea level rise. Some sensible-sounding climate scientists predict a global rise of 0.7–1.2 metres by 2100. Nearly a million homes in England and Wales could be at significant risk of tidal flooding by the 2080s. Increased frequency and velocity of storms may exacerbate erosion, and the violent storms over the winter of 2013/14 certainly focused minds on the problem of coastal protection.

In December 2013 a storm surge along the east coast pushed the tide higher than the great storm of 1953 when 307 people lost their lives in England. This time, although homes fell off the dunes at Hemsby in Norfolk, there were no fatalities and far less flooding, largely because of hard defences erected after the 1953 floods. In January and February 2014 the coasts of south-west England and Wales bore the brunt of storms that reduced Isambard Kingdom Brunel's marvellous railway line to something like a rope bridge where it snakes around the cliffs at Dawlish. Homes, beachside cafes, promenades and sea walls were destroyed and so were natural features we might assume to be immutable – the rock arch at Porthcothan Bay, Cornwall, and the great stack of rock on the south side of Portland, in Dorset.

As a species, we struggle to accept demonstrations of our own powerlessness and take time to adjust to changes in a landscape we imagine is dependably permanent. When I descended the dunes to my local beach, Wells-next-the-Sea, in Norfolk, after the storm of 2013, I couldn't comprehend what I saw. I expected the beach huts to be smashed up, and some were, but there was a void on the horizon where the outermost sand dune had always stood tall. I had played on its marram top as a boy; it was where I proposed marriage; and now it was gone. I felt disconsolate and turned away, wishing the beach of my memory could return.

Denial is a natural human reaction and it defined the government's response to these storms. Ministers at first pledged to repair all damage and insisted that everything would be defended against flood water and sea water, and there were no hard choices to make. 'We have got to force the sea back and keep it out,' cried one Conservative backbencher in Parliament, 'not retreat from it like we have been for years.' The government's approach was clear: patch up and protect, or 'hold the line' in the jargon of the shoreline management plans which define how the authorities defend our coast. As long as we remain a relatively wealthy nation, this is justifiable and sensible in some areas. London, for instance, is terribly vulnerable to rising seas but will be protected by the Thames Barrier and its successors until the apocalypse. In the north, more than 300,000 people and some £7 billion of assets currently reside on low-lying land around the Humber Estuary so it makes sense to protect it with 146 miles of flood banks.

Follow the logic of traditional sea defence and we would swaddle the coast in concrete. If we don't defend everywhere, however, we make some spots more vulnerable by blocking erosion which would naturally spread deposits of sand or shingle along our shores. Protecting seaside towns makes less developed areas more fragile and there are fewer financial imperatives to justify expensive defences on the Neptune coast.

There is also a growing awareness that hard defences are not as effective as they first appear: scientific studies show a dramatic lowering of beaches in front of them. Sand dunes will naturally roll landwards and re-form, unless they are constrained by defences, which cause them to rapidly erode. Similarly, salt marshes, superb at dissipating wave energy and preventing erosion, quickly disappear if constrained by sea defences. And once sand or shingle is washed away, it is often gone for good. Managed realignment does result in increased local erosion but that may benefit other sections of the coast, slowing the crumbling of the coast or allowing the accretion of sand and shingle elsewhere.

I saw a vivid illustration of the futility of conventional sea defences at Orford Ness. The peninsula is eroding by four metres each year, which is fast but still slower than other Suffolk edgelands such as the lost port of Dunwich. The sea in front of the Ness and the river behind want to turn the peninsula into an island by punching through the narrowing ridge of shingle that tenuously connects its north end to the mainland by Aldeburgh. It is inevitable that the Ness will eventually be surrounded by water; when this happens depends on us. Estuary and sea are only 30 metres apart in places, separated by low marsh and the naturally formed shingle bank. Here, immediately beyond where decaying concrete, wood and rock sea defences ended, spring storms almost swept through the shingle ridge in 2013. The Environment Agency repaired this breach with shingle that summer, but by December the sea had pulled the bank apart again. Using a bulldozer to create a shingle ridge is not as effective as a naturally formed bank because it lacks the very fine particles which form an impermeable cement within a natural ridge. But the Environment Agency's policy is to protect the Ness for the next quarter-century unless such repairs are judged unsustainable, so their engineers once more poured shingle into the breach in January 2014. A month later, the ridge required repair again after another storm. This was a perfect example of what Phil Dyke, the National Trust's coast and marine adviser I had met on the Carrick Roads, called the 'sea defence cycle': construct, fail, reconstruct. When do we decide this kind of defence is unsustainable?

Coastal change is a challenge for anyone who lives by the sea. For someone owning 742 miles of coast, it is particularly vexatious. Phil Dyke explained to me how the charity once fortified its properties against the sea but over the past decade has embraced a radical programme of adapting to coastal change, in consultation with local people. 'Are we just going to be applying more sticking plasters on things that will pull off again and again?' he asked. 'Or are we going to take a proper look at vulnerable places and think about rollback, adaptation and realignment, and allow the undeveloped parts of the coast to function more naturally?' Phil argued that recreating a naturally functioning shoreline would free us from that expensive 'sea defence cycle'. As well as the cost, the Trust was also instinctively opposed to most conventional defences on aesthetic and environmental grounds: they are ugly, intrusive and destroy fragile and valuable coastal ecosystems.

In places such as Orford Ness, the ultimate decision whether to maintain expensive sea defences is taken by the Environment Agency. On parts of the Neptune coast, however, the National Trust is now responsible. The Environment Agency withdrew from the defence of Northey Island several years ago and left the Trust in charge of its decaying sea walls and difficult decisions about how, and for how long, they will be maintained.

Northey's managed realignment occurred on its southern flank. The Environment Agency removed a section of the sea bank, exposing two acres of pasture to the sea, but protected the rest of the island from incursions with a new bank inland. In two decades the sea had returned the exposed pasture to salt marsh: small creeks formed across the tawny grass and sturdy, oval-leaved sea purslane had established itself all over the field. Now the sea wanted more.

Along the road that hugged Northey's sheltered western side, a hairline fracture had appeared during the winter I visited, about 10cm wide, 50cm deep and 15m long. The blackthorn scrub that edged the road was falling onto the shore and dying where its roots touched salt water. A dirty white polystyrene coffee cup lay at the base of the hedge where a high tide had reached three weeks before.

I followed the old sea bank up the western edge of the island. Its northern salt marshes re-formed after an 1897 storm smashed up the old sea walls and caused the abandonment of most of Northey's grazing pasture. Old maps showed that Northey had been protected by banks before 1774 but the latest Ordnance Survey depicted a four-metre-high broken bank encircling half the island at best. The reality, in 2014, was far less. The remaining fragments of sea bank were barely two metres high and were dissolving before my eyes, great sods of earth collapsing onto the salt marsh below. I tried to reach the northern tip of the island but the bank had disintegrated, allowing the sea to open up a 100m-wide bay. As a hundred lapwings rose from the muddy edge of the Blackwater, I turned back, unable to go further on this disappearing salt marsh, one of the last true wildernesses of southern Britain.

Left alone, Northey would not exactly be abandoned to the sea, but it would slowly revert to its medieval state: salt marsh and summer grazing only. There were only two properties on Northey and local people held no traditional rights such as grazing or wildfowling on the island as happens on many other salt marshes. This was as simple as realignment got because there were so few people affected but a retreat from the sea was never straightforward. On Northey the National Trust had a moral duty to protect the family who still lived on the island and who had generously given it to them. Left to nature, the houses would probably become inaccessible by road shortly after this book's publication. Should the Trust spend money every year to protect the lane or build a new road over higher ground? Should it patch up existing sea walls or build a new one around the two houses, to safeguard them for another twenty or thirty or fifty years? How best could it protect the pastureland that nourished the overwintering geese? The Trust was supposed to guard inalienable land for the public, for ever, so why let any of this unique and beautiful island slip into the sea?

At first glance, Northey looked so solid but we derive a false sense of security from terra firma, geological time and the long lulls between extreme storms. A while ago, the Trust undertook consultations with the local community over the fate of Northey and people concluded it should be let go. Two years later, they checked again and residents said it should be defended. Phil Dyke had done his job for long enough to expect such a volte-face. At Mullion, a classic Cornish cove on the Lizard Peninsula, the landed gentry built a harbour in 1895 to import coal from South Wales. Its fine stonework became an effective sea wall and part of the beauty of the place, which attracts 150,000 visitors each year. But the harbour was never sustainable and is now besieged by the sea. The harbour is owned by the National Trust and, rather awkwardly, protects a few privately owned homes from the waves. In collaboration with the local community, the Trust devised a plan to maintain the harbour walls until 'catastrophic failure', at which point local people agreed that the Trust could roll back the harbour, rebuilding its arms at their next strongpoint. This strategy was agreed in 2007 and more than £1 million has been spent repairing the wall since, but there remains the problem of who defines 'catastrophic failure'? And since the agreement was reached, new residents have moved in while others have changed their minds. The Trust is finding that hard-won deals with local people over the shores of the future are as impermanent as dunes, cliffs and sea walls. Phil Dyke felt that violent storms like those of 2014 made us more realistic about what could be defended but only for a short while. 'People definitely get it straight after a storm and then you have collective memory loss,' he said. 'The further you are away from an extreme event you start to think, "Maybe we could build a defence."'

Seaside residents appreciate the peace-of-mind created by tangible defences. The current favourite is rock armour, hefty lumps of stone, usually imported from Norway, which are more effective at dissipating wave energy than solid concrete barriers and less unsightly. But there are even more environmentally friendly forms of protection too. Orford Ness coped with the 2013/14 storms better than expected because of nearly two miles of new ditches, alongside sluices and lagoons created by a €1 million wildlife project funded by the EU. This was designed to assist rare birds during droughts but, ironically, the measures also alleviated flooding. The effectiveness of such softer defences, making space for the sea by allowing once-defended arable land to become salt marsh, for instance, showed how managed realignment was not simply 'giving up' and leaving people defenceless against the mighty ocean.

Governments excel at crisis management and short-term fixes such as hard sea defences. Unfortunately they are far less effective when operating within geological timescales. Nudging voters towards an acceptance of coastal change requires cash for things other than conventional defences. Further along the vulnerable East Anglian coast from Northey, I visited one place that undertook a shift back from the sea with vanishingly rare financial assistance from the authorities. Happisburgh (pronounced 'Haysbrough') in Norfolk is famed for its rapidly eroding sandy cliffs which recently exposed 800,000-year-old footprints belonging to one of our ancestors. After a section of defunct sea defence was removed, Happisburgh lost more than 40 metres of land between 1998 and 2007. Several dozen properties disappeared; others were left dangerous and worthless.

Malcolm Kerby, a retired businessman, became a campaigner for thousands of seaside residents when the authorities removed the dilapidated wooden groynes which had protected Happisburgh for half-a-century. His efforts helped create the experimental Pathfinder scheme whereby the government offered £11 million for communities to 'adapt' to shifting shores. North Norfolk district council won a £3 million grant to help Happisburgh and the community devised a solution. Cliff-edge residents were offered planning rights to build a replacement home on the landward side of the village, and a small amount for their worthless homes. Or, they could sell this planning right to the council and receive almost 50 per cent of what their house would be worth were it not threatened with imminent collapse. In the end, nine affected families sold their planning rights to the council and their homes were removed from the collapsing cliffs. Derelict ground was tidied up and a new beachside car park was created, generating money for the village. More importantly, the council could now sell the planning rights it bought from the residents to developers and amass a contingency fund for Happisburgh's next adaptation to the sea. 'It's a sustainable model,' said Kerby: Happisburgh will continue to exist, slowly migrating inland, rather than being abandoned like the drowned villages all around our coast. During the storm surge of 2013, neighbouring communities lost homes and businesses but Happisburgh didn't make the news at all: it was now, in the favoured cliché of coastal engineers, resilient, although the one unfortunate cliff-top resident who refused to sell up lost her bungalow to the storm.

The Happisburgh solution would be too expensive for large coastal communities but it could help residents of smaller villages. Unfortunately, the scheme was only an experiment and Kerby believed the government was not in favour of developing it further because it came perilously close to looking like compensation. 'Every time we lose more coast, the success of Pathfinder is underlined but the government doesn't want it because it might cost them a shilling or two,' he said. 'It simply won't fund adaptation. In some cases, these communities desperately need assistance.'

We're inclined to regard coastal change as loss. The storms of 2013/14 stripped many Cornish coves of their sand and Phil Dyke feared that increased storminess could permanently turn much-loved sandy idylls into beaches of rock and stone. But he accepted that evolution was a perpetual feature of the coast. 'The character and ecology of the coast is driven by change,' he said. 'Most of the things that live on the coast need the erosion and the bare ground to flourish.' The handsome dunes of Sandscale Haws, a National Trust reserve on the Cumbrian coast, were recently judged to be too stable and thus in an unfavourable condition for pioneer plants and insects such as mining wasps which should thrive in such ecosystems. When I spoke to Phil after the storms, however, he said they had exposed new blowouts and lowered the front of the dunes, creating a better habitat for rare seaside species.

Even when landowners such as the National Trust accept coastal change and propose adaptations to it, they have found nature cutting across their best-laid plans. 'Suddenly what we thought would be difficult decisions to be made in ten or fifteen years' time are actually difficult decisions we are going to have to start making now,' said Phil Dyke. 'The luxury of time has been taken away from us.' At crumbling Birling Gap, East Sussex, the Trust refurbished a dilapidated hotel and turned it into a stylish cafe and education centre in the summer of 2013, very much with coastal erosion in mind. The modular clifftop building was designed to leapfrog over itself away from the cliffs in the coming decades. After the storms of 2014 caused seven years' worth of erosion in two months, the Trust had to make its first move backwards, dismantling its newly vertiginous sun lounge and ice-cream parlour.

The sea had moved more quickly than I expected on Northey too. During the course of my gentle meander around the island, the Blackwater stiffened its flow and an old black Thames barge that had been marooned in mud was suddenly surrounded by water. The causeway back to the mainland was supposedly above the tide until 3 p.m. but a blustery wind rose up and the sea raced in more quickly than tide-tables predicted. When I reached the causeway at 1.45 p.m., it was reduced to a narrow sliver of dark rocks, water swallowing it in the middle. I was cut off. I splashed across in a brisk trot just before the sea went over my boots.

As I looked back at the island from the safety of the mainland, I had a sudden sense that Northey would endure for a while yet. Salt marsh was the land's cleverest accommodation with the sea and the island would still be here, fraying at the edges, its eight-metre-high peak secure for decades to come. Its land was already perfectly adapted to its situation. What was increasingly untenable on Northey were its human elements – the road, the house, the blackthorn hedge, the pasture, the sea bank. When we discussed our country's vulnerability to climate change, we meant us. Human Northey would disappear within my lifetime.

Assuming we do not retreat to the relaxed planning regimes of the 1930s, the biggest coastal conservation challenge in the future will be marine preservation, for so long the Cinderella of the environmental movement. The visible landscape has been guarded far more effectively than what lies beneath the waterline. An awareness of a need to protect the biodiversity of the sea arrived in the mid-1960s, at the same time as Enterprise Neptune. Unfortunately, the National Trust's campaign to protect the coast has been virtually powerless to save sea and shore life because almost all land in Britain below the tideline is owned by the Crown Estate, whose vision has historically extended only as far as exploiting this resource – for gravel extraction, gas facilities and now for renewable energy. When I met marine biologist Sue Gubbay, she recalled a meeting with the head of the Crown Estate when she worked for the Marine Conservation Society, Britain's marine charity. She wanted to lease some land from them to protect it and was asked what she would do with it. 'Nothing,' she had said. The official looked puzzled. 'We can't lease you something you're going to do nothing with,' he replied.

A few years ago, the British government announced the creation of the biggest 'no take' zone in the world – in the Chagos Islands. In the vast waters around Britain, fishing is barred from just three square miles off Lundy. The government has been unwilling to confront the 'stakeholders' who oppose the protection of our land below the water. The concept of marine nature reserves was established in British law in 1981, but until 2013 Britain boasted a grand total of three Marine

Nature Reserves: Lundy, Skomer and Strangford Lough, less than 0.12 per cent of British territorial waters within the standard 12-mile limit. While the tiny 'no-take' zone off Lundy has been declared a resounding success by marine biologists monitoring the sea life there, I have described how all kinds of fancy conservation classifications failed to protect the seabed of Strangford. Fishing may be controlled within these reserves but it has not been barred, and nor is it prohibited in the twenty-seven Marine Conservation Zones belatedly established by the government in 2013. These cover 9,700 square kilometres in England, much of it adjacent to Neptune holdings, including Lyme Regis, Beachy Head, the Blackwater Estuary and Chesil Beach, but it is a fraction of the 127 zones recommended after an epic consultation process. Earlier discussions about marine conservation failed because of what the government called 'inadequate stakeholder consensus'. This timorous, bureaucratic phrase is the requiem for our age, declares Richard Girling in *Sea Change*, his impassioned book about the failure to protect sea life. Many conservationists believe the twenty-seven new zones have been created not where they are most needed but where they are most acceptable: in other words, where 'stakeholders' have fewest economic interests. Critics have called them 'paper parks' because they do not protect aquatic wildlife from fishing and other forms of exploitation. A proposal to have small 'no take' areas of 'scientific reference' was dropped by the authorities after vehement opposition from fishermen and others who eke a living from the coast. This frustrates marine biologists. 'You don't go picking flowers in a terrestrial reserve but somehow, because it's a "natural livelihood" for a few people, it is seen as acceptable to do so in the sea,' marine biologist Sue Gubbay told me.

For all the scientific evidence that 'no take' zones can benefit fishermen working around the areas by providing sanctuaries that become nurseries for shell fish, Gubbay felt that no amount of scientific pressure would create a successful marine conservation movement. 'It's not the science that's going to win it,' she said. 'These conservation areas will be created only if society really wants them. On land, society has accepted that it is worth having these refuges. There just isn't that recognition in the marine environment. There's no feeling that we've got anything like the National Trust for the sea.'

Although the Marine Conservation Zones in England, Wales and Northern Ireland left a lot to be desired, Bob Brown, the marine biologist who had devoted much of his career to attempting to save the seabed of Strangford Lough, felt that marine conservation was finally making real progress. Similar protected areas created around the Scottish coast had a far better scientific basis than the English, Welsh and Northern Irish zones, he said. 'The trouble is that all around our coast the seabed bears no resemblance to what it would've done three hundred years ago. It's completely changed.' Without a thriving seabed ecology, big fish cannot survive, just as deer or badgers would struggle if the English countryside was turned into desert in the space of a few generations. 'The fish brought in by fishermen are tiddlers. We are getting less and less fish for more and more effort, and more and more damage is being caused. There are no seabed areas that can truly be described as pristine any more.'

By far the most unstable element within the coastal environment is man, and it is impossible to predict how we will develop or imperil it fifty years from now. The campaigners who launched Enterprise Neptune in 1965 were not unduly concerned about marine conservation or coastal erosion but were terrified that the coast would be strangled by shacks. The biggest human development over the last fifty years, however, and the one likely to make the biggest impact on our coast in the next fifty, is derived from our hunger for energy. The 1960s was the era of nuclear power, and saw the construction of industrial behemoths which dominate the seaside for miles in Suffolk, Kent, Cumbria, Somerset and Lancashire. While most of the early nuclear power stations are entering the final years of their productive life, there are proposals for a new generation. Power stations – nuclear and now wind and tidal – are the biggest construction projects on our shores today.

Like any industrial development, nuclear plants offer jobs that impoverished coastal communities dependent on seasonal tourism often crave. The 72,000 hectares of Anglesey contained 70,000 people. 'We keep losing our youngsters and getting in retired people,' said Bryn Thomas, the witty, Welsh-speaking National Trust ranger who took me on a tour of the island. 'It's a poor state of affairs from an economic point of view if you're heavily dependent on tourism. They do say that's Anglesey's primary purpose – to see the mountains.'

So islanders were keen on projects like Wylfa, the nuclear power station at Cemlyn, 'the only fairly serious carbuncle we've got on the unspoilt northern coast,' as Bryn put it. Wylfa provided good jobs when it was built in the 1970s and locals hoped that a new generation station would be sited next door, beside a piece of coast protected by the National Trust. 'New Wylfa' could bring 3,000 construction jobs to Anglesey. 'The local community wants work. We want to protect the landscape and some interest in the area – not only plants and animals but cultural things as well,' said Bryn as we walked beside Wylfa on Cemlyn nature reserve, a shingle bar and dark lagoons containing islands where Arctic terns nested. It was here that Bryn would bump into R. S. Thomas, in the last years of his life, watching birds. They would train their binoculars on the wading birds and discuss what else they had seen, and talk about the Welsh language. 'He was a grumpy old git,' recalled Bryn, 'but if you caught him with some interest, he was very interesting.'

The local council had designated Anglesey an 'Energy Island' in the hope of creating more jobs but there was currently no clear policy on wind farms. Bryn called turbines 'windmills', so I assumed he was not a fan. He explained the various unintended consequences of energy projects, from pylons to the problem of the planning system. Getting a wind farm through planning was rightly difficult and expensive but this only made it possible for big schemes backed by global corporations to succeed, halting community generation on a human scale which more directly benefited the local area. 'Economic development is a risk to what we're trying to sell here – this landscape, seascape and nature conservation,' said Bryn. The National Trust could not stop New Wylfa but it could exert some pressure on developers to ameliorate the most damaging aspects of its construction. 'With luck it won't harm the Arctic terns,' said Bryn. 'But when you realise the scale of construction that's not going to be an easy job.'

As dusk fell, we followed a path to Felin Cafnan, a ruined stone water mill. Although the bright sodium lights of Wylfa lay directly ahead, we could only hear running water from a little stream. The view took in stones, black rocks and the darkening sea. 'Wylfa is good for switching the lights on, but Felin Cafnan Mill is good for the soul,' said Bryn. Its tranquillity, and simple sea view, would vanish for ever if New Wylfa's proposals for a bulky new sea wall and lagoon for supplying water for the power plant came to pass.

Bryn was not particularly enamoured with nuclear or wind but we are told we are facing an energy crisis and must build new forms of generation. 'What would be the solution?' He grinned as he answered his own question. 'Use less energy.'

Whether new nuclear stations are built or not, wind power is currently transforming our coast more than any other form of energy. Putting aside debates over their efficiency, like most nature lovers I instinctively prefer wind farms to fossil fuels. Wind turbines can be graceful, and even where they are intrusive perhaps a certain scenic degradation is an acceptable price for clean, safe, sustainable power. Onshore turbines usually mobilise fierce opposition and so a massive programme of development is occurring offshore, mainly on the sandbanks of the North Sea.

My view of wind power shifted when I stayed on Scolt Head Island. On my first evening there, I scaled the dunes and surveyed the peace of the empty beach. There were no human interventions in my entire field of vision except if I raised my binoculars and picked out a speck that was the amusements at Butlin's on the distant Lincolnshire dunes. Turning inland, there was nothing but an old-fashioned wind-mill and a couple of church towers. Out at sea, however, an earlier haze was clearing and two wind farms now came into view: I could count fifty-four turbines at Lynn and Inner Dowsing to the north-west and eighty-eight at Sheringham Shoal to the north-east. The Lynn operation was the biggest offshore wind farm in the world when it was completed in 2008 but bigger operations have rapidly sprung up elsewhere; Sheringham Shoal materialised on the horizon in the summer of 2011.

These two power plants were distant and tolerable. At the moment, as long as I didn't focus on my peripheral vision, I could look north, straight out to sea, and not see anything man-made, just an eternal horizon. Already-approved plans for more wind farms would soon blight this last peaceful horizon on the North Norfolk coast. At night, the existing turbines were illuminated with blinking safety lights; they made what was a perfectly black horizon for the first thirty-five years of my life now appear to house several offshore airports.

What price an uncluttered horizon? What price a dark horizon? To me they were priceless, but to the remorseless logic of our economic system they were worthless without a price. Writing about Land's End in 1908, W. H. Hudson hoped to save it from development by 'men so devoid of sentiment and imagination that they would not hesitate to stamp out the last beautiful thing on earth'. But he presciently deplored the language of early conservationists, who described places like Land's End as the country's best 'asset' or the 'goose that lays the golden eggs' or other similarly 'abominable' phrases. These arguments only appealed to human 'greed and cunning', he said. Unfortunately, this language of monetary values is exactly the diminished battle-ground on which many modern conservationists fight. Wild land-scapes are feted for the 'ecosystem services' they provide us: so salt marsh, for example, is praised (as I have just done too) for its utilitarian function of defence from the sea. Wild land is discussed in terms of job creation and tourist revenues. Conservationists will even put a price on a suburban street tree the better to save it.

In some ways, even hailing natural landscapes as a way of making ourselves happier and healthier, as I have in this book, is another expression of our need to find a 'use' for the wild. In his essay *The Tree*, John Fowles criticised the narcissistic way we turn nature 'into a therapy, a free clinic for admirers of their own sensitivity'. He argued that our desire to derive some personal yield from nature was actually the subtlest of our alienations from it. 'We shall never fully understand nature (or ourselves), and certainly never respect it, until we dissociate the wild from the notion of usability – however innocent and harmless the use,' he wrote. 'For it is the general uselessness of so much of nature that lies at the root of our ancient hostility and indifference to it.'

In a world where consumption is celebrated with increasing fervour, it becomes braver to make the case for beauty or wilderness; for spirit, soul and for species other than ourselves. I can adapt to a horizon cluttered by wind farms and, as conservationists' concept of 'shifting baselines' acknowledges, my children, who have never known any different, will comfortably accept them as an eternal part of our seascape. We don't *need* an unbroken horizon and this is the weakness of any appeal to an aesthetic value in today's society: we don't need any of it. And yet we lose some richness of our lives, to say nothing of the richness of the planet, each time we destroy an unbroken horizon, add crude structures to landscapes where once there were none or lighten the sky at night so we cannot see the stars. Every such development subtly degrades our lives and deepens our estrangement from the natural world.

I am not quite as pessimistic as Fowles and I am convinced we can and do cherish landscapes, their atmospheres and their forms of life even when they appear 'useless' to us. Surely, a love of wild things for their own sake forms part of the motivation of the eminent professor who studies the mud snails of Scolt Head Island for forty years, and it's part of why we as a society facilitate such an endeavour. We have an inalienable passion for natural places, and to give organisations like the National Trust credit, even when they have been accused of fogeyish attitudes, they have long been prepared to make an aesthetic case for conservation and talk about beauty or spirit of place.

In sensible, pragmatic terms, the problem of wind farms is one of scale and balance. Scores of offshore wind farms around Britain are fine but hundreds are not, and it would be tragic if they filled every horizon. At some point, we must take courage and campaign to preserve an empty horizon simply because it gives people a peace and a pleasure they cannot explain.

I know I am part of the problem and staying in the Hut on Scolt was instructive when I began thinking about energy. It showed me how little power it was possible to use in an era when domestic energy consumption is rising by a scary 6 per cent each year. As the Anglesey ranger Bryn Thomas remarked, we should start by using less power. We could all be micro-generating and everything should be metered to destroy the illusion that the energy we so carelessly consume is virtually free. If power was more expensive and we all knew the exact cost of charging a mobile phone, we would all live more carefully. We can adapt to low-energy lives. But people including me struggle to practise restraint or consider the implications of our behaviour much beyond our children's generation, let alone in geological time.

It was after 9 p.m. when I descended to the beach on Scolt. In summer, the sun set over the sea in North Norfolk and, as a boy, I loved waiting for it drop into the horizon. Now, it would be disappearing behind the wind farm. I watched it through my binoculars, the wind turbines marking its surprising lateral descent beyond the horizon. As the sun's final quarter slipped away, it was as if someone had built a golden temple over Skegness. Watching it so closely made me feel slightly giddy, as if we were all at sea on a giant ocean liner which appeared to be shifting slowly but was actually going at speed. In one slow moment, I could see how quickly time itself was moving. Any sunset is marvellous and this sunset over a wind farm was still stunning. And yet I hope we will fight the idea that a wind turbine will frame every view of the sun dropping into the ocean.

I could have continued my journey around the Neptune coast for another three years, or another lifetime. Just as the coastlines of England, Wales and Northern Ireland become longer in measurement if you use a smaller ruler, so these wiggly lines expand infinitely the more closely you look at them. The more I travelled, the more I noted down, the more I became aware of the mysteries, stories and science still to discover. Every day, there is something surprising, joyful and new to be found beside the sea. And we can never fully capture its essence in our thoughts or feelings or in any of the ways we arrange these in words, photographs, songs or paintings, which is probably why we keep coming back.

My final pilgrimage to the Neptune coast was to Antrim, which vies with North Cornwall for offering our craggiest cliff spectacle. It was March but the air possessed the hazy serenity of September, an unusual stillness, a pause before spring burst forth. Bright yellow gorse bloomed on the hillsides, wagtails bobbed on beaches of white rock and my progress along the scenic road that hugged Northern Ireland's north-east shore was interrupted by constant repair works: workmen helping the road retreat from the sea.

Fellow visitors were an event in this gloriously empty landscape and I met just one other person when I walked around Murlough Bay in the far north-eastern corner of Northern Ireland. 'I had this place to myself all morning,' said the solitary walker. To the north loomed the great bulk of Fairhead, where the Antrim plateau met the ocean in mighty basalt-topped cliffs. These formed an amphitheatre for four buzzards, whose high-pitched cries were the only sound as they circled high, broad wings braced against a thermal. Below the crags were birches, stunted and purple, and copper bracken; across the quiet, pond-like blue water, I could just make out Rathlin Island in the haze. On a clear day, Scotland would materialise on the northern horizon in the shape of the Mull of Oa and the Paps of Jura, a triumvirate of rounded mountains.

The emptiness was almost eerie. Perhaps that part of the Antrim coast was so unpeopled because everyone was at the Giant's Causeway. 'It's like the beginning of the world,' commented William Thackeray, just one of millions of awestruck visitors to this cathedral of natural worship, which attracts 600,000 paying visitors each year, far more than any other National Trust house or coastal property. The Causeway's three-, four-, five-, six-, seven- and eight-sided columns of basalt are polished smooth by millions of feet and by all the gossip that accumulates around celebrity places. When I arrived, towards the end of the day, foreign students were taking photographs of themselves as teenagers performed handstands on the stones, and a girl sat on the highest point and played the fiddle.

The challenge of managing these pilgrims to the Causeway's 40,000 basalt columns has been cleverly met by the creation of a cavernous green-roofed visitor centre and car park, both of which invisibly merge with the natural sweep of the land from every aspect. But as I stood on the roof of the new centre and looked west across the unspoilt farmland of Northern Ireland's north coast, Cliff Henry, the Trust's formidably knowledgeable (and appropriately named) ranger here, pointed to where a vast new golf course, luxury hotel and shopping and holiday village will be built, in full view of this unique World Heritage Site. Despite legal challenges by the National Trust, the development has been approved by Northern Ireland's environment minister.

At the end of his excellent celebration of the National Trust's coast on the twenty-fifth anniversary of Neptune, Charlie Pye-Smith noted that so many of Britain's peaceful shores were once noisy, busy and dirty. It was tempting, he wrote, to see the speed at which our industrial activities are buried by the constantly changing coastline as proof of the resilience of nature. He felt, however, that contemporary threats – nuclear power stations, rapacious development, dousing farmland with pesticides and chemicals – could be ruinous not merely for decades but for centuries. There was still a need, he concluded, for the Neptune campaign.

Twenty-five years on, for much of my journey around the 742 miles of Neptune coast I felt that the battle against unsightly housing and tourist developments by the sea had been won. Old fears that our shores would be swamped by shacks or caravans seem quaint today. Our planning laws and conservation designations should stop the crude developments of the past. The government has followed the spirit of Neptune by funding the creation of a coast path for Wales and, soon, for England. But the belief that the coast has been saved is still too complacent in some regions. As long as we flock to the seaside and house prices continue to rise, developers scent a killing. Cornwall council is planning to build 47,500 new homes in the county by 2030; not all will be inland. And conservationists were certainly working in a subtly different climate in Northern Ireland.

Apart from the massive resort planned close to the Giant's Causeway, new bungalows in the kind of scenic positions not permitted on the English coast since the 1930s were popping up along the north coast and around Strangford Lough. Northern Ireland's planning laws were more generous than those in England and Wales. 'There's a strong feeling among politicians and probably most of the people in Northern Ireland that we are still catching up with wealthy Britain,' a senior civil servant working in environmental protection in Northern Ireland told me. 'The economic argument always wins. The unemployment rate is higher here and so is the cost of living. It's jobs, it's advancement.' The marine biologist Bob Brown agreed. 'There is a nascent Northern Irish psychology which says as a premise, "We're economically backward." Our politicians say, "If it means jobs, it's okay." But what is the basis of Northern Ireland's wealth? Its environment is a big determinant of quality of life.' Tourism was one answer to those who feared that economic growth must always be at the expense of the environment, but it was not the solution to this conundrum and it would not be the answer everywhere. There are still plenty of preservation battles for Neptune to fight.

My final hours in Northern Ireland were spent five miles east of the Giant's Causeway, at White Park Bay, a magnificent three-mile arc of sand between a pair of rocky headlands. I descended through a ferny-bottomed blackthorn thicket, past the whitewashed ruins of an old youth hostel and onto one of Antrim's most celebrated northern beaches. Despite its conspicuous beauty, there was not a soul on the beach on a sunny day. Instead, there loafed fourteen cows, Belted Galloways, their long coats like the black seaweed on the rocks.

White Park Bay's sand was washed in purple and gold by the workings of the green North Atlantic and it was so fine it squeaked. I climbed on a damp rock not far from a virtually invisible ringed plover and considered the waves. There was a crash when they broke and then they advanced in silence before hissing as they slid up the beach, rolling each grain as they arrived.

Joseph Conrad said that the sea was very old. To me, on that day, it looked ageless, unmarked by time or by humankind. I don't want to belittle it by comparing it to our affairs but I suddenly imagined it was the most successful chain store in the world: wherever we encountered it, in all its different forms, it was familiar and full of bounty. This encouraged us to exploit it and here the analogy collapsed because, unlike a shop, even if the sea is emptied, or overheated, or acidified, or turned permanently stormy, it will always give us free gifts, sensory pleasures and peace.

The sea frightens us and reassures us; it sedates and awakens us; it nourishes and strips us bare; it imperils and heals us; it smashes things up and smooths things over; it emphasises our insignificance and reminds us of our responsibilities. This great nothingness and enormous presence is for both faithful and faithless; it is an ever-changing mirror that reflects our every changing mood: romantic, enraptured, angry, grieving, resigned, content, childlike. The sea is for all of us.

So too are generous lengths of Britain's shores, thanks to the efforts of social reformers, preservationists, conservationists and ordinary local people. We make no mark on the ocean – any injuries we cause it are usually internal – but we scribble lines all over the coast. Our wildest land is a gateway to the untameable water, and the seaside has become a bustling memorial to all those who have spent time here: their loves and passions, their greed and violence, their charity and poetry. We enclose and exploit almost all the land we live on but we seem to recognise that our shores are too important to be packaged up for private enjoyment. They are a temple where we experience something greater than ourselves. They show us our tiny place in the world – which can be a realisation of profound comfort and great joy.

I was given both that day by the sea. I picked up a small stone and rolled it, cool and sure, in my palm. I dug a dam of sand across a beach rivulet and watched how quickly my creation was undone by the current. I sat down and then lay down and closed my eyes. The waves broke in perfect stereo, running into my right ear and out of my left, washing away jagged thoughts. It felt as though water was flowing through me. If this was the end, I would be blessed. It was monotonous, intoxicating, exhilarating, tranquil. There was nowhere I would rather be.

> *There is a rapture on the lonely shore,*
> *There is society where none intrudes,*
> *By the deep Sea, and music in its roar:*
> *I love not Man the less, but Nature more,*
> *From these our interviews, in which I steal*
> *From all I may be, or have been before,*
> *To mingle with the Universe, and feel*
> *What I can ne'er express, yet cannot all conceal.*

George Gordon Byron

## Explorations of Neptune

Like other tiny islands, **Northey** is perfect for a gentle meander rather than an epic route-march. The most important thing is to check the tides and call the local National Trust office (01621 853142) to obtain a permit to step onto the island. To reach Northey by car, use the postcode CM9 6PP on satnav or drive south out of Maldon on the Mundon road. A quarter of a mile after Maldon's last roundabout, turn left onto a track. This wiggles through a farmyard and there is space to park on the left just before the sea bank. Then you can walk across the causeway onto Northey. A nice stroll is to circle the bottom half of Northey in an anticlockwise direction by turning right and following the old sea bank around the south-eastern corner of Northey. This loops round the frayed perimeter of Northey offering views of the Essex marshes as well as the historic first spot where 'managed realignment' took place in 1991. Eventually the bank leads you past Northey's two houses (which are private) and here you join the island's only road. Where this turns sharply south again, you can strike out north along the old sea bank that runs up Northey's east side. The salt marsh soon becomes impenetrable; you can then retrace your steps and follow the road south to the causeway. Treat the marshes with respect (they can be dangerous), don't disturb wading birds and keep an eye on the tide – it races in fast, and you'll need to get back across the causeway sooner than you think.

### OS Map
Explorer 176, Blackwater Estuary
### Nearest railway station
North Fambridge, 6.5 miles
### Website
www.nationaltrust.org.uk/northey-island/

The North Antrim coast is as spectacular as the finest bits of Cornwall or Wales and, apart from **the Giant's Causeway**, a lot less busy. I'm not a fan of crowds and I'd never visited the Causeway before. Like bumping into a celebrity in real life, it looks familiar and yet its popularity is justified: it is a visually staggering place and the feeling it triggers of communal worship, the sense that we are following in the footsteps of generations before us, is a lovely one. The National Trust's state-of-the-art visitor centre can swallow an enormous number of tourists without feeling oppressive too. The North Antrim Cliff Path is an excellent five-mile clifftop walk east from the Causeway, following every cove and craggy headland of this mighty coastline around Benbane Head to the ruins of Dunseverick Castle. It is part of the longer Causeway Coast Way. Further east, the National Trust also looks after one of the most stunning beaches in the country, **White Park Bay**, and the thrilling rope-bridge to **Carrick-a-Rede** island, near Ballintoy, which was traditionally erected by salmon fishermen to gain access to the island. Forty years ago it was treacherous; the modern, much sturdier incarnation cost £16,000 and is fashioned from wire rope and Douglas fir. If you want to do something banned almost everywhere in Britain, you can drive your car onto the beach at **Portstewart Strand**. I did and it feels naughty, like smoking in a restaurant. Conservationists hate cars on beaches but this long tradition, much cherished by daytrippers from Belfast, is not thought to be damaging the firm sand on this big surf beach. It is certainly less environmentally disastrous than putting a car park in the sand dunes. Portstewart is a popular beach but it is easy to walk two miles west to its tranquil, car-free end and explore the flowery dune system behind the strand. For lovers of the loneliest of walks, head to the north-east corner of the Antrim coast beyond the main coast road. You can take the tough walk to the top of the 200m-high basalt cliffs of **Fair Head**, Northern Ireland's tallest cliffs, from Ballycastle, three miles to the east, or you can park in the council car park at the top of Fair Head Road and walk to the cliffs and down to **Murlough Bay** and Benvan (which can be confused with the equally impressive but very different Murlough national nature reserve, a gigantic 6,000-year-old sand dune system, also protected by the National Trust, which is an hour's drive south of Belfast).

## *The Giant's Causeway*
44 Causeway Road
Bushmills
County Antrim BT57 8SU
## *Map*
OSNI Activity Map (1:25,000), The Causeway Coast and Rathlin Island
## *Websites*
www.nationaltrust.org.uk/giants-causeway/
www.nationaltrust.org.uk/white-park-bay/
www.nationaltrust.org.uk/carrick-a-rede/
www.nationaltrust.org.uk/portstewart-strand/

## Further Reading

Joseph Conrad, *The Mirror of the Sea*, Little Toller, 2013
James Hamilton-Paterson, *Seven-Tenths – The Sea and its Thresholds*, Faber & Faber, 2007

# BIBLIOGRAPHY

James Acheson, *John Fowles*, Macmillan, 1998

Blanche Atkinson, *Ruskin's Social Experiment at Barmouth*, James Clarke & Co., 1900

James R. Aubrey (ed.), *John Fowles and Nature*, Associated University Presses, 1999

Jane Austen, *Mansfield Park*, Wordsworth Editions, 1993 (originally published 1814)

Jane Austen, *Persuasion*, Penguin Classics, 2006 (1817)

Denys Val Baker, *Britain's Art Colony by the Sea*, Sansom & Company, 2000 (1959)

Sabine Baring-Gould, *The Vicar of Morwenstow*, Methuen & Co., 1899 (new and revised edition)

Bella Bathurst, *The Wreckers*, HarperCollins, 2005

Michael Bird, *Art in Cornwall*, Alison Hodge, 2012

J. T. Blight, *A Week at the Land's End*, Alison Hodge, 1989 (1861)

Ronald Blythe, *The Time by the Sea*, Faber, 2013

Piers Brendon, *Hawker of Morwenstow: Portrait of a Victorian Eccentric*, Jonathan Cape, 1975

Robert Brown, *Strangford Lough – The Wildlife of an Irish Sea Lough*, Queens University Belfast, 1990

James Canton, *Out of Essex*, Signal Books, 2013

Hugh and Mirabel Cecil, *In Search of Rex Whistler: His Life and His Work*, Frances Lincoln, 2012

Pierre Chaplais, *Piers Gaveston: Edward II's Adoptive Brother*, Clarendon Press, 1994

Robert Chesshyre, *When the Iron Lady Ruled Britain*, 2012 (original edition, 1987)

Bob Chestney, *Island of Terns*, Quiller Press, 1993

Charles Clover, *The End of the Line*, Ebury Press, 2004

Rose Collis, *Death and the City: The Nation's Experience Told Through Brighton's History*, Victorian Secrets, 2013

Joseph Conrad, *The Mirror of the Sea*, Little Toller, 2013

Peter Conradi, *John Fowles*, Methuen, 1982

Alain Corbin (trans. Jocelyn Phelps), *The Lure of the Sea – The Discovery of the Seaside in the Western World 1750–1840*, Penguin, 1995 (1988)

Nicholas Crane, *Coast: Our Island Story*, BBC Books, 2010

G. M. and R. C. Davis, *Trial of Error – The Court Martial Arising from the Loss of HMS Montagu, Lundy, 1906*, G. M. & R. C. Davis, 1983

Daniel Defoe, *A Tour Through the Whole Island of Great Britain*, Penguin, 1978 (1724–7)

Daphne Denaro Brooke-Smith and Susan Mears, *Brook – A Village History*, Crossprint, 2010

Wesley Dougill, *The English Coast: Its Development and Preservation*, The Council for the Preservation of Rural England, 1936

Jo Draper, *Dorset, the Complete Guide*, Dovecote Press, 1986

Colonel P. T. Etherton and Vernon Barlow, *Lundy – The Tempestuous Isle*, Lutterworth Press, 1950

Kathryn Ferry, *Sheds on the Seashore*, Pen Press, 2009

Margaret Forster, *Daphne du Maurier*, Chatto & Windus, 1993

Keir Foss, *The Book of Newtown*, Halsgrove, 2004

John Fowles, *A Short History of Lyme Regis*, Dovecote Press, 1991 (1982)

John Fowles, *The French Lieutenant's Woman*, Jonathan Cape, 1969

John Fowles (ed. Charles Drazin), *The Journals: Volume 2*, Jonathan Cape, 2006

John Fowles, *The Tree*, Aurum Press, 1979

Elain Franks, *The Undercliff*, The Promotional Reprint Company, 1993

Arabella Friesen, *Stackpole and the Cawdors: Evolution of a Landscape*, The National Trust, 2005

Felix Gade, *My Life on Lundy*, F W Gade UK, 1979

John Gaze, *Figures in a Landscape*, Barrie & Jenkins, 1988

Richard Girling, *Sea Change – Britain's Coastal Catastrophe*, Eden Project Books, 2007

James Hamilton-Paterson, *Seven-Tenths – The Sea and its Thresholds*, Faber & Faber, 2007

Thomas Hardy, *A Pair of Blue Eyes*, Wordsworth, 2010

Paddy Heazell, *Most Secret: The Hidden History of Orford Ness*, The History Press, 2010

Caspar Henderson, 'Hypnagogia', *Archipelago* Magazine, Issue 5, Spring 2011

Eileen Hopper, *Easington Through the Years*, Summerhill Books, 2011

Polly Howat, *Tales of Old Norfolk*, Countryside Books, 1991

W. H. Hudson, *The Land's End*, Wildwood House, 1981 (1908)

Robert Huffaker, *John Fowles*, Twayne Publishers, 1980

Paul Hyland, *Wight: Biography of an Island*, The Dovecote Press, 1997

Institute of Estuarine and Coastal Studies, University of Hull, *Historical Study of Natural Sea Wall Failures in Essex*, English Nature Research Reports No. 15, 1992

Stan Jarvis, *East Anglia Shipwrecks*, Countryside Books, 1990

R. Gerallt Jones, *A Place in the Mind – A Boyhood in Llŷn*, Gomer, 2004

Jack and Johanna Jones, *The Isle of Wight – An Illustrated History*, The Dovecote Press, 1987

Andy King, 'Lordship, Castles and Locality: Thomas of Lancaster, Dunstanburgh Castle and the Lancastrian Affinity in Northumberland 1296–1322, *Archaeologia Aeliana*, Fifth Series, Vol. XXIX, 2001

Sophia Kingshill and Jennifer Westwood, *The Fabled Coast*, Random House, 2012

Keith Lane, *Life on the Edge*, John Blake, 2010

A. F. Langham, *The Island of Lundy*, History Press, 1994

Peter Laws, *A Guide to the National Trust in Devon & Cornwall*, David & Charles, 1978

Lena Lencek and Gideon Bosker, *The Beach – The History of Paradise on Earth*, Pimlico, 1999

Lloyd's Salvage Association Reports 1866–68

J. R. Maddicott, *Thomas of Lancaster, 1307–1322: A Study in the Reign of Edward II*, Oxford University Press, 1970

Philip Marsden, 'Land's End', *Granta* 102, 2008

G. Masselink and P. Russell, 'Impacts of climate change on coastal erosion', *MCCIP Science Review*, 2013

H. J. Massingham, 'Hawker of Morwenstowe', *Out of Doors*, Vol. 13, No. 10, January 1952, via http://www.robertstephenhawker.co.uk

Daphne du Maurier, *Frenchman's Creek*, Penguin, 1964 (1941)

Daphne du Maurier, *Jamaica Inn*, Virago, 2003 (1936)

Daphne du Maurier, *Vanishing Cornwall*, Book Club Associates, 1981

Ian McEwan, *On Chesil Beach*, Jonathan Cape, 2007

Frank Meeres, *The North Norfolk Coast*, Phillimore, 2010

Fred Mew, *Back of The Wight*, The County Press, 1934

John Michell, *A Short Life at the Land's End: J. T. Blight FSA, Artist, Penzance*, The Compton Press Ltd, 1977

The National Trust, *Properties of the National Trust*, 4th revised edition, 1988

Paul Newman, *The Tregerthen Horror: Aleister Crowley, D. H. Lawrence & Peter Warlock in Cornwall*, Abraxas, 2005

# BIBLIOGRAPHY

Alastair Oswald and Jeremy Ashbee, *Dunstanburgh Castle*, English Heritage, 2007

Richard Perry, *A Naturalist on Lindisfarne*, Lindsay Drummond, 1946

J. B. Priestley, *English Journey*, William Heinemann, 1934

Charlie Pye-Smith, *In Search of Neptune*, National Trust, 1990

Jonathan Raban, *Coasting*, Collins Harvill, 1986

Jenny Randles, *UFO: Crash Landing? Friend or Foe?*, Blandford, 1998

Derek Ratcliffe, *The Peregrine Falcon*, T & AD Poyser, 1993

Byron Rogers, *The Man Who Went Into The West*, Aurum Press, 2006

Ian Scott and Richard Worsley (eds), *The Return of the Tide*, JJG Publishing, 2010

Jeremy Seal, *The Wreck at Sharpnose Point*, Picador, 2001

W. G. Sebald, *The Rings of Saturn*, Vintage, 2002

Maurice Smelt, *101 Cornish Lives*, Alison Hodge, 2006

Maurice de Soissons, *Brancaster Staithe – The Story of a Norfolk Fishing Village*, Woodthorpe Publishing, 2003

St Levan Local History Group, *The Book of St Levan*, Halsgrove, 2004

David J. Starkey, Chris Reid and Neil Ashcroft, *England's Sea Fisheries – The Commercial Sea Fisheries of England and Wales since 1300*, Chatham Publishing, 2000

Paul Stradling, *Horden, The First 100 Years*, Horden Millennium Committee, 2011

Alison Symons, *Tremedda Days*, Tabb House, 1992

D. J. Taylor, *Bright Young People: The Rise and Fall of a Generation: 1918–1940*, Chatto & Windus, 2007

David Temple, *The Collieries of Durham*, Volume 1, TUPS Ltd, 1994

Paul Theroux, *The Kingdom by the Sea*, Penguin, 1983

R. S. Thomas, *Collected Later Poems*, Bloodaxe, 2004

R. S. Thomas, *Collected Poems, 1945–1990,* Phoenix/Orion, 2000

Hugh Thomson, *The Green Road into the Trees*, Preface Publishing, 2012

Kate Tristram, *The Story of Holy Island*, Canterbury Press, 2009

E. L. Turner, *Birdwatching on Scolt Head*, Country Life, 1928

Dominick Tyler, *Uncommon Ground*, Guardian Faber, 2015

Eileen Warburton, *John Fowles – A Life in Two Worlds*, Jonathan Cape, 2004

Merlin Waterson, *A Cornish Bastion: The Work of Michael Trinick*, The Trustees of the Michael Trinick Memorial Fund, 2006

Merlin Waterson, *A Noble Thing: The National Trust and its Benefactors*, National Trust, 2011

James Wentworth Day, *Rum Owd Boys*, East Anglian Magazine Limited, 1974

Laurence Whistler, *The Laughter and the Urn*, Weidenfeld and Nicolson, 1985

Kyffin Williams, *A Wider Sky*, Gomer, 1991

Dixe Wills, *Tiny Islands*, AA Publishing, 2013

Virginia Woolf, *To the Lighthouse*, Wordsworth Editions, 1994 (1927)

M. Wynn Thomas, *R. S. Thomas: Serial Obsessive*, University of Wales Press, 2013

# ACKNOWLEDGEMENTS

Anyone who feels queasy when encountering too many thank-yous, please look away now. This book would not have been written without Mike Collins of the National Trust, whose original idea it was. Mike is the best press officer I've ever encountered, a factory of ideas working out of Bath and Swindon who has been hugely supportive throughout the long process of writing *Coastlines*.

I was allowed to write exactly what I wanted, independently of the National Trust, which made the kindness of Trust employees even more notable. I leaned heavily on the goodwill of many rangers and other Trust folk who put me up in strange places or accompanied me, sometimes for several days, on fascinating and hugely informative tours of their local patches. These rangers are the lifeblood of the Trust, and they are hugely impressive. Some have popped up in the book but many equally entertaining and informative individuals haven't: thank you to Phil Davidson for her generosity and enthusiasm over three days in Northern Ireland; Jon Brookes for an insightful perspective on Penwith; John Walton for the same in Northumberland; Robin Lang for his remarkably broad knowledge (and books) on the Isle of Wight; Crispin Scott for his wit and wisdom along the coast of Kent and Sussex; and Tony Flux for his ideas and inspiration along the Dorset coast.

I hope the following people are thanked via their appearances in the book but I would like to thank them again for all the time they spared and stories they shared – in particular Phil Dyke for a splendid evening in Cornwall and for tirelessly discussing the National Trust's changing approach to the coastline; and Richard Neale in North Wales for grasping exactly what I was looking for and first telling me the story of Plas Newydd as well as alerting me to many relevant works, including Byron Rogers's superb biography of R. S. Thomas. Grant Lohoar and David Fincham were supremely informative on Orford Ness; Gareth Wilson and Wayne Appleton similarly so on the Durham coast; and Reuben Hawkwood and John Lamming on Brownsea. David Steele was excellent value on the Farne Islands as well. Thanks to Bryn Thomas for opening my eyes on Anglesey and Stuart Banks for joining me on Northey. I would also like to thank Katie Bond, the National Trust's publisher, and her predecessor, Grant Berry. Thanks also to my friend Matthew Oates, who accompanied me on some Isle of Wight adventures and is a perpetual inspiration.

Beyond the National Trust, many other people have contributed to this book, particularly John Whittow, David Pinder, Keith Lane and Charles Duff. Thank you. Des Hannigan in Penwith was splendid company and a source of many fruitful leads and ideas. Chris Thain of Dorset Wildlife Trust was an amusing addition to the Brownsea informants. Thanks to Derek Green at the Landmark Trust on Lundy and a particular thanks to Michael Rooney of Natural England who allowed me to stay on Scolt Head Island. It was an unexpected treat to find that the seasonal warden on Scolt was Neal Lawson, who was a young warden when I took childhood holidays by the sea at Holme Dunes nature reserve. Thank you Neal for your grand tour of Scolt and the terns.

My first draft was as choppy as the North Sea on a bad day and so my heartfelt thanks go to Laura Barber, my brilliant editor at

# ACKNOWLEDGEMENTS

Granta, for bringing flow to the structure, for providing so many big and small ideas, for labouring long into the night to spruce up my sentences and for supporting me at every stage of this book. John English saved me from embarrassment with his forensic line edit; corrections and improvements were also gratefully received from Phil Dyke, Mike Collins, Tony Flux, Bob Brown, John Walton, Phil Davidson, Michael Rooney, Reuben Hawkwood, David Pinder, Peter Newson, John Barkham and Suzanne Barkham. Thank you. Mistakes that remain are my own.

Thank you to everyone at Granta Books for their help and hard work: Sigrid Rausing, the publisher; the superb (and ever-patient) Christine Lo and Sarah Wasley; Iain Chapple, Aidan O'Neill, Sara D'Arcy, Ka Bradley and the rest of the team.

I'd like to thank my agent, Karolina Sutton at Curtis Brown for her time as well as her ninja negotiating skills. Thank you to her assistants Norah Perkins and Lucy Morris too.

At the *Guardian*, I'd like to thank my managing editor, Sheila Pulham, for her tolerance and wisdom, and Suzie Worroll for her superb professionalism. Thanks also to the two Johnnies: John Crace for his friendship and John Sutherland for this book's title.

Writing a book is a bewildering experience for any close observer (how can it take *that* long?) especially if they happen to be a toddler, so thank you Camilla and Esme Barkham for your love and inspiration, and thank you Ted Barkham for being a joyful person since being born a year ago. Writing a book while three children are still in nappies (thankfully no longer) has only been possible because of the amazing support Lisa and I have had from Jan and Rob Palmer, Laura Peck, Teresa Norton and Suzanne Barkham and John Barkham. I owe my mum and dad a huge debt for their love and support which included everything from correcting facts to financial assistance during the gestation of this book. Thank you.

Last but obviously not least: thank you Lisa Walpole for your excellent humour, love, patience, talent and acceptance, especially when I kept deserting the family for a few days hard graft in coastal nirvana.

# Index

# INDEX